AFRICA AND THE WEST

Recent Titles in
Contributions in Afro-American and African Studies
Series Advisers: John W. Blassingame and Henry Louis Gates, Jr.

Philanthropy and Jim Crow in American Social Science
John H. Stanfield

Israel in the Black American Perspective
Robert G. Weisbord and Richard Kazarian, Jr.

African Culture: The Rhythms of Unity
Molefi Kete Asante and Kariamu Welsh Asante, editors

Writing "Independent" History: African Historiography, 1960-1980
Caroline Neale

More Than Drumming: Essays on African and Afro-Latin American Music and Musicians
Irene V. Jackson, editor

More Than Dancing: Essays on Afro-American Music and Musicians
Irene V. Jackson, editor

Sterling A. Brown: Building the Black Aesthetic Tradition
Joanne V. Gabbin

Amalgamation!: Race, Sex, and Rhetoric in the Nineteenth-Century American Novel
James Kinney

Black Theatre in the 1960s and 1970s: A Historical-Critical Analysis of the Movement
Mance Williams

An Old Creed for the New South: Proslavery Ideology and Historiography, 1865-1918
John David Smith

Wilson Harris and the Modern Tradition: A New Architecture of the World
Sandra E. Drake

Portrait of an Expatriate: William Gardner Smith, Writer
LeRoy S. Hodges, Jr.

AFRICA AND THE WEST

THE LEGACIES OF EMPIRE

EDITED BY
ISAAC JAMES MOWOE
AND
RICHARD BJORNSON

Prepared under the auspices of the College of Humanities, The Ohio State University

Contributions in Afro-American and African Studies, Number 92

GREENWOOD PRESS
New York • Westport, Connecticut • London

Library of Congress Cataloging in Publication Data

Main entry under title:

Africa and the West.

   (Contributions in Afro-American and African
studies, ISSN 0069-9624 ; no. 92)
   Bibliography: p.
   Includes index.
   1. Africa—Civilization—Occidental influences—
Addresses, essays, lectures.   2. Humanism—Addresses,
essays, lectures.   3. Africa—Colonial influence—
Addresses, essays, lectures.   I. Mowoe, Isaac James.
II. Bjornson, Richard.   III. Ohio State University.
College of Humanities.   IV. Series.
DT14.A343   1986   960   85-5618
ISBN 0-313-24109-0 (lib. bdg. : alk. paper)

Copyright © 1986 by the College of Humanities, The Ohio State University

All rights reserved. No portion of this book may be
reproduced, by any process or technique, without the
express written consent of the publisher.

Library of Congress Catalog Card Number: 85-5618
ISBN: 0-313-24109-0
ISSN: 0069-9624

First published in 1986

Greenwood Press, Inc.
88 Post Road West, Westport, Connecticut 06881

Printed in the United States of America

The paper used in this book complies with the
Permanent Paper Standard issued by the National
Information Standards Organization (Z39.48-1984).

10 9 8 7 6 5 4 3 2 1

To Diether Haenicke, whose vision, support, and sense of humane values made possible the symposium which inspired this volume

and

to Jane Wemhoener, whose commitment, ingenuity, and grace under pressure made that symposium a success.

Contents

Preface	ix
1. Introduction RICHARD BJORNSON AND ISAAC JAMES MOWOE	3
2. Africa in World History PHILIP D. CURTIN	13
3. Cultural Forces in African Politics: In Search of a Synthesis ALI A. MAZRUI	33
4. Man in African Religion JOHN MBITI	55
5. African Traditional Religion: Monotheism or Polytheism? KWESI A. DICKSON	69
6. The Revolution of 1889 and Leo Frobenius LÉOPOLD SÉDAR SENGHOR Translated by RICHARD BJORNSON	77
7. On the Question of an African Philosophy: The Case of French Speaking Africa V. Y. MUDIMBE	89
Appendix A: Tempels' Philosophical School	114
Appendix B: Milestones in African Philosophy	114

8. Contemporary Thought in French Speaking Africa 121
   ABIOLA IRELE

9. Political-Cultural Schizophrenia in Francophone Africa 159
   VICTOR T. LEVINE

10. Colonialism, Media Imperialism, and the
    Survival of African Culture 175
    NJOKU E. AWA

11. Judicial Process and Legal Development in Africa 189
    TASLIM O. ELIAS

12. Perspectives on African Musicology 215
    J. H. KWABENA NKETIA

    Selected Bibliography 255

    Index 259

    About the Contributors 269

Preface

In late May 1982, over three hundred scholars, clergymen, representatives from the public sector, and private citizens from three continents gathered in Columbus, Ohio, to participate in a three-day symposium on "Africa and the West: The Challenge of African Humanism," sponsored by the College of Humanities of The Ohio State University. The majority of the essays in this volume were originally presented, in a somewhat different form, at that symposium. The unifying thread which links them together is a common concern for the lingering social, political, economic, and cultural consequences of the European penetration of Africa as seen a quarter of a century after most countries of Africa achieved their independence.

During our work on this volume and the symposium which preceded it, we were assisted in so many different ways by so many different people that it would be very tedious to mention them all by name; nevertheless, we would like to express our appreciation to a few whose contributions proved indispensible to the success of this project. Our deepest gratitude is expressed in the dedication, but the support and encouragement of William E. Nelson, Michael Curran, E. Garrison Walters, Robert Stull, Jonathan Green, Bruce Mathews, and Earl Vance were also crucial at various points along the way; Jan Adams, Phyllis Newman, Dorothy Shoemaker, Connie Dantuono, Edie Waugh, and Shari Lorbach also provided invaluable assistance, as did Aija Bjornson and Bobbie Clarke. On many occasions we benefited greatly from the advice and counsel of a planning committee comprised of Otto Beatty, Jr., Hugh Dorrian, Larrilyn Edwards, John Elam, Tullia Hamilton, Jerry Hammond, Dave Kaylor, Tom Maroukis, Ruth Schildhouse, Calvin Smith, Jerri Wasserman, Okechukwu Onyejekwe, Deborah Toler, Frank Chiteji, Okechukwu Odita, and Marilyn Waldman. Financial and other support was generously provided by the College of Humanities of The Ohio State University, the Ohio Humanities Council, the Ashland Chemical Company, the United States Information Agency, the African-American Institute, the Mid-West Consortium for International Assistance/Women in Development, and the Greater Columbus Arts Council. Our sincere thanks also to Dr. G. Micheal Riley, Dean, College of Humanities, for his very generous support of our efforts.

>Richard Bjornson
>Bayreuth, Federal Republic of Germany
>
>Isaac James Mowoe
>Columbus, Ohio

AFRICA AND THE WEST

1

RICHARD BJORNSON
ISAAC JAMES MOWOE

Introduction

The geo-political map of contemporary Africa has unquestionably been drawn along lines determined by a four-hundred-year history of Africa's relationship to Europe. This history has frequently been marked by a violent conflict between cultures that are posited on quite different assumptions about the nature of the universe, the purpose of human existence, and the moral values that ought to govern an individual's relationship to the world and the other people who inhabit it. During the greatest part of this history, most Europeans who concerned themselves with Africa premised their attitudes upon the conviction that they were bringing "civilization" to a backward and primitive part of the world. Partly to disseminate Christianity and partly to create a literate elite capable of performing subordinate but necessary functions in colonial administrations and commercial enterprises, a small number of Africans were taught to read and write in European languages. Because Europeans tended to believe that the transfer of culture necessarily moved from the "civilized" parts of the world to "uncivilized" ones, they generally assumed they had little to learn from their pupils, except in a curious, antiquarian fashion.

However, the impact of European language literacy upon Africans did not always follow the anticipated lines. It did not, for example, produce a universal or unqualified acceptance of European customs and modes of thought. On the contrary, it made many Africans intensely aware of values like justice, liberty, and fair play that seemed to be cherished by Europeans in their own countries. Why, they asked, were these values not being applied to them? In addition, their literacy in European languages often provided educated Africans with an opportunity to reflect seriously upon the beauty, wisdom, and social usefulness of their own traditions. As they gained insight into their own cultures, they began to revive attitudes and social practices that had all too often been summarily dismissed by European observers; indeed, nearly all ideology in contemporary Africa reflects the fusion of humanistic ideals drawn from Western and indigenous sources. Ironically, when Europeans introduced education as a means of consolidating their dominance on the continent, they created a new class of Africans who understood, perhaps even better than they did, the vulnerability of the colonial system; among its members were most of the leaders who led the struggle for national liberation in the 1950s and formulated the policies of the newly independent African states in the 1960s.

Nevertheless, the transition from colonialism to independence was not an easy one. There were wide divergences of opinion among Africa's literate elites. Personal ambition, corruption, unforeseen economic difficulties, and increasingly intense pressures from major world powers frequently produced conditions that disappointed millenarian dreams and fragmented the solidarity generated during the rush toward independence. A new reality had come into existence, and a new ideology was needed to cope with it. One of those who recognized this imperative more clearly than most was Kwame Nkrumah, who advocated "consciencism" as a way of incorporating traditional African humanism with principles borrowed from European and Islamic models which, he felt, had also become part of Africa's heritage. "With true independence regained," he proclaimed, "a new harmony needs to be forged, a harmony that will allow the combined presence of traditional Africa, Islamic Africa and Euro-Christian Africa, so that this presence is in tune with the original humanist principles underlying African society. Our society is not the old society, but a new society enlarged by Islamic and Euro-Christian influences." According to Nkrumah, the new ideology needed to foster harmonious growth and development in this situation would emerge from the productive encounter, within the African consciousness, of "the three strands of present African society." But it has not been so. More often than not, natural catastrophes, economic setbacks, pervasive governmental corruption, and a growing sense of public resignation have constituted the hallmarks of much of contemporary Africa. But there have also been a number of extremely positive developments in independent Africa. Among them is the emergence of a mature and self-confident humanistic scholarship that seeks to comprehend African history and culture from a holistic, non-ethnocentric perspective. Problems of individual and national identity have tended to recede into the approaches to reality. Whether he himself ever succeeded in transforming the principles of consciencism into practical realities remains questionable. What is undeniable, however, is that he gave utterance to a theme that continually resurfaces in the following pages: Africa does possess a significant humanistic tradition, and it will undoubtedly influence any viable system of values that emerges to sanction social and political organization on the continent, but such a system of values will also, it seems, invariably contain elements imported from abroad.

The intellectual landscape of Africa has changed considerably since the late 1950s and early 1960s. As Ali Mazrui suggests in his essay on cultural forces in African politics, "the euphoria of the early years of independence has been replaced by the agonies of failure. Political instability is widespread, food production has declined, numbers of refugees are expanding. As the saying goes, the old revolution of rising expectations has indeed been replaced by a new revolution of deepening frustrations." Against this background, Africans and non-Africans alike have begun to forge a new synthesis from disparate elements in the African past and present. Western ethnocentric arrogance (like Hugh Trevor-Roper's casual dismissal of African history before colonization as being unworthy of serious interest), paternalistic pronouncements on nation building, and naive anti-colonialist rhetoric have given way in many quarters to the dispassionate pursuit of a balanced understanding of the African experience within its global context. The essays collected in this volume provide eloquent testimony to the rigorous growth of this tendency in recent scholarship.

The initial idea for this collection took shape during a conference on "Africa and the West: The Challenge of African Humanism" that took place on The Ohio State University campus in May 1982.

Many of the contributors were present at that conference, and they agreed to revise their presentations for an interdisciplinary volume that would enable readers to gain some insight into the present state of humanistic scholarship on Africa. As organizers of the conference, we took it upon ourselves to solicit additional essays in areas of specialization that had not been fully represented in the conference sessions. Taken together, these essays span a wide spectrum of disciplines from history and political science through religion, philosophy, musicology, and literature to communications and jurisprudence. Yet, whatever the disciplinary orientation might be, each of them reflects the belief that contemporary Africa must be understood as an extraordinarily complex, culturally rich continent which exists within a world that it has helped to shape. Indeed, as Léopold Sédar Senghor points out in his personal essay on the origins of *Négritude*, the West may well have contributed technological advances to Africa, but Africa itself has much to teach the West, if the West would only listen and learn.

In his opening essay "Africa in World History," Philip Curtin repeatedly illustrates the value of adopting a global perspective. The world's leading authority on the slave trade, he has developed an overall view that recognizes how the catastrophic depopulation of the New World created a vacuum that was filled by one of the largest folk migrations in history. According to him, the movement of Africans to the New World was part of this folk migration to repopulate the Americas; if their participation was constrained rather than voluntary, it was in part because much of Africa had long remained isolated from what he calls the "intercommunicating zone," an area of urban culture in which frequent exchange helped disseminate the technological advances of the agricultural and industrial revolutions. When Africans entered the intercommunicating zone, they were as adept as any other people in military organization, commercial enterprise, and technological innovation; but at the moment of the first European incursions, many parts of Africa had not yet become part of the intercommunicating zone. (Curtin cites the drying up of the Sahara in about 1,500 B.C. and the high incidence of disease as primary barriers to the inclusion of Africa in this area.) For this reason, its people were thus particularly vulnerable to exploitation. An adequate historical understanding of the slave trade cannot be based on oversimplified stereotypes,

Introduction

Curtin concludes, and he goes on to suggest that the roles of capitalism, imperialism, and industrialization in the evolution of contemporary Africa will only be understood when viewed from the same global, non-ethnocentric perspective he has applied to the slave trade.

Ali Mazrui would certainly agree with Curtin's pleas for a holistic appraisal of African history, but his approach to the problem is entirely different; rather than worldwide demographic movements, he focuses upon the network of cultural symbols by means of which Africans define their own reality. He regards African history as an ongoing war of the "gods"—a war which figuratively represents Africa's quest for a new civilizational synthesis. For him, these gods exist on different levels; they are indigenous, Muslim, and Christian, and they include values that have largely been kept alive by ethnicity (the extended family, a shared concern for the aged and the young, collective responsibility, and hospitality) or introduced by widespread yearnings for national integration, pan-African solidarity, and economic development. There is a cultural congruence throughout much of Africa, he contends, and it creates a prior sense of Africanness in many of the people who live there; furthermore, ideas and ideologies, music, literature, and development aspirations have diffused throughout the continent. Despite common values, dreams, and points of reference, however, "the gods of African culture are not yet at peace with each other." But they could be, and as a brilliantly persuasive advocate of African unity, Mazrui makes concrete suggestions about how a continentwide cultural synthesis might be achieved. Whether such a reconciliation of the "gods" ever takes place, it is obvious for Mazrui that the true significance of man's experience in Africa is inscribed in the interplay of cultural forces and must be read on that level to be understood.

One of the best examples of Mazrui's cultural congruence lies in the area of religion, the subject of complementary essays by John Mbiti and Kwesi Dickson. As Mbiti points out, there are striking similarities in indigenous belief systems throughout the continent; virtually identical images of God, concepts of man's place in the universe, ideas about how human beings participate in the invisible, desires for harmony with the cosmos, and moral precepts can be found from Senegal and Ethiopia to South Africa. An understanding of this complex belief is crucial to an understanding of contemporary

Africa, he continues, because there as elsewhere "the political, economic, cultural, and scientific activities of man are all developments within the religious framework of the image of man." Unfortunately, this image of man has often been distorted when described within the framework of Western conceptual categories. In Dickson's essay, this point is clearly made on the basis of specific examples drawn from the Asante of Ghana. Although labels like "monotheism" and "polytheism" might both be applied to Asante religious practices by a Western observer, they obscure rather than clarify the true nature of Asante belief. As a result, Dickson concludes that African religions can best be understood when they are allowed to speak for themselves and not when they are shoehorned into inappropriate Western categorization schemes. What is required is a new vocabulary, and much humanistic scholarship on post-independence Africa has been devoted to the search for this vocabulary.

The essays by Senghor, Valentin Y. Mudimbe, Abiole Irele, and Victor LeVine all revolve around the intellectual life of francophone Africa—an area that has received far less attention than it deserves in the scholarship of the English speaking world. One of the founders of the *Négritude* movement and a former president of Senegal, Senghor has for decades been the pivotal figure in this intellectual world. His writings have crucially influenced the debates that have taken place there since independence, for (as Irele and Mudimbe demonstrate) even those who disagree with him have felt obliged to use his intellectual position as a point of departure. In "The Revolution of 1889 and Leo Frobenius," Senghor himself reveals how he and Aimé Césaire received some of the impetus for their articulation of a new African worldview when they discovered the work of the German ethnologist Frobenius, who had broken decisively with the racist, nationalistic, positivistic assumptions that had guided most Western anthropological research in Africa up to that time. After reading Frobenius, Senghor knew with certitude what he had only vaguely sensed before—that every human society has its own culture, the values of which were not inherently inferior to those of other cultures; that Negro culture everywhere shares certain common features; that discursive reason was not the only or even the best instrument for understanding other cultures, because a deeper vision was necessary to grasp the characteristic style of any culture and it requires a reliance on intuition.

In the process of describing the influence of Frobenius upon himself, Senghor provides a rare insight into his own most cherished principles. Like Dickson, he faults Western observers for applying their own mental constructs to complex African realities; like Curtin, Mazrui, and Mbiti, he is consciously seeking a global perspective. But his ultimate goal is perhaps more visionary than theirs, for at the end of his essay he envisages a new world order—"la civilisation de l'universal"—in which each culture would be respected and allowed to contribute its characteristic virtues to the rest of humanity. Only by listening to Africa, he implies, will the people in the West begin to regain their lost capacity to plumb the real by intuitively projecting themselves into the lives of others. Senghor is not overly sanguine about the possibility of achieving this "civilisation de l'universal," but like Mazrui and Mbiti, he is convinced that progress in other domains is contingent upon a broader understanding of African culture. "There will be no new economic order," he argues, "if a new cultural order is not established first."

By providing a concise overview of francophone African thought, V. Y. Mudimbe's "On the Question of an African Philosophy" contributes to a global, contextualized understanding that might be regarded as a first step toward the new cultural order envisaged by Senghor. His reevaluation of Placide Tempels' *Bantu Philosophy* within a context of religious and anthropological writing and his careful delineation of competing philosophical trends in contemporary Africa result in a new, non-ethnocentric way of categorizing works that range from commentaries upon traditional belief systems through Western-style academic philosophizing to ideologically committed analyses of African social and political realities. From this perspective, "all of them are part of a history of African philosophy in the making."

As a literary and cultural critic, Abiola Irele looks at some of the same works discussed by Mudimbe, but his approach to them is quite different. He relates the works of thinkers like Senghor and Cheikh Anta Diop to the rise of cultural nationalism and the desire to assert a viable sense of identity in the face of a colonialist countermyth. After independence, however, there was a reaction against the concept of African identity as formulated by Senghor and Diop. According to Irele, it was the radical West Indian Frantz Fanon who established a new precedent for the younger generation of radical writers by stripping traditional culture of its sentimental appeal, by introducing a new realism into an understanding of the white man's domination of the black man, and by diverting attention away from Senghor's and Diop's preoccupation with the need to define and affirm a viable African identity. Influenced by Fanon, writers like Marcien Towa and Paulin Hountondji insist upon the use of critical reason (even though it might be intimately linked with Western thought and the colonialist enterprise), because they are convinced that it is the only mode of thought that will ever enable Africans to become self-determining rather than remaining forever subjected to the determinations of others. Yet, as Irele points out, Towa and Hountondji may not be as radically divorced from Senghor as they claim to be; in fact, they possess precisely the self-confident sense of identity which their predecessors strove so hard to define. In other words, if francophone African thought is placed within a larger perspective, young radicals can be seen as the further evolution of a movement they themselves claim to repudiate.

In his essay on "Political-Cultural Schizophrenia in Francophone Africa," Victor LeVine looks at a different and highly controversial aspect of intellectual life in francophone Africa—the relationship between African elites and French culture. Far more than in anglophone areas of the continent, French speaking Africans were encouraged to identify with the language, culture, and political institutions of the colonizing power. Before independence, this situation engendered a certain ambivalence; as late as 1958, a large percentage of francophone African elites desired integration in a French "community" even more than they wanted national autonomy, but because they were black, they suspected they could never be fully assimilated into the alien culture. After independence this ambivalence was compounded because the new national leaders had, in a sense, taken over the dominant roles previously filled by Frenchmen. Furthermore, they continued to enjoy numerous advantages as a result of their close ties to the government in Paris; at the same time, they could never become surrogate Frenchmen, because the ideology of nation building required them

Introduction

to espouse new myths of African identity. Consequently, on both political and cultural levels, many francophone Africans remain entrapped in a dichotomous personality that is not, according to LeVine, altogether different from the condition of schizophrenia.

One of the ways in which cultural-political schizophrenia is perpetuated throughout Africa involves the images that are created and reinforced by the public media. Newspapers, movies, and television programs profoundly influence the way people perceive the world, and Njoku E. Awa's essay on media imperialism discusses the way in which the major industrial powers have monopolized the flow of information through these channels, thereby imposing upon Africans a distorted picture of their own societies. Focusing specifically on recent UNESCO debates over the freedom of reporting, he establishes an ingenious comparison between free trade and the free flow of information in order to reveal the speciousness of Western arguments against demands by Third World countries for a more equitable share in the control over news that emanates from them and circulates within their borders. After discussing the further ramifications of the differences between information-rich and information-poor societies, Awa concludes with a plea for a new cooperative world order, contending that it is essential for the "survival of African culture."

Like LeVine and Awa, Taslim O. Elias (president of the International Court of Justice in The Hague) discusses a situation that arose in part as a result of the colonial presence in Africa. Drawing upon a broad spectrum of judicial decisions, he examines the relationship between English legal precedent and the actual practice of law in the Commonwealth nations of the continent. During the colonial period, English precedents were of course authoritative in African courts; now they have only persuasive value. But the British common law concept has, he argues, proved more adaptable to African social realities than codification, because it is flexible and hence allows the incorporation of customary law into a growing body of national or local case law. Conversely, idiosyncratic practices of customary land tenure can be modified and rendered more equitable by the application of English common-law principles. Elias even foresees the emergence of a separate common law in each of the Commonwealth nations of Africa. At the present time, however, African judges still find themselves confronted with complex and frequently contradictory sets of laws, statutes, and customary practices. Under such circumstances, Elias declares, each judge needs to develop an underlying philosophy that will help him fulfill the ultimate purpose of the judicial process—"to effect a dynamic compromise between law and society, between the technicalities of legal science and the requirements of social justice." For him, then, the judicial process is, at its best, a fundamentally humanistic enterprise.

For similar reasons, the professional study of African music is a profoundly humanistic endeavor for J. H. Kwabena Nketia. In his "Perspectives on African Musicology," he outlines for the first time the history of African scholarly interest in African music. Like Dickson and Senghor, he feels that Western observers have sometimes misrepresented the nature of African music, because they judged it according to the values of European musical traditions rather than placing it into its own sociocultural context. Like Irele, he finds that cultural nationalism and the questions of identity that preoccupied African students of music in the 1950s and 1960s have given way to a more rigorous professional attitude toward the analysis of musical phenomena. Ideally, he concludes, the activities of African musicologists will enable them to renew their identification with their own people, while at the same time remaining part of the international community of music scholars. Eschewing facile stereotypes, he too exemplifies an impulse toward the holistic, nonethnocentric perspective that invites dialogue—the same perspective that informs much of the best that has been thought and written about Africa during the past twenty-five years.

2   *PHILIP D. CURTIN*

Africa in World History

Human experience in Africa was not so different from that on other continents, but historians elsewhere were slow to take it into account. It was the last of the major continents to have a recognized history. A serious burst of interest in the study of African history began only in the 1950s, mainly in response to the new conditions of the post-war world. The new universities in Africa set up courses in African history. It became clear in Europe and America that Africa was going to be important in the post-war world, and Africa was clearly moving toward independence. Graduate study in it had begun in the recent past—especially in France, Britain, and Belgium, which had African colonies.

By the end of the 1950s, African history began to reach the major American universities as well, both as undergraduate courses and in formal seminars for graduate training. When the African Studies Association was founded in 1959, only twenty-one of its American and Canadian members listed themselves as specialists in African history. By 1970, the number had risen to more than three hundred and fifty, and it kept going up; but the 1960s was the crucial decade, when five percent of all history Ph.D.'s in the United States were in African history. History in general was also changing, with a much greater interest in new problems and new areas of study. But some parts of the profession still remained curiously parochial. Many historians tended to regard their study as a semi-private turf, relevant to their own nation but of no real concern to anyone else. This is one reason why the place of Africa in world history remains problematical.

Africa's acceptance in all historical circles is still in doubt. One of the most spectacular and frequently quoted attacks on African history in the post-war years came from Hugh Trevor-Roper, the Regius Professor of History at Oxford, in 1963. In a public lecture he categorized African history as the study of the "unrewarding gyrations of barbarous tribes in picturesque but irrelevant corners of the globe." Now the statement sounds pretty ignorant, but it wasn't just a matter of ignorance. Trevor-Roper went on to give the basis of his opinion, saying: "We study . . . history in order to discover how we have come to be where we are."[1] History, in short, was supposed to be relevant only to the time and place of the historian and his audience. Followed to its logical conclusion, European history would have no more meaning for Africans than African history had for Europeans.

Although this kind of ethnocentrism still exists in some historical circles, it has been under serious attack—and not just from Africanists. Today, many, if not most, historians would claim that we study history not to discover how we came to be as we are but to discover how the world in general came to be as it is. A fair number would go further and claim that history's central question is to discover the processes of change in human societies in general.

It was partly this change of attitude that made it possible to look again and in detail at the history of Africa, not merely to see how Africa got to be as it is today, but to see how African development fits into the development of a broader world. But this effort has to begin with the legacy of pseudoscientific racism handed down from the nineteenth century. It has to combat an even more deep-seated cultural chauvinism that accepts the allegation that sub-Saharan Africa, at least, was somehow a "primitive" place, "barely out of the stone age," a region of the world that had contributed little to the main stream of "civilization"—little or nothing that could be held up as a major creation in music, arts, or letters. This contention is by no means dead, even if its main reinforcement comes through Tarzan movies, cartoons of the missionary in the stew pot, or American television series like "Daktari" or "Roots." The fact that "Roots" belongs among the negative pictures of Africa shows how persistent some of the old myths can be, since Alex Haley was proud of his own African heritage and wanted to support Afro-American feelings of self-respect and dignity. His account is nevertheless drawn more from the old stereotypes than it is from the new image of Africa being formed by the scholarship of the post-war decades.

Consider the picture he paints of life along the lower Gambia at the middle of the eighteenth century. Here were people who seemed to be living a simple, somewhat idyllic, rural life. At first glance, that hardly seems an anti-African view, however inaccurate. On consideration, however, here we have simple villagers, whom we know from other evidence to have been in commercial contact with Europeans since the middle of the fifteenth century. Yet they seemed to have no firearms. People would have to be stupid indeed to trade with other people as dangerous as the Europeans over three centuries, yet not even bother to buy some guns for self-defense.

In fact, the picture in "Roots" is completely false for that time and place. The Africans of the kingdom of Niumi, where Jufure was located, were very well armed indeed. The French official in charge at their trading post of Albreda, next door, reported in 1775 that the king of Niumi could arm one hundred large canoes with forty to fifty musketeers as paddlers in each. In 1768, a similar fleet attacked the English fort on James Island opposite Jufure and very nearly captured it, in spite of the English artillery.[2] In fact, rather than being innocent victims of chronic raids from European ships, the people of Niumi were very heavily involved in the slave trade; and Europeans who wanted to trade in the Gambia did so on terms the Niumi dictated. The Gambians may or may not have been moral (though it is hard to judge morality across cultures and across centuries), but they were certainly ingenious in their ability to make the most out of their geographical position, and in the face of European power that was potentially much greater—though not generally great in local terms.[3]

What Haley presumably adopted unconsciously was part of an ancient myth about African abilities—a myth that credited people of African descent with unusual docility, with a natural superiority in the Christian virtues of humility and submission; while Europeans were thought to be unpleasantly aggressive and violent, but nevertheless more intelligent. The most famous and dramatic statement of this stereotype is, of course, Harriet B. Stowe's *Uncle Tom's Cabin*.[4]

One place to begin looking for the most general perspective on Africa in world history is to risk oversimplification by trying to take the longest but most generalized view of how human societies have changed through time. Most authorities now agree that the first humans evolved somewhere on the African continent, probably somewhere in the eastern African highlands. The earliest people lived as hunters and gatherers. Except for some fishing people, this kind of life called for fairly small communities that became widely scattered in their pursuit of game. As they scattered, they tended to lose touch with other communities, and, as a result, their ways of life tended to change. Over time, they became more and more different. The general pattern for hundreds of thousands of years was therefore one of cultural divergence.

During all these millenia, Africa, on the basis of the archaeological records, was no better and no worse off than any other region of the world. Everyone used stone tools that changed gradually over time, improving slightly but giving no particular region a marked superiority.

On this point, however, a warning is necessary. It is very difficult to measure the superiority of one culture over another. Especially in the fields of art, letters, or religion, different people have their own standards of judgment, and these standards are deeply rooted in the culture. I may believe that a European cathedral is more beautiful than an Indian temple, but I have no way of convincing anyone else of that fact through rational demonstration. Judgments within a single cultural framework may find broad agreement. Those that cross cultures or long stretches of time are particularly difficult and unconvincing.

One kind of human achievement, however, is more susceptible to rational comparisons, and this is technology—the means for doing something rather than the thing that is done. It is possible to judge the efficiency of means to a particular end without judging whether the end itself is good or bad.

Keeping to this standard as much as possible, about 10,000 years ago, people began to discover that they could plant seeds and grow crops under human care. If they did this, far more people could live in a small space. Larger communities were possible, and the world could sustain a much larger human population.

About 3,500 B.C., successive improvements in agricultural technology made possible the early urban culture in Mesopotamia. As people came to live more densely together, specialized occupations were possible. A discovery by one person would soon be known by others. A fairly efficient agriculture soon led to new developments in metallurgy—first bronze, later iron. The invention of writing was still more important. It helped preserve knowledge, once gained, and it helped speed the diffusion of knowledge from one place to another.

This early urban culture was not available to everyone. First, it could only be practiced in particular geographical environments that were best suited to the earliest agricultural techniques. It began in river valleys, first Mesopotamia, later the Nile valley in Egypt, the Indus valley in what was to be Pakistan, and the Yellow River valley in northern China. Historians sometimes talk about these regions as the first civilizations, and the value judgment in their favor and against the barbarian cultures around them is often explicit. Whatever the term used, these little nodes of urban culture were able to expand fairly rapidly in their own regions. With comparatively dense populations, the fact that they could communicate among themselves more easily than their less numerous neighbors made it possible for them to expand. It also made it possible to achieve an even more rapid rate of innovation in technology. Over time, these little zones of intercommunication not only expanded, but they also came into contact with one another, quite early for the large region stretching from Egypt to the Indus valley, but extending to a regular communication between there and China before the beginning of the Christian era. The nascent American civilizations were still out of contact, but by the time of Christ, it is fair to speak of a general inter-communicating zone where the pace of technological change was rapid—surrounded by a zone of less active inter-communication, where technological change was less rapid.

Before trying to see where Africa fits into this schema, let me carry this broad generalization to the present. The first proposition was that human cultures tended to diverge from the beginning of human life down to the agricultural revolution. After that time, many cultures—at least those of the inter-communicating zone— tended to become more alike, as they borrowed ideas and techniques from one another. Thus the pattern of cultural divergence changed to one of cultural convergence, at least for those societies that were within the inter-communicating zone.

As a second general proposition, human cultures changed comparatively slowly before the agricultural revolution. After that, those in the inter-communicating zone changed much more rapidly. This new and more rapid change was especially obvious in the field of technology.

As a third proposition, the rapidity of technological change was to alter once more with the industrial revolution, beginning toward the end of the eighteenth century for the first societies to industrialize but continuing at something like the new pace right down to the present. Thus, in the longer run of human history, one major discontinuity comes with the agricultural revolution; a second comes with the industrial. Perhaps these major breaks should not be called "revolutions" at all—not, at least in the model of a political revolution. A political revolution is a period of very rapid change, preceded and followed by periods of more regular and ordered evolutionary change. These two technical revolutions were not like that. They represent permanent alterations in the pace of technological change—two successive accelerations, without a marked slowdown afterward.

With that broad pattern in hand, we can move back in time to see how Africa fitted in. Stone-age technology in Africa was not notably different from stone-age technology elsewhere. Nor did the early phases of the agricultural revolution occur differently in Africa. The Middle-Eastern crops and the idea of agriculture itself probably reached the northeast corner of Africa about 5,000 B.C. From there, they diffused southward at least into the Ethiopian highlands, though Ethiopia had its own local agricultural practices as well. Further moves into the rest of tropical Africa had to stop at this point, since the Middle-Eastern grains were not suited to the climate further south. By about 2,000 B.C., however, plant domestication had begun south of the present day Sahara. At least nine different cereals were domesticated in tropical Africa, including the sorghums and millets now grown much more widely. This development was so successful that sesame seed, of African origin, was already found in Mesopotamia before 2,000 B.C.; and other African grains soon afterward had diffused as far as India. To this point, in short, African participation in the agricultural revolution fitted into the normal pattern of southwest Asia.

Then, beginning about 2,500 B.C. and continuing for about one thousand years, the region that was to become the Sahara desert began to dry up, changing from something like the open savanna country that now lies south of the desert edge into the desert we know today. This meant that, as urban civilization began to spread into Egypt and Egypt became part of the inter-communicating world, further communication with the south and southwest became difficult. The Nile, of course, provided one route across the desert. The Red Sea was another, and these water corridors are part of the explanation of why Ethiopia managed to stay in contact with the outer world. The barrier line was not precisely the Sahara but rather the western Sahara and then a swing around the Ethiopian highlands and east to the Indian Ocean in about northern Kenya or southern Somalia.

This is not to say that the barrier was total. It was not. Some techniques managed to cross it after a delay; others did not. Most of sub-Saharan Africa, for example, missed the Bronze Age, for which the technology was slow to arrive, but iron technology came with only a moderate delay. The first effective techniques for making iron and steel were apparently invented in Anatolia about 1,500 B.C. By 250 B.C., they were known quite generally just to the south of the desert. By 500 A.D., they were known all over the continent.

Nor was the barrier static, between tropical Africa and the inter-communicating zone. A series of changes in the available technology of transportation gradually eroded the effectiveness of the barrier over time. The earliest civilization in Mesopotamia and later in Egypt used cattle for pulling and donkeys for carrying. Neither animal was much good for crossing deserts or for military purposes. Then, between about 1,700 and 1,400 B.C., horse-drawn chariots were introduced into the inter-communicating zone by invaders from the steppes of central Asia, who used them to conquer all of the inter-communicating zone from Egypt to China. Sometime in the last millenium B.C., chariot-using, Berber speaking people from northwest Africa managed to set up some kind of chariot route across the western Sahara. The main evidence for this is a series of stone engraving of chariots, still to be seen along these routes. It may, indeed, have been through some such device that the knowledge of iron work crossed to West Africa. Sub-Saharan Africa nevertheless remained notably isolated during the period when the Mediterranean basin and northwest Africa came to be included in the inter-communicating zone—unified politically as well by the Roman Empire. Chariots or not chariots, there is no evidence of any regular trade across the Sahara in Roman times, nor did the Romans leave any written evidence that they even knew secondhand what might be found there, though they knew the Nile Valley and the east coast.

It would appear that the chariot phase brought some communication, but little or no regular trades depended on a second kind of new technology. Sailing ships had used the Indian Ocean for many centuries, but in about the second century B.C., traffic became much more regular as sailors began to use the seasonal alternation of the monsoonal winds. This meant, for one thing, that Roman traders and shippers reached India in important numbers. It also meant that "Roman" shippers—actually, Greek speaking Egyptians—could now reach down the east African coast as far as central Tanzania. This trade continued in Arabian hands after the fall of Rome. By the twelfth century, trade routes and scattered commercial towns stretched down the east African coast as far as the mouth of the Zambezi River and the most valued trade was the gold already being drawn from the Zimbabwe gold fields. The intensity of commerce all along this coast reached a peak in the fifteenth century, when the ships came south not only for gold but for such low-value, high-bulk products as mangrove poles for building houses on the nonforested shores of the Persian Gulf.

One might expect this trade to have linked the whole of eastern Africa into the inter-communicating zone, but it did not. Except for the gold and occasional copper from the interior, most of exports were from the coast itself. The settlers from Arabia who lived in the coastal towns rarely or never went into the interior. While we have many Arabic reports of the coast over these centuries, surviving reports of the interior are no more informative than the Roman reports of West Africa. The reason in this case is not so much an arid belt like that of the Sahara, as the fact that the bush country inland from the east coast was infested with tsetse flies which carried sleeping sickness dangerous to humans—even more important, they carried a variety of trypanosomes that were fatal to cattle and horses. The only way to move goods into the east African interior before the coming of the railroad was head porterage.

Meanwhile, the introduction of camels had finally broken the barrier of the Sahara. The first camels to influence Africa appeared in Arabia about 1,000 B.C., where they helped to link southern Arabia with the northern urban centers. Their use spread across the Red Sea into Egypt, then westward along the southern desert fringe, reaching the vicinity of Lake Chad by the first century A.D. Camel nomads then extended their range across the desert to reach late-Roman North Africa in about the fourth century A.D.

We know little about the early trans-Saharan trade, but camel caravans were extremely efficient in cost-per-ton mile. They linked North Africa and the Sahel until the end of the nineteenth century, in direct and successful competition with shipping to the coast. They dominated the trade from the Mediterranean to northern Nigeria until this century, when the railway reached Kano from the coast.

It was the camel caravans which brought the west African savannas into contact with the inter-communicating zone, now represented by the Muslim civilization of North Africa. Merchants from the north came down to the main towns on the desert edge, where they exchanged their goods from North Africa for those brought from the south by sub-Saharan merchants—by donkey, by pack oxen, or by boats on the Niger and Senegal rivers. Along with their goods, the North Africans brought their religion. The local merchants, their opposite numbers, began to convert to Islam and to carry the religion on their voyages further south. Since Muslims are "people of the book," this meant that they gained literacy in Arabic and, in time, took up the custom of pilgrimage to Mecca. By about 1,000 A.D., a Sahelian ruler had already converted to Islam. By the fifteenth century, when the Portuguese voyages began to reach the Guinea coast, at least a few Muslim merchants were already in the habit of coming that far south overland. By then, in short, West Africa was already in contact with the inter-communicating world, though not yet part of it. The point here is that the arrival of European traders was not a significantly new development of African history, merely another important step in a series of changes—and barriers still remained.

One reason why tropical Africa was comparatively slow to join the wider world was its peculiar disease environment. Before the development of effective tropical medicine in the present century, tropical Africa had what can probably be characterized as the worst disease environment of any comparable region. Rates of infestation with schistosomiasis have been estimated at as high as 90 percent for tropical Africa as a whole. Most of tropical Africa was an endemic region for falciparum malaria, the kind most frequently fatal. All children therefore fought a life-or-death struggle with this disease. If they lived past six, they gained a kind of false immunity. That is, they were still infested with the parasite, but clinical symptoms rarely appeared. And the disease list can go on through yellow fever, leprosy, river blindness, Guinea worm—to say nothing of trypanosomes that made travel inland from the east African coast so difficult.[5]

However difficult this disease environment was for Africans themselves, it was even deadlier for outsiders who entered without the immunities they might have gained from an African childhood. This applied to North African merchants who came across the Sahara as well as Europeans who came to live on the African coasts. In the eighteenth or early nineteenth century, a newly arrived European stood more than a 50 percent chance of death from disease within the first year, and the risk continued at nearly this level in the succeeding years. No wonder, then, that comparatively few Europeans came as residents to the African coast. And no wonder the African interior was the least known to people from the inter-communicating zone of any major land area and remained so until the late nineteenth century when the technological wonders of the industrial age began to be available.

Another unique aspect of African history in the preindustrial age was the role of the slave trade. Sub-Saharan Africa in the eighteenth century, and the first half of the nineteenth, exported a greater value of slaves than of any other product. Historians used to be complacent about their understanding of the slave trade. Most explanations turned on the assumption that Africa was a "primitive" place, and primitive people might be expected to sell their fellow men—or historians assumed that if civilized people stood ready to buy slaves, the uncivilized could certainly be expected to sell them. They were strangely uncurious about the awkward fact that in a peak year of the eighteenth century, tropical Africa actually exported 100,000 people. No genuinely primitive society could have had the organization to capture that many people, move them to the coast, and hold them ready for sale to the European shippers.

In the past few decades, historians, not necessarily in agreement with one another, have begun to ask new questions and to get some new answers.[6] Their recent research, however, makes it possible to see the slave trade as a migration that can be examined in world perspective alongside other migrations. In that perspective, first of all, it was very large indeed—certainly the largest intercontinental migration over such a distance up to that time.

Well into the nineteenth century, the size of the stream of Africans moving overseas exceeded that of the Europeans moving out to settle in the Americas, Siberia, and Australasia. The sheer size and the distance and the fact that it was coerced, all combine to make migration out of Africa appear to be unique in human history. It had, nevertheless, similarities to other migrations. To understand its place in world history, we have to set it alongside other associated movements of people.

Although the out-migrations of the Africans had certain special and unique features, it overlapped with three other simultaneous migrations. One of these was the repopulation of the tropical Americas after the death of the Indians. A second was a preindustrial means to concentrate people for work in certain labor-intensive occupations. The third was a pattern of slavery and the slave trade peculiar to Muslim societies in the Middle East, sometimes called "service slavery."

In its first aspect, the Atlantic trade belongs to a whole complex that Alfred Crosby has labelled *The Columbian Exchange*.[7] Once the maritime revolution of the fifteenth century broke the isolation of the American continents, people, crops, and diseases moved across the Atlantic in ways that profoundly influenced world history. The native Americans had no childhood-acquired immunities against the common diseases like measles or whooping cough which became the frequent killers of nonimmune adults. Smallpox, plus the malaria and yellow fever of the Old World tropics, had also been unknown in the Americas. This combination of European and African diseases was most disastrous for the tropical lowlands. Most lowland peoples in Brazil or the Caribbean were simply wiped out in the first century after contact. Even the highland populations of Mexico or Peru suffered population losses that seem to have been at least half. Estimates of the total loss have to allow a wide margin for error, but the Americas lost somewhere between half and three quarters of the native American population in the first century and a half after Columbus. The world as a whole may have lost something like 15 percent of its total population, as many who died between 1500 and 1650 left no descendents.

Even before tropical plantations became important in the Americas, people of the Columbian exchange began to replace the dying Indians—partly Spanish and Portuguese, but even more Africans recruited through the slave trade. By 1600, Africans already outnumbered Europeans in Mexico, Peru, and Brazil, the main centers of European activity up to that time. The European part of this migration differed in that the element of coercion was much less, but it was not absent. The African slave trade, then, can be seen as one part of a larger movement to repopulate the New World, by far the largest part until the second half of the nineteenth century.

In its second aspect, people were required not only to replace the native Americans, but even more for economic development. Gold mining needed far more people than were likely to be found in the region of a major gold strike. Thus, while the older mines in Mexico and Peru were kept going by forced Indian labor, new gold discoveries tended to look to Africa for labor. This was especially true for the most important gold rush of all, in Minas Gerais in Brazil at the end of the seventeenth century.

Even before the new gold strikes, sugar plantations began to produce for the European market. Sugar cane was a very labor-intensive crop. It needed workers for the cane fields and still others for the sugar mill and the boiling house where sugar was semi-refined for shipment. Where a small farmer must use several acres just to grow enough food for himself and his family, a sugar plantation needed about one worker for each acre of cane land—still more for food production.

Wherever sugar was planted in the era of European colonial empires, some form of coerced or semi-coerced labor seemed to be required. Sugar and slavery in the Mediterranean basin were associated even before African slaves were widely used. Much of it was supplied by slaves from Africa, not only in the Americas but also in the Mascarene Islands in the southern Indian Ocean. African slaves were also sometimes used on plantations under African control, like the clove plantations of Zanzibar and Pemba, but all coerced labor in tropical plantations was not from Africa.

After the African slave trade was abolished, contract workers from India and China served in the sugar fields of countries as widely scattered as Peru, Hawaii, Fiji, and some of the Caribbean colonies previously worked by African slaves. Thus, the slave trade was part of an even larger movement of people all around the tropical world. It was a movement intended to redistribute labor from the places it was plentiful to those where it was scarce, a movement that almost always included a large degree of coercion—if not to force a worker to sign a labor contract, then to keep him at work against his will after the contract was signed—and a movement that included the African slave trade as a phase between two others where Africans were not much involved.

The third aspect of the African slave trade was largely confined to Asia and North Africa. For reasons that seem more cultural than economic, many Muslim societies preferred alien slaves to local people as soldiers. Slave soldiers from Africa were used in almost every Muslim country from Morocco to India. They were valued because they could be trained from childhood and lacked kinship ties in the local society—ties that might compromise their absolute loyalty to the ruler. Another preferred occupation for alien slaves in Muslim societies was domestic service, especially domestics whose service required a special degree of intimacy with the master—such as concubines and harem guards.

But here again, the African slave trade was only one source of service slaves for the Muslim world. The Ottoman Empire drew slaves from the Balkans, from the Caucasus, and from the wide region between the Black Sea and the Caspian. Though the slave trade across the Sahara and the Indian Ocean was significant, the black African contribution to Muslim service slavery was almost certainly less than half of the total.

Seen in this light, then, the slave trade from Africa was part of three different patterns of migration, each of which included migrations by other people—some coerced, some not. But they all belong in the context of migration studies. Historians, along with sociologists, economists, and geographers, have come some way with comparative migration studies in recent decades. The two key questions to be asked comparatively are first, who moved, from where, to where, and why? Second, what was the impact of their arrival on the society they entered? These questions are as important for the study of the North Atlantic migration from Europe as they are for the tropical Atlantic migration from Africa, and historians are working on both.

For the African migration across the Atlantic, historians now have a fairly good approximation of who moved where and when. The other question has generated more disagreement, in some cases with profound ideological overtones. One view has been especially popular with Third World historians. It would hold that the economic complex of slavery and the slave trade fed enormous profits to Europe, and these profits provided the initial capital which financed the industrial revolution. If this view could be confirmed by a series of careful quantitative studies, it would give Africa a really important role in world history; the industrial age itself could be shown to have been caused by African sacrifice. In fact, it has not held up very well in several efforts actually to measure the quantitative weight of slave trade profits.[8] It also carries a family resemblance to a similar view of Indian historians early in this century, which credited the drain of profits from British India for the birth of the industrial age in Britain. That thesis has not held up very well either, but both have a certain attraction in the Third World. In 1978, Amadou-Mahtar M'Bow, a former historian as well as the director general of UNESCO, gave the link between the slave trade and the industrial revolution a form of official blessing when he opened a UNESCO sponsored conference with the claim that the slave trade was decisive to the industrialization of countries that were to become the developed countries of the twentieth century.

A similar controversy has to do with the influence of the slave trade in Africa. It goes back in Western scholarship to the arguments for and against the abolition of the slave trade. No one would argue today that the slave trade was good for Africa, but there is plenty of room for differences of opinion about how serious the damage may have been—to Africa as a whole or to individual regions. In recent decades, African scholars have entered this controversy with two clear lines of opinion. One appears most frequently in anglophone circles, though it may not be dominant even there. It tends to hold that Western scholars have exaggerated the influence of Europe on Africa. The African scholars of this opinion sometimes argue that the overemphasis on external causes is most serious in regard to the slave trade—this being the only aspect of the precolonial African economy that Europeans really cared about.

A nearly opposite body of opinion sees the slave trade as having overwhelming importance and as being entirely negative. Without the slave trade, they would argue, Africa would today be developed economically on a par with Europe or Japan. This view has its greatest following in francophone West Africa and among Africans living in Paris, though it has some following elsewhere as well. It is worth noting that both views are part of the revisionist tendency in African historiography. Both are part of the post-war effort to see African history in a new light—reasserting African pride in reaction to the old European attitudes of racism and cultural chauvinism. Clearly, the same result can be sought in ways that are diametrically opposed one to the other.

Similar concerns about the African image are raised by recent assessments of Africa's role in world history since the beginning of the industrial age. It is clear that Europe conquered most of Africa between about 1880 and World War I, just as it conquered most of the rest of the world. Then, after 1960, Europe withdrew its political control, leaving only the important but informal kind of influence sometimes labelled "neo-colonialism."

One issue for the historical interpretation of the past century is semantic but important. Historians write and talk about major entities that bear names like "capitalism," "imperialism," and "industrialism" without very clear agreement about what these large aggregates really consist of at any point in time and without any clear agreement about how each is related to the other two.

It is clear that the last two centuries saw the beginning of the industrial age, first in Europe, then in America, Japan, and elsewhere. It is equally clear that this development first took place in economies that can be thought of as capitalist—though some will argue about the true nature of capitalism and its geographic spread in the present day world. Finally, there is no doubt that Europe conquered most of the world in these same two centuries and profoundly influenced the cultures of those places it did not conquer.

Historians of the West have not reached agreement about whether one of these three—imperialism, capitalism, or industrialism—may have been the independent variable that caused the others. The earliest industrialism certainly came to capitalist economies, but economic historians of Europe do not agree that capitalism was a necessary cause of industrial development. Nor do they agree that capitalism caused imperialism. The case for industrialism as cause of imperial conquest is somewhat stronger. It made cheap conquest tempting, whatever the motives of the policymakers who decided that imperial advance was desirable. And European conquests overseas were exceedingly cheap up to the time of World War I. After that, machine guns began to turn up in non-Western hands and the costs altered dramatically.

For the non-Western world, the interrelations of capitalism, industrialism, and imperialism over these past two centuries pose one of the most serious problems for the understanding of world history. In some places, like North America, overseas Europeans or settlers conquered and occupied most of the continent in a movement that was clearly capitalist, industrial, and imperialist all at the same time. Elsewhere, as in Africa, these three factors seem more often to appear separately or at least with one or the other clearly dominant.

In West Africa, for example, even before the slave trade had ended, Europeans came to buy peanuts and palm oil. The economic demand was clearly an offshoot of European industrialization, but the Africans who began to fill the demand did so without any clear shift to capitalist modes of production and without falling under European empires for six to eight decades after their new commercial relations with Europe had begun. The result was an important period of political, economic, and social change, as people produced in old ways but also began to consume vastly increased quantities of products from other parts of the world economy.

Among the continents, Africa was one of the last to be conquered. This meant that some of the new industrial technology was available in Africa before either capitalism or imperialism had become important. The most important new technology was the new weapons, which made African empire building possible wherever one African state got the new techniques and its neighbors did not. This phenomenon is sometimes called "secondary empire," because the empire builders were not themselves the source of the new techniques of warfare. It is usually associated with the rapid changes in European gun types in the second half of the nineteenth century, but secondary empire building began as early as the 1820s with Muhammad Ali's conquest of the Nilotic Sudan. His troops used the common muzzle-loading muskets that Europeans had used since the 1690s, but they were trained in close-order drill and volley firing; and that European tactic gave them the edge over Sudanese armies. Additionally, the northward movement of the vortrekkers from the Cape in the 1830s and 1840s can be thought of as secondary empire building, carried out this time by tactical innovation of mounted infantry fighting against people who used well-trained, disciplined infantry but had few guns of any kind.

Most secondary empire building, however, came after about 1860 and was even more clearly associated with industrial changes in Europe, where the standard infantry weapon changed every few years with new combinations of cartridges, rifling, breach loading, and automatic reloading—ending with the effective introduction of machine guns in the 1880s. African rulers in this period changed the political map of eastern and central Africa beyond recognition. Scores of expanding new states appeared, not only on the coast but in the far interior from Katanga to Kisangani in the Congo basin, reaching northward until they made contact with the Egyptian secondary empire moving up the Nile. Menelik's Ethiopia and Leopold's Congo Independent State are other variants on this theme.

Secondary empires were less important in West Africa, largely because that region was very heavily armed with the older muskets. But the empire created by Samori Toure—stretching in the 1880s from upper Guinea-Conakry eastward to the present northern Ghana—was a clear example of the pattern found in east or central Africa.

These secondary empires not only remade African boundaries; they also tended to destabilize the African political, social, and economic institutions in ways that made imperialism a tempting alternative for the European powers. If one wanted to generalize about the various roles of imperialism, industrialism, and capitalism in nineteenth century Africa, it would seem clear that Europe reached Africa first through its new demand for African products and the supply of weapons. In schematic terms, it was the unintended influence of industrialism that opened the way for imperialism, which in turn brought capitalism in its wake.

But capitalism did not follow by necessity. It penetrated to some parts of Africa in the colonial period, but not to all. One notable example would be the pattern of economic development in the French colony of Ubangui-Shari, now the Central African Republic. There, the French found the colony so far from the sea that none of its crops could be sold profitably on the world market. They therefore introduced an elaborate system of forced cultivation, requiring each peasant to grow a minimum acreage of cotton, even though it was unprofitable for him to do so. They managed to get the cotton sold by subsidizing European capitalist traders, who otherwise would also have found the trade unprofitable.[9] But the scheme failed even as a fiscal device. It was so unpopular that it provoked an armed revolt. The military costs of suppression far outweighed the fiscal benefits.

European capitalist forms were far more prevalent in most colonies, but this case can be taken to illustrate a more fundamental point. In Africa, capitalism and imperialism did not necessarily go together, just as the influence of industrial Europe was able to penetrate for several decades before either European conquest or capitalism had made its appearance. A better understanding of Africa in world history during the past two centuries will take careful research—especially research that can help us straighten out the relationships between these three major variables that so clearly dominated the African scene in these centuries.

NOTES

1. *The Listener*, November 28, 1963.

2. M. Le Brasseur, "Questions sur nos possessions de la Côte d'Afrique, avec les reponses de M. Le Brasseur," Archives Nationales, Paris C6/17; Charles O'Hara to Sec. of State, 15 September 1768, Public Record Office, London, CO 267/14.

3. See Philip D. Curtin, *Economic Change in Pre-colonial Africa* (Madison, Wis.: University of Wisconsin Press, 1975), pp. 122-25, 196-97.

4. For the broader ramifications of the myth see J. C. Furnas, *Goodbye to Uncle Tom* (New York: W. Sloane, 1956).

5. The study of historical epidemiology is only just beginning. New research should provide better evidence, but meanwhile see Gerald W. Hartwig and K. David Patterson, eds., *Disease in African History* (Durham, N. C.: Duke University Press, 1978).

6. P. D. Curtin, "The African Diaspora" in Michael Cranton, *Roots and*

Branches—Current Directions in Slave Studies (New York: Pergamon Press, 1971).

7. A. Crosby, *The Columbian Exchange* (Westport, Conn.: Greenwood Press, 1972).

8. Stanley Engerman, "The Slave Trade and Capital Formation in the Eighteenth Century," *Business History Review*, 46 (1972): 430-43.

9. UNESCO, *The African Slave Trade from the Fifteenth to the Nineteenth Century* (Paris: UNESCO, 1979).

3
ALI A. MAZRUI

Cultural Forces in African Politics: In Search of a Synthesis

Hegel regarded history as, in a sense, the autobiography of God—the unfolding of the Absolute Spirit. The history of Africa is the history of its own changing gods, culminating in the modern period in a triple heritage of indigenous worship, Islamic prayer, and the Christian creed.

The gods have secular as well as religious faces. Their secular manifestations are differing civilizations—indigenous African, Islamic, and Western civilizational traditions. If to Hegel human history is the unfolding of the Absolute Idea, then African history is the unfolding of the Cultural Essence. Central to this process of unfolding is the interplay between cultural forces and practical politics in the arena of day-to-day human experience. If there is a religious factor within the civil wars of Chad, that is one theatre of combat in the war of African gods. If there is pronounced ethnicity in the periodic electoral politics of Nigeria, that is the secular face of competing gods. If Robert Mugabe emerges as a Shona leader in spite of himself, or Joshua Nkomo becomes a symbol of Ndebele defiance in spite of himself, that is another arena of the interplay between culture and politics in Africa's experience. And if European medicine competes with African witchcraft in the struggle to control biological forces, that too is a battlefield of the gods, an interplay between culture and biology.

Of special concern in this essay are four major areas of interaction between culture and politics in Africa—first, the quest for a civilizational synthesis among indigenous, Islamic, and Western traditions; second, a quest for national cultural integration in every African country; third, a quest for cultural convergence at the continental level; and fourth, a search for a developmental ideology compatible with African culture. Let us explore each of these cultural areas in turn.

THE TRIPLE HERITAGE OF AFRICA

Kwame Nkrumah, independent Ghana's founder president, identified the three elements of the African soul as being indigenous traditions, Islam, and what he designated as the "Euro-Christian" legacy. The distribution of the three traditions over the African continent has not been even. The most universally present is the indigenous religious and cultural legacy, alive in varying forms all over the African continent. Less deeply but still widely distributed is the Western tradition, discernible among at least the elites of the different African societies, but with the trickle-down effect on other strata of African populations. More deeply rooted than Western traditions, but less widely distributed geographically, is the Islamic tradition within the African continent. The greatest concentration of Islam in Africa is of course in Arabized North Africa, where the great majority of the population is Muslim. Next in Islamic concentration is West Africa and the Horn of Africa, where countries like Senegal and Guinea (Conakry) are also illustrations of an overwhelming Islamic majority presence.

Nigeria is in a class by itself, the largest of the African countries by far, with a population which makes one out of every four black Africans a Nigerian. At the very minimum Nigeria has a plurality of Muslims over Christians and may even have a majority of Muslims in the population. Whenever Nigeria has been under civilian rule, with a government chosen through the electoral process, the pinnacle of governmental power has been Muslim so far.

Another country which may have a plurality of Muslims over Christians, but in this case is ruled by a Christian president, is Tanzania under Julius Nyerere. Ethiopia's population may be half Muslim and half Christian, though centuries of a Christian theocracy have made Muslims a functional minority even if not a numerical one.

Countries like the Ivory Coast, Ghana, Uganda, and Kenya have Muslim minorities.

Countries like Angola, Zimbabwe, and the Republic of South Africa have almost no indigenous Muslims, though there are immigrant Muslims from South Asia and Southeast Asia in some of these countries.

But whatever the distribution of the three legacies of Africa, can they be integrated or synthesized? Again, this was one of the questions that Kwame Nkrumah confronted, quite early in the post-colonial era in Africa. Nkrumah suggested that a new synthesis was needed to lend coherence to the tripartite nature of Africa's soul.

> With true independence regained . . . a new harmony needs to be forged, a harmony that will allow the combined presence of traditional Africa, Islamic Africa, and Euro-Christian Africa, so that this presence is in tune with the original humanist principles underlying African society. Our society is not the old society, but a new society enlarged by Islamic and Euro-Christian influences.[1]

Nkrumah's advocacy of a new synthesis of the triple heritage was designed to be what he called "Philosophical Consciencism":

> . . . the theoretical basis for an ideology whose aim shall be to contain the African experience of Islamic and Euro-Christian presence as well as the experience of traditional African society, and, by gestation, employ them for the harmonious growth and development of that society.[2]

But a major question presents itself obstinately and insistently. Are these three legacies compatible with each other? At the logical level, are they mutually consistent? At the political level are they reconcilable? At the level of faith can they be synthesized?

Sometimes there are problems of compatibility even within the same legacy. For example, both Christianity and Marxism are part of the Western bequest to Africa. But can an African be both a Christian and a Marxist? Nkrumah himself had no doubt about the answer. He has told us in his autobiography: "I am a Marxist-Leninist and a non-denominational Christian and I see no contradiction in that."[3]

Can an African be a Muslim and a Marxist? Again there are many illustrations in Muslim Africa of this endeavor to synthesize.

In places like Somalia and the Sudan, Muhammad, Marx, Mullahs, and Mahdism have from time to time interacted.

Can an African be a Christian and a follower of African traditional religion? The answer is emphatically in the affirmative. The continent accommodates millions of African Christians who combine their Christian religious experience with beliefs in the powers of the ancestors and the efficacy of primordial symbolism.

Can an African be both a Muslim and a follower of African traditional religion? Again the continent accommodates millions of such Muslims. Indeed, because Islam does not have a formal priesthood and is less structured in authority than either the Roman Catholic Church or the Church of England, who is to outlaw syncretism? Who is to ban a mixture of Islamic usages with ancestral African practices? Indeed, the Prophet Muhammad himself had attempted to find areas of reconciliation between Islam and the ancestral idolatry of pre-Islamic Arabia. After all, Mecca was the holy place of Arab pagans before it became the holy place of Muslims the world over.

But can an African be both a Muslim and Christian? Here we seem to be confronted with a more obstinate boundary. Allegiance to these two universalistic religions appears to be mutually exclusive. It may not be entirely accidental that Africa did not experience religious wars until these two mutually exclusive religions started competing for the African soul.

But an even more complex problem of cultural exclusivity may lie in the question as to whether an African can be both a Marxist and a follower of African traditional religion. At first sight the logical exclusivity may not seem as sharp as in the hypothesis of trying to be both a Muslim and a Christian. But there are cultural contradictions involved in the dichotomy between Marxism and African traditional religion. For the time being it seems to be a sociological impossibility for an African to be a sophisticated Marxist without being at the same time substantially Westernized. I personally have never met an African Marxist who was not at the same time considerably Westernized. A major reason is linguistic. To be a sophisticated Marxist requires considerable familiarity with Marxist literature—both the primary literature of the founding fathers of the Marxist tradition and the voluminous secondary literature of commentary, explication, argument, and elaboration by Marxist and non-Marxist commentators. Familiarity with this body of literature is for the time being impossible through an indigenous African language. Only fragments of the works of Marx are available even in such major African languages as Kiswahili and Amharic.

And so, for an African to become a sophisticated Marxist, he needs to have acquired considerable familiarity with a Western language. And Africans do not learn their first Western language the way Westerners learn an African language—as a mere linguistic skill. The acquisition by a colonized African of the language of the colonizer has almost invariably been a major experience in cultural transformation, an immersion into the wider civilization of the imperial language. It is because of this that for the time being it remains a sociolinguistic impossibility for an African to be a sophisticated Marxist without being at the same time substantially assimilated into Western culture.

Even those Africans who learn their Marxism in the Soviet Union or in the Peoples' Republic of China are selected to go to those Communist countries after they have passed through a Western type of schooling in their own countries or beyond. Neither Moscow nor Peking recruits for either the Patrice Lumumba University or the University of Peking from among the non-Westernized villagers of Mozambique and Benin. Education for Africans in socialist countries begins with the credentials of Western schooling.

Given this link between a high level of intellectual Westernization and sophisticated Marxism among Africans, it becomes unlikely that an African who is a sophisticated Marxist would at the same time be a follower of African traditional religion. The mutual exclusivity may not be as sharp as that between adherence to Christianity and adherence to Islam, but there is still a basic cultural tension between Marxism and African traditional religion, at least at some levels.

CULTURAL SYNTHESIS AND NATIONAL INTEGRATION

All these issues are of relevance to the tasks of giving coherence to the new forms of nationhood in Africa and integrating the diverse cultural sub-units of the African scene. Northern Nigeria, for example, is a striking illustration of the fusion between Islam and African traditions. The emirates of the North have been among the more impressive Afro-Islamic institutions which have survived into the post-colonial era.

On the other hand, the British policy of Indirect Rule tended to keep out of the North that third legacy of Africa's triple heritage— the Western legacy. Fearful of upsetting Muslim sensibilities and anxious to make use of the elaborate Islamic institutions which had already evolved in Northern Nigeria, the British discouraged the Christian missionary penetration of the North and also discouraged Western education, at least for a while. Northern Nigeria remained an illustration mainly of the dual heritage rather than the triple heritage, an interplay between Islam and indigenous culture without the new mediating role of Western traditions.

It is arguable that, by keeping the third legacy of the West out of Northern Nigeria for so long, the problem of national integration in Nigeria was compounded—even if the problem of cultural imitation of the West was simultaneously reduced. In Nigeria's case a full realization of the triple heritage within the heavily populated northern part of the country might have reduced some of the sense of insecurity in the North after independence and therefore facilitated a faster rate of national integration. After all, under the British impact, the concept of education became increasingly equated with the acquisition of Western values and educational symbols. Western linguistic and literary skills became the basis of a new intelligentsia. The North of the country produced fewer specimens of this new breed of intellectuals and clerical personnel. The North, numerically preponderant, became educationally deficient. The stages were set for regional insecurity, a North-South cleavage in Nigeria, and diverse ethnic rivalries.

The problem was compounded by the fact that Eastern Nigeria was also an illustration of duality rather than a triple heritage—but Eastern Nigeria had a combination of the indigenous and the Western without the Islamic, whereas Northern Nigeria had a combination of the indigenous and the Islamic without the Western. Theoretically and hypothetically the Islamization of the East, as well as the Westernization of the North, would have deepened processes of cultural integration in Nigeria and might have reduced certain areas of suspicion, condescension, and mutual distrust.

Of the three main regions of the First Republic of Nigeria after independence, only the West, Yorubaland, came closest to illustrating the triple heritage in a rounded form. But the West was inevitably sucked into the political confrontation between the North and the East, a confrontation which exploded first into a military coup in January 1966, then into communal riots and slaughter between Hausa and Ibo in May 1966, and finally into a civil war from 1967 to 1970.

In East Africa the most important area of interaction between Islam and indigenous African culture has been outside the realm of theology and worship. It has been more in the secular visage of African gods rather than in their sacred masks. The cultural area in question in this case is that of language. Kiswahili is preeminently a product of the interplay between Islamic civilization and indigenous African culture. Even today the great majority of the Waswahili, native speakers of the language, are Muslims. But the great majority of speakers of Kiswahili are no longer those who speak it as a mother tongue. Kiswahili has become preeminently the second language for millions of Africans in Eastern Africa, a *lingua franca*, a medium of communication across cultural and ethnic boundaries. The great majority of speakers of Kiswahili now are not Muslim at all, even if those who speak it as the language of the cradle, the Waswahili, still remain predominantly Muslim.

Of course Hausa civilization is also a product of Islamic and indigenous traditions, but native speakers of Hausa constitute a much larger proportion of speakers of the language than do native speakers of Kiswahili. There remains a heavier correlation between language and religion in the case of Hausa than in the case of Kiswahili. Kiswahili was born out of the marriage between Islam and indigenous culture, but it has ceased to be identified with any particular religion. Hausa has also spread beyond Muslim West Africa, but to a more modest extent than Kiswahili has spread beyond Muslim East Africa. In any case both languages remain instances of an Afro-Islamic dual heritage, still working out a future relationship with the third legacy of the triple heritage, the Western legacy.

In East Africa Kiswahili has sometimes been used to help indigenize Western institutions. Until 1974 the Kenyan Parliament, for example, was heavily British in style and orientation, from the garb of the speaker to the details of protocol and procedure. And then in 1974 President Jomo Kenyatta ordered that discussions and debates in Parliament should be conducted in Kiswahili with almost immediate effect. The utilization of Kiswahili instantly transformed the nature of the institution.

With one stroke parliamentary experience which had been so overwhelmingly Anglocentric was transformed into a platform of African oratory. Speakers who had previously been mediocre when addressing the House in English now metamorphosed into Kiswahili Churchills. On the other hand, great parliamentary performers in the English language were now reduced to halting proportions in Kiswahili. The Kenyan Parliament became substantially Africanized simply by being linguistically Swahilized. Kiswahili had itself been, as we indicated, a progeny of a marriage between Islam and indigenous African culture. Kiswahili had now been recruited to serve in a marriage between African political culture and an imported Western institution. The triple heritage of the African continent was still unfolding.

There were indeed anomalies in this Africanization of the Kenyan Parliament. Although the debates and discussions during the last years of Kenyatta's rule were indeed conducted in Kiswahili, the legislation came before Parliament drafted in the English language. The language of Kenyan mass politics had indeed become Kiswahili, but the language for interpreting the Kenyan Constitution was still English. The language of electioneering for Parliament had become mainly Kiswahili, but the constitutional requirements for standing for election demanded competence in English but not in Kiswahili. The triple heritage in Kenya was imperfectly amalgamated, but the process of integration was still under way.

In Kenya and elsewhere in Africa the most important preservative of the indigenous element in the triple heritage has been ethnicity. Indeed, ethnicity has served as a kind of refrigerator for African culture throughout the continent, keeping at least some African values relatively fresh and enduring. The colonial experience had indeed destroyed many of the organized institutions of African societies. It had undermined traditional structures. But colonialism had fallen short of destroying substantial areas of

African culture. Ethnicity, or allegiance to one's ancestral ethnolinguistic unit, has at times been deepened rather than destroyed by the aftermath of colonialism and the impact of the new territorial boundaries upon ethnic rivalries for scarce resources.

On the one side we do witness the negative consequences of ethnicity in the face of ethnic nepotism in the sharing of African resources and ethnic malpractices in politics and the economy. On the other hand, there is still what Kenya's Tom Mboya used to call "positive tribalism"—the resilience of the African heritage, the values of collective responsibility and the principles of sharing, the traditions of respect for the aged and concern for the young, the imperatives of hospitality and the bonds of the extended family. Ethnicity has been the underlying preservative of these residual cultural orientations.

But not all ethnic cultures will survive in Africa. Indeed, the great majority of them are probably under sentence of death, challenged both by the corrosive power of Western culture and the pull of more dominant indigenous cultural units. Many of the smaller African languages are similarly condemned to die out. In East Africa, for example, Kiswahili might well facilitate this demise of smaller languages. Many such languages will fail to attract publishers for whatever works they may produce. Investment in the printed word will increasingly favor the wider linguistic markets. Smaller linguistic civilizations are bound to fall by the wayside.

But that itself may be a process of integration. The minimum stage in the process of integration is the stage of bare coexistence, when two cultural or ethnic units are bounded together within the same political community or country but hardly know about each other. There may be small "tribes" in Northern Nigeria, for example, that know almost nothing about specific small "tribes" in Southern Nigeria.

The next stage in the process of integration is that of contact. In this stage of contact the groups are beginning to be at least aware of each other and are evolving some minimum communication between each other. Such communication can take a wide variety of forms, ranging from remote trading relations to migratory patterns.

Contact at a certain level begins to unleash the forces of competition. This is itself a distinct stage in the integrative process, often involving deeper political and economic interpenetration.

The fourth stage is that of confrontation, when competition is acute and defensive mechanisms in the two cultures or two peoples have been invoked at different psychological and practical levels.

The confrontation could lead either to cultural conquest, on one side, or to cultural compromise. In the case of cultural conquest, one of the cultures asserts supremacy and begins to eliminate, subjugate, or incorporate the "lesser" cultures. Kiganda culture in Uganda was beginning to have that effect on the subordinate culture of the Basoga when the British arrived towards the end of the nineteenth century.

A compromise stage in integration is a kind of cultural *modus vivendi*. The competing cultures have found a new basis of living with each other on the principle of "live and let live." Compromise can sometimes occur after a period of partial conquest.

The final stage in integration is coalescence, when the cultures merge and become indistinguishable over time, creating a new collective synthesis.

At the level of national integration most of Africa is at the pre-compromise stage, but instances of the different stages are discernible in regional and local contexts. The gods of African cultures are not yet at peace with each other.

CONTINENTAL CULTURAL CONGRUENCY

What should continue to be borne in mind is that integration in Africa is not merely a local, regional, and national process; it is also a continental phenomenon. This continental integration is aided on one side by cultural congruence, or prior similarity in cultural traits among African peoples, and on the other side by cultural diffusion, the spread of certain cultural traits from one African people to another.

Ethnic consciousness, for example, is a case of cultural congruence all over the African continent. The Baganda have not learned to be ethnically conscious as a result of the influence of, say, the Yoruba; yet the ethnic consciousness helps to make the Baganda understand the Yoruba better as a people similar to themselves. The elder tradition in Africa is also one of the survivors of prior similarity in African cultures, with particular respect to the aged. In politics it has sometimes helped to strengthen the legitimacy of a particular leader, if other circumstances permit. For example, Jomo Kenyatta in Kenya managed to use the sanctity of the elder tradition to strengthen reverence for himself. The very title of *Mzee*, meaning elder or old man, became a title of reverence and a term of respectful affection for the head of state from 1963 when Kenya became independent to 1978 when Kenyatta died. The elder tradition manifests itself in other ways in different parts of Africa, though sometimes it is undermined by the rise of the Westernized intelligentsia with its new credentials and quest for influence in situations of cultural fluidity.

Often closely related to the elder tradition is the patriarchal tradition. But there are important differences. The elder tradition is, in the final analysis, an elevation of the accumulated wisdom of age as against youth. The partriarchal tradition includes such an elevation, but it is also an elevation of the judgment of men as against women in public affairs. The elder tradition is a form of positive discrimination on the basis of age; while the patriarchal tradition is sometimes a case of discrimination on the basis of gender. Again patriarchy is a matter of cultural congruence all over Africa and, of course, in much of the rest of the world.

The warrior tradition idealizes martial virtues and the culture of combat. It is arguable that military coups in Africa have sometimes resulted in a partial resurrection of the warrior tradition in African political culture. Beneath the uniform that an African soldier wears as a member of a modern army there may be a rustic ethnic warrior, influenced and conditioned at least as much by the culture of combat of his traditional ancestry as by any vestige of Sandhurst pretensions.[4]

The sage tradition is also a case of cultural congruence. This is the elevation of the virtues of the mentor, or *marabout*, or what in Indian culture is the *guru*. One of the more striking illustrations of the sage tradition in Africa concerns the role and status of Mwalimu Julius K. Nyerere of Tanzania. The very little *Mwalimu* means mentor or teacher. On the one hand the title echoes Nyerere's previous career as a school teacher, but, more importantly, it signifies both reverence and political affection for him as a guide and mentor of his people. Nyerere has often converted the whole nation into a classroom and the political process into a blackboard to illustrate telling lessons. Léopold

Senghor of Senegal (a contributor to this volume) was also a good illustration of the sage tradition at work in African politics.

Once again a cultural trait drawn originally from the indigenous part of the triple heritage is now wearing the guise of the Western part of that heritage. Even the urge that African presidents have sometimes shown of being philosopher kings is itself an illustration of the sage tradition. Founder presidents especially have at times indulged in extensive theorizing and philosophizing. Illustrations of Africa's philosopher presidents include not only Nyerere and Senghor but also Nkrumah of Ghana, Kenneth Kaunda of Zambia, Sékou Touré of Guinea, and for a while Milton Obote of Uganda.

Also illustrative of the sage tradition is the partiality which some African presidents have shown not only for receiving honorary doctorates but also for using them as day-to-day titles. Dr. Obote, Dr. Kaunda, Dr. Nkomo, and Dr. Nkrumah are all illustrations of honorary doctorates used as day-to-day titles of learned authority.

An important exception is that of General Yakubu Gowon, former head of state of Nigeria. A recipient of a doctorate from the University of Cambridge, *Honoris Causa*, Gowon nevertheless decided, upon being overthrown from power, to pursue academic education in its own right. He went to Warwick University in England as an undergraduate in political science, to the consternation and derision of many of his more status-conscious compatriots in Nigeria. Pictures of Gowon carrying a tray in a cafeteria queue at Warwick were interpreted by some as an insult to the honor of Nigeria. But this political figure of immense personal humility persevered in his pursuit of undergraduate studies even when he was later accused of being implicated in the attempted coup which led to the assassination of his successor as head of state, General Murtala Mohammed.

In 1981, on Nigeria's independence day, Gowon was granted a pardon by President Shehu Shagari. But Gowon delayed his return to Nigeria, partly because he was then working for his Ph.D. at the University of Warwick.

In 1982 I received a message from a Polish professor who had interviewed Gowon that Gowon was interested in reestablishing contact with me academically. My conversation with him in July 1982 revealed, among other things, that he was still serious in completing his doctoral program at Warwick before returning home to Nigeria. He was convinced that if he returned before completing his thesis on the Economic Organization of West African States (ECOWAS), he would never find time to complete it later. This remarkable leader, who had once been honored as head of state by the University of Cambridge with an honorary doctorate, was now about to vindicate himself academically with a Ph.D. Whether Gowon still has political ambitions and his academic credentials are designed to strengthen his image as a sage remain among the more tantalizing questions about his future in Nigeria.

Less easily compatible with humility is the monarchical tradition in African political culture. This royal tendency has manifested itself even among rulers drawn from ethnic groups which did not have kings before the colonial period. The tendency includes a display of pomp and splendor in presidential styles, a quest for aristocratic effect, a leaning towards ostentatious consumption and behavior, and an effort to both sacralize authority and personalize power. Even such relatively radical African leaders as Kwame Nkrumah betrayed this monarchical tendency, combining both pomp and royal piety. His very title, the *Osagyefo* (the redeemer), was part of the effort to sacralize authority and imply a divine right within the presidency.

Rulers like Felix Houphouët-Boigny of the Ivory Coast have built palaces in royal style. The extreme case of the monarchical tendency in post-colonial Africa was the phenomenon of Central African Emperor Jean-Bédel Bokassa who literally attempted to establish a new royal house in modern Africa with a coronation of Napoleonic proportions. Less literally, Kenyatta's family in Kenya came to be known as "the royal family."

These then are some of the cultural traits which constitute cultural congruence between the ways of life of different African societies. These are some of the prior similarities which have helped to put a stamp of shared Africanity among groups separated by huge geographic distances.

CONTINENTAL CULTURAL DIFFUSION

But cultural integration and convergence on the continental scale are not only based on prior similarities; they are also based on cultural diffusion before colonial rule, during colonial rule, and since independence. Sometimes the diffusion is as a result of conscious policy. The novels of Chinua Achebe of West Africa and Ngugi wa Thiong'o of East Africa are read and studied in schools from Maiduguri to Mombasa.

But there is also cultural diffusion independent of policy. Africans are dancing to the music of Zaire from Lusaka to Lagos. One sees West African dress in the streets of Dar es Salaam. And Nigeria's playwright, Wole Soyinka, has championed the adoption of Kiswahili as Africa's continental *lingua franca*.

There is indeed cultural pan-Africanism already under way. Africans are reading each other's books, performing each other's plays, borrowing each other's ideas, wearing each other's dress, and sharing each other's feelings on at least some issues.

But if Africa does want this cultural diffusion to be less accidental and more purposeful, less a product of blind social forces and more of a response to policy, Africa would have to be selective on a rational basis. Which of Africa's different dress cultures should be encouraged and disseminated all over the continent? There seems little doubt that the best, most sophisticated, and sometimes most elaborate indigenous dress culture in Africa is West African. It would make sense to disseminate West Africa's dress heritage more purposefully to other parts of the continent. This diffusion of at least West African shirts is already taking place, from Dodoma to Durban. But a concrete policy of adopting West African dress culture as pan-African would help to disseminate what is best in Africa's patterns of attire.

In popular music within Africa it would also make sense to build on strength. The music of Zaire has, as we indicated, already spread its influence to other parts of the continent. Should that music now be adopted as pan-African music, encouraged in dance halls and schools, in concert halls and on radio waves, from Blantyre to Ougadougou? There is a case for letting Africa respond to the rhythms of Zaire.

Eastern Africa has already produced the most pan-African indigenous language to have emerged so far—Kiswahili. Should we now respond to Wole Soyinka's trumpet call—and adopt Kiswahili as a language of continental communication? Should every African schoolchild from Harare to Cotonou be encouraged to learn

Kiswahili? Should there be a speedy training of teachers for that purpose all over the continent?

Southern Africa's contribution should in fact be technology. This is partly because parts of Southern Africa are today the most technologically advanced areas of Africa but also because the history of technological sophistication in Southern Africa did not begin with the coming of the white man. Those ancient walls of Zimbabwe are still standing there, bricks without mortar defying the elements for over six hundred years, a unique achievement in engineering.

But while these ancient Shona kingdoms demonstrated accomplishments in civil engineering, nineteenth-century Zulus demonstrated accomplishments in military organization and innovation. Technological credentials of Southern Africa therefore extend from the structures of the Shona to the conquests of Shaka. The emergence of superior European technology became almost an extension of a preexistent indigenous innovativeness in Southern Africa. It is for this reason that the Africa of the future should look especially to its southern tip for technological leadership, the pan-Africanization of scientific know-how.

This is not to deny the ancient technological achievements of West Africa, the region nearest to a major technological take-off, which became the major hunting ground for European slave trade. The relative devastation of those stages of European penetration and the considerable depopulation of West Africa in the wake of three centuries of slave raiding probably aborted the technological take-off presaged by early West African utilization of metal. Whatever the cause of technological abortion in West Africa, subsequent centuries gradually tilted the technological balance in favor of Southern Africa. It is therefore arguable that while European penetration of West Africa was dysfunctional to the technological development of the region in the final reckoning, European penetration of Southern Africa helped to lay the foundations of future technological leadership by the region. The two elements of the triple heritage of Africa, the indigenous and the Western, may in time fuse technologically against the shadow of great Zimbabwe and against the background of the historical achievements of the Zulu.

There has of course been a moral and human cost in Southern

Africa. While West Africa was indeed the region which suffered most from the slave trade, Southern Africa has been the region most humiliated by racism. However, while slave raiding is totally destructive of the region subjected to it, European settlers' racism has constructive as well as destructive consequences. Industrially and economically it has been those countries most intensely subjected to settler colonialism that have been the most "advanced." In the Maghreb this has meant Algeria; in East Africa this has so far meant Kenya; in Southern Africa this has meant South Africa and Zimbabwe; in Portuguese speaking Africa this has meant Angola. The correlation is persistent that settler colonialism contributes to greater industrialization, with a political and moral cost because of settler racism. The positive legacy of white settler colonialism is also part of Africa's triple heritage, part of the Western component within that heritage. Its technological manifestation in Southern Africa should be given a chance to yield pan-African dividends.

As for North Africa, what parts of its heritage should in fact be pan-Africanized? Karl Marx started from the premise that man has to eat in order to live. From this he drew the conclusion that economics is the primary force in human behavior. Starting from the same premise that man has to eat in order to live, the gourmet may conclude that, if economics is the heart of civilization, a good cuisine is its stomach. An elegant food culture becomes the very spice of life.

Of all the cuisines of the African continent, perhaps the one which most deserves to be continentalized is the North African cuisine. As it is diffused to other parts of the African continent, it may have to incorporate new elements distinctive to the other different regions, new variations. But on the whole it is arguable that every African culture should recognize two cuisines, its own local one and the North African variety.

But North Africa is also strong in architecture, bearing the stamp of succeeding conquerors but also betraying a distinctiveness of its own. In addition to the cuisine, there may be a case for letting North African architecture compete more extensively with the rest of the African continent, responding to local variations and adjustments while maintaining a pan-African consistency. If in technology the fusion is between the indigenous and Western legacies of Africa's triple heritage, in architecture the fusion might become an interplay between the Islamic and indigenous branches of the triple heritage.

These then are the different dimensions of continental convergence in Africa, the different forces of cultural pan-Africanism yearning for a coherent policy. Were those policies to be adopted, future generations of Africans might at least have the option to dress West African, speak the tongue of the East, dance to the rhythms of the center, enjoy the cuisine of the North against the splendor of its architecture, and be productive under the stimulation of a technological tradition which will one day mate the achievements of white South Africans with the prior triumphs of the walls of Zimbabwe.

LUGARD VERSUS LENIN

But culture is not merely concerned with identity and its many levels; it is also concerned with a sense of direction and with development. Particularly important in post-colonial Africa has been the dilemma of development and the search for an ideology of transformation. The euphoria of the early years of independence has been replaced by the agonies of failure. Political instability is widespread; food production has declined; numbers of refugees are expanding. As the saying goes, the old revolution of rising expectations has indeed been replaced by a new revolution of deepening frustrations.

In the face of these negative tendencies, there has been a groping for alternative strategies of development, a search for ultimate answers. At least among the intelligentsia in Africa socialism has become increasingly attractive as a way out of the present morass.

There have of course been socialist and even Marxist experiments already in different parts of Africa. One of the more striking factors is that in the first twenty years of Africa's independence not a single former British colony went Marxist. On the other hand, virtually all former Portuguese colonies went Marxist at least for a while after independence. The former French colonies were somewhere in between. The first one to acquire independence, Guinea (Conakry) tried to be Marxist-Leninist under President Sékou Touré.

One question which arises is why former British colonies, in some cases endowed with a bigger working class than either French speaking or Portuguese speaking countries, have nevertheless fallen considerably shorter of radical socialism than have the countries once ruled by Latin imperial powers. Could it be that one of the consequences of the British approach to colonial rule was to make former British colonies less hospitable to Marxism than they might otherwise have been? Has the legacy of Lord John Frederick Lugard, the architect of Britain's policy of Indirect Rule, made the lure of Vladimir Lenin more resistible?

Two African countries which may be the least likely to go Marxist voluntarily in a free election are probably Nigeria and Uganda. Those two countries are also the best illustrations of Britain's policy of Indirect Rule and the most directly affected by the life and service of Lord Lugard. After all, Lugard directly participated in ruling both countries. The question which arises is whether this apparent resistance to socialism manifested in both Nigeria and Uganda is part of Lugard's legacy or whether the correlation is accidental.

There is evidence to suggest that the policy of Indirect Rule helped to consolidate, on the one side, indigenous organized institutions of governance and, on the other side, deepen ethnic consciousness in British colonies. To put it in another way, Indirect Rule both helped to preserve neofeudal institutions and helped to sustain ethnic nationalism. In Nigeria and Uganda the preservation of neo-feudal institutions and ethnic consciousness both militated against future attempts to inaugurate socialist movements.

In Uganda the neofeudal institutions included the monarchical offices of Buganda, Bunyoro, Ankole, Toro, and to some extent Busoga. In Nigeria the neofeudal institutions included the emirates of the North and the elaborate chiefly offices of Yorubaland. Indirect Rule was Britain's attempt to utilize preexistent native institutions, many of which in Nigeria and Uganda were neofeudal.

These neofeudal institutions were themselves a contributory factor to ethnic consciousness, although there were also other factors behind ethnic identity and ethnic nationalism in places like Buganda, Yorubaland, and Hausaland.

Ethnic consciousness in Africa has often militated against class consciousness. A Yoruba peasant is a Yoruba first and a peasant second when the political chips are down in Nigeria as a whole. Similarly, a Buganda peasant is a Buganda first and a peasant second when the country is in a tumult. All attempts to mobilize the underprivileged of either Nigeria or Uganda on the basis of class have, on the whole, failed in the wake of ethnic rivalries.

Chief Obafemi Awolowo of Yorubaland adopted socialist rhetoric and attempted to rally all the underprivileged of Nigeria behind his banner of fundamental social transformation. But when he turned back to look who was following him, it turned out they were all fellow Yorubas regardless of social class—rather than all the underprivileged of Nigeria regardless of ethnic background.

Milton Obote of Uganda attempted a move to the left in his first political incarnation before Idi Amin's military coup. On balance, Obote's socialist experiment from 1969 to 1971 enjoyed little support in Uganda outside his own immediate ethnic supporters and a few intellectuals from other ethnic groups.

Among the most opposed to socialism in both Uganda and Nigeria are precisely those groups among whom Britain's policy of Indirect Rule was at its most successful. Both the Buganda in East Africa and the Hausa-Fulani in West Africa are among the strongest bulwarks against socialism. Lugard's Indirect Rule had helped to preserve in both countries their inner African authenticity. And it may well be precisely this residual and to some extent fundamentally resilient authenticity which has created a problem for the legacy of Lenin as contrasted with the legacy of Lugard. On the issue of socialism and ethnicity two of the traditions of the triple heritage are in opposition with each other. Radical Westernism and ancestral Africanity are to some extent part of the war of the gods in Africa.

On examining the role of religion more closely in this opposition to socialism, an intriguing contrast emerges between Northern Nigeria and Buganda. In Northern Nigeria part of the distrust of socialism emanates from the Islamic tradition and its own suspicion of radical alien ideologies. The music of the muezzin is more compulsive than the trumpet call of the Marxist.

But in Buganda, socialism's greatest constraint is not devout Islam but pious Christianity. The atheistic element in Marxism is sometimes inflated in the interplay between politics and religion in Uganda. A tradition among the churches in Uganda to denounce socialism as dangerously ungodly made things difficult for Obote when he attempted a move to the left before he lost power to Idi Amin, and it may have contributed to his attempt to play down socialism in his second political incarnation after the fall of Amin.

Paradoxically both Islam in Northern Nigeria and Christianity in Buganda are part of the dialectical legacy of Lord Lugard and Britain's policy of Indirect Rule. They are two strands in Africa's triple heritage but both in alliance against radical forces of transformation. The ghosts of Lord Lugard and Vladimir Lenin have looked at each other, eyeball to eyeball, in a tense confrontation over the destiny of former British Africa. For the time being it has been Lenin who has blinked, wavered, and at least temporarily floundered.

CONCLUSION

We have attempted in this essay to identify some of the cultural forces which have been at play in Africa's tumultuous political evolution, especially since independence. A central part of the picture is the triple heritage of Africa encompassing the legacy of indigenous values and beliefs, the legacy of Islamic civilization, and the legacy of the Western impact. Africa's history is partly the autobiography of its culture, the self-revelation of its gods both in conflict and in concord. In recent times there has been the quest for a civilizational synthesis, as Africanity, Islam, and Westernism have sought a point of fusion.

But against the background of newly invented nation-states there has also been the fundamental agony of malintegration. Cultural forces have sought to narrow the gap between African nationalism and African nationhood, between the state as a system of authority and the nation as a principle of identity.

There has also been the trend towards continental convergence and pan-African integration and the need to define cultural policies which range from pan-African dress to pan-African architecture, from a pan-African language to pan-African music, from a pan-African cuisine to a pan-African technology.

Finally there is the need for a developmental ideology; and yet the need is constrained by the contradictions of the triple heritage, including the dialectic between the legacy of Lugard and the legacy of Lenin.

If history is the autobiography of God, could culture be the autobiography of Man?

NOTES

1. Kwame Nkrumah, *Consciencism* (London: Heinemann, 1964), pp. 68-70.

2. *Ibid.*

3. Kwame Nkrumah, *Ghana: The Autobiography of Kwame Nkrumah* (Edinburgh and New York: Nelson, 1957).

4. See Ali A. Mazrui, ed., *The Warrior Tradition in Modern Africa* (The Hague: Mouton, 1978). See also Ali A. Mazrui, *Soldiers and Kinsmen in Uganda: The Making of a Military Ethnocracy* (London: Sage Publications, 1974).

4
JOHN MBITI

Man in African Religion

USE OF THE TERM "AFRICAN RELIGION"

"African Religion" is used here to refer to the indigenous religious system and life of African peoples. It developed gradually, without particular founders, systematic doctrines, or written scriptures. African religion is fully integrated into the total life of the people so that it exerts its influence and presence in their total worldview. Each African society has its ways of life, some of which differ from, or resemble, those of other African peoples. For this reason we find a number of common elements of African Religion in many societies; we also find certain differences. I will use the singular, religion, in order to embrace the basic religiosity which has its diversities and commonalities. Scholars who wish to speak in the plural, African religions, have my sympathies. One can compare African Religion to the baobab tree—an enormous tree with many branches, but with a single trunk which is sometimes difficult to see when the tree is in full foliage.

This chapter under separate copyright © 1985 by John Mbiti. Permission to quote from *Prayers in African Religion* by John Mbiti given by Orbis Books, Maryknoll, N.Y., and SPCK (Society for Promoting Christian Knowledge), London. "The Fulani Creation Story" first appeared in *Black Orpheus* No. 19, March 1966. It was reprinted in *Poems of Black Africa*, edited by Wole Soyinka, and is quoted here with thanks to Martin Secker and Warburgh, Ltd., London.

MYTHOLOGICAL ORIGIN OF MAN

According to African myths of origin, man appears first on the world scene as a religious being. I use the term "man" generically to include male and female. Man does not emerge as a politician, nor as a scientist, nor as an astronaut. These other aspects of his being and his life developed later. We have thousands of myths all over Africa, depicting the emergence of man and his early state of existence. I wish to quote one of these myths as an illustration of this point. It is the Fulani creation story. The Fulani people live in a number of West African countries, including Senegal, Nigeria and Cameroon.

> At the beginning there was a huge drop of milk.
> Then Doondari (God) came and he created the stone.
> Then the stone created iron;
> And iron created fire;
> And fire created water;
> and water created air.
>
> Then Doondari descended the second time.
> And he took the five elements
> And he shaped them into man.
>
> But man was proud.
> Then Doondari created blindness, and blindness defeated man.
>
> But when blindness became too proud,
> Doondari created sleep, and sleep defeated blindness;
> But when sleep became too proud,
> Doondari created worry, and worry defeated sleep;
> But when worry became too proud,
> Doondari created death, and death defeated worry.
> But when death became too proud,
> Doondari descended for the third time,
> And he came as Gueno, the eternal one,
> And Gueno defeated death.[1]

According to this myth, man is a physical composition of stone, iron, fire, water, and air. But these five elements are put together by God (Doondari) to shape man. There is no question here and in other African myths that man is a created being, created by God—however that notion of God may be formulated or understood. We observe, further, that man has an integral relationship with the physical environment—man is tied to the material world around him—the earth, the soil, the minerals, the fire, the water, and the air. He has an inbuilt dependence on these elements.

Another major aspect of man's nature is his moral being. That is brought out forcefully in this Fulani myth when it says, "But man was proud," and so were his experiences of sleep, and worry, and death. Man's moral responsibility is driven home in these images of what happened to these otherwise normal activities of his body. This finality of man's life is death—but death is ultimately put under subjection by God who, accordingly, descends the third time, and defeats death. This assumes, then, that man is set free from the forces which defeated him, namely, blindness, sleep, worry, and death, whose original cause is man's pride, man's moral and spiritual sickness.

MAN AS A RELIGIOUS BEING DEPENDENT ON GOD

This Fulani myth illustrates clearly and beautifully the view in African Religion that man emerges as a religious being, that his experiences in life are basically religious, and that the world in which he lives is also religious. African Religion underlines the humanness of man vis-a-vis that other reality from which he derives his origin, as well as his continuing well-being. That reality is named God in African societies. I have not come across a single African people who do not have knowledge of God. In many African languages the word for God means Creator, or Father, or Mother, or Originator, thus emphasizing the nature of God as the Origin of all things including man.

This humanness of man, in contrast to the otherness of God, is well illustrated in a statement of the Fang people of Cameroon and Gabon. They say:

> Nzame (God) is on high, man is below!
> Nzame is Nzame, man is man:
> Each to himself, each in his dwelling.[2]

However, man is entirely dependent on God for his life and well-being. This comes out clearly in a prayer statement from the Zulu of South Africa, by means of which the wisdom of the forefathers is taught to the subsequent generations.

> The Source of being is above,
> Which gives life to men;
> For men are satisfied,
> And do not die of famine,
> For the Lord gives them life,
> That they may live prosperously.[3]

From these illustrations, a portrait of man as a religious being emerges. His mythological origin is religious—created by God, however the creation stories may vary. His continuing existence is religious—he depends on God. He has ethical responsibility in the world, since he is a human being and not an automaton. These basic concepts of man in African Religion come out beautifully in a prayer used by the Adhola people of Uganda, when they make a sacrifice to God. They pray:

> O God of our forefathers:
> All our lives depend on you
> And without you we are nothing.
> It is you who look after wealth:
> Give us plenty of good harvest,
> Rain and wealth and children.
> Without you we can't live
> Because we shall have neither food to eat
> Nor water to drink.
> You are the source of life.
> You protected us on our journey to this fertile land.
> Where we came from we don't know but you know.
> You are the God of wars and fights:
> Protect us against anyone who wants to harm us,
> Especially here in my home.
> Here is your present![4]

MAN IN SOCIETY

Relationships

The image of man as a religious being is not just an abstract image. It has living and ongoing ramifications in society. We look at these further.

Man is man in society, the center of which is the family. The concept of the family has both horizontal and vertical dimensions. Relationships are counted on the basis of blood, marriage, and sometimes ritual or mystical establishments (such as membership in initiation groups, people bound together by oath or other solemn acts, or "blood brotherhoods" formed through ritual exchange of blood between individuals). Consequently a person can have several fathers, mothers, brothers, uncles, wives, husbands, and so on, in accordance with the wide network of kinship. For example, in my language Kikamba, which is spoken by about two million people in Kenya, we have more than one hundred kinship and relational terms. When two people meet for the first time, they go through the intriguing exercise of working out the kind of kinship relationship existing between them. They assume that they are somehow related to each other as human beings. Once they establish what form of relationship exists between them, they begin to relate to each other within the framework of that relationship. So, they may tease each other, they may call each other brother or sister, they may regard each other as mother and child, or as in-laws, and the rest of their conversation with/and attitude toward each other, will be framed accordingly. Through these kinship links, they establish the humanity which exists between them. There is not only a social but also a moral relationship between them.

The Departed Or The Living Dead

According to African Religion, the family is composed of three levels of man's being, that is, the departed members, the living, and those yet to be born. Without these three levels the individual is not complete and society is not complete. The individual exists because others existed before him. The individual is tied by a mystical chain to the departed and to those yet to be born. The departed still exist through those who are living as well as in the world of the departed. Among most African people it is held that the departed are present in the physical surroundings of their living relatives. They have been buried in the ground on the compound or sometimes in the houses where they have lived and died. So the living are literally walking on the graves of the departed. The living acknowledge the presence and continuity of the departed through various acts of remembrance and fellowship—like libation, donation of small bits of food, mentioning of their name, invocations and rituals, naming of children after the departed, and endeavoring to fulfill requests made by the departed before or after their death. The relationship between the living and the departed members of the family is generally a very active one, though more noticeable among farming communities than among pastoral and nomadic communities.

What is said about the Yoruba of Nigeria can be said about many other African peoples. For the Yoruba,

> the ancestors constitute the closest link between the world of men and the spirit-world and they are believed to be keenly interested in the welfare of their living descendants. They exercise protective and disciplinary influences on their children. The ancestors expect their descendants to care for them by making offerings of food and drinks. They are regarded as presiding spiritually over the welfare of the family. The living have the confidence that they live in a world in which their ancestors are interested and over which they are watching.[5]

Whether this relationship between the living and the departed is understood literally or symbolically is neither here nor there. The important point about it is that man has a participation in the invisible dimension of reality, and that his humanness is not destroyed by the forces of death. The affection, the care, the concern, the love, and the generosity of the living reach out not only to the fellow human beings in the horizontal dimension but also to those who have entered the vertical dimension—the departed who are kept alive in the memories and affection of their descendants. For this, among other reasons, I coined the term "the living dead" to describe that invisible population of society, according to African Religion. Man has roots, and these roots are living roots; they are not dead; they have not withered.

Those Yet To Be Born

The family is also at the level of those who are not yet born. These are the buds, the flowers, the seeds in all of us. They are planted in our loins, in our reproductive system. They have a right to participate in full humanness. As long as they are still in the loins, they have no shape, they have no form, they have not come into actual existence. For this reason, the living must unlock their reproductive system to free the unborn, to let them take shape and form, to let them participate in the community of human beings. The living have a duty to get married and to bear children. Otherwise there is no society. True humanness means participation in the continuation of life; it means letting others live, letting others become human beings. The Zulu believe that, after creating man, God commanded him to increase upon the earth. God told the first human beings:

> Let there be marriage among men,
> That there may be those who can intermarry
> That children may be born
> And men increase on earth![6]

Marriage and procreation are absolutely integral to the image of man. They are moral obligations for everyone, even if in actual reality not everyone can fulfill these obligations, but society finds means of ensuring that the obligations are fulfilled to a very high degree. Thus, society, as a corporate expression of humanness, fulfills these obligations and is thereby perpetuated.

The Individual

The individual also has his place in the wider community. Many African societies observe rites of passage which focus on important phases of individual life. Nevertheless, these rites are moments of renewal and rebirth for the wider community since it is the community and not the individual alone which observes them. Nature brings a child into the world, as an individual. But the community turns the child into a member of society, into an integral part of its own being. This process of making the individual a member of the human society begins even before the actual birth of the child.

In some societies, the first pregnancy of a wife is regarded as the final seal of marriage, the sign of her complete integration into the family and relations of her husband, as well as the integration of the husband into the circle of her kinship network. Pregnancy is not a private affair; it is a community concern. Each African people has its customs and observance surrounding the pregnant woman. One of these is that sexual relations cease between the husband and the expectant wife—in some cases immediately after pregnancy is noticed, in others only some months before delivery. There are taboos concerning the type of work an expectant wife may or may not do, the foods she may or may not eat, and the people with whom she may or may not communicate directly. Prayers may also be offered to God, to ensure the safety of the wife and baby; and in some societies she may carry protective religious objects. All these measures are physical, social, psychological, and ritual precautions to safeguard the expectant mother and baby. Thus, pregnancy involves husband and wife, family members and relatives, the community of the living and the departed, as well as God Himself.

The process of integration into the community of human beings accelerates after birth. For example, in many societies the placenta receives special handling: thus, it may be buried carefully in an uncultivated field, or it may be thrown into a flowing river, or it may be buried inside the house where the birth actually takes place. In some societies the umbilical cord is dried up and later tied around the neck of the child or kept carefully in the home. These different practices symbolize the physical separation of the child from the mother, in order that the child may now begin the process of belonging to the wider circle of human beings. The child, in effect, now dies to the mother's womb in order to be made alive in the community.

In some African societies this process is symbolically instituted after the birth of a baby. The mother and baby are kept in seclusion in the house or somewhere else, for periods ranging from a few days to a few months. During this period of seclusion, the mother and child are seen by only a few people, and great care is taken over them. When the period is over, they are brought out into the public at an occasion of great communal festivity and celebration. Seclusion has obvious physical value. But it is to give the wider community an opportunity to publicly receive the new baby—for the baby to be born afresh to the community, to be seen by its many mothers and fathers, its many aunts and uncles, brothers and sisters, to the nth degree of relationships.

Man in African Religion

The naming of the child is a further step in the process of integration. This is usually done at a ceremony at which relatives, family members, neighbors, and even passers-by may get together. It is an occasion for rejoicing and celebrating. Some names mark the weather conditions prevailing at the time of the child's birth; some names relate to the activities of the parents or of the community at the time; other names may link the child with departed members of the family; and other names may express prevalent feelings of the parents or family, such as thanksgiving and praise to God. As a rule, African names have specific meanings or reasons for their use, and most of these are profoundly religious.

In many African societies, there are initiation rites which take place before, or during, or immediately after adolescence. In these initiation rites the child or young person is actively participating in the process of integration into the community. These rites usually have a deep impact upon the young and have profound meanings for the community.

One of the commonest of the initiation rites is circumcision which is carried out on boys and in some cases on girls as well. Where this custom is observed, nobody can become a full member of society until the circumcision rite has been performed. The whole community gathers together for this important occasion, men for boys and women for girls; after the ceremony, the initiated young people are normally taken into seclusion. This may be in the forest or woods nearby, where special huts have been constructed for the use of the initiatees and their instructors. The period of seclusion may vary from a few days to even a year or slightly longer.

Initiation and seclusion are symbolic acts of cutting off the child from the life of childhood and physiological inactivity. The end of seclusion is the birth into the new life of adulthood and productivity. In some societies the young people even lose their original names and acquire new names. During seclusion they learn many things in preparation for responsibility in the community and in adulthood, such as history, religious rituals, matters of sex and marriage, and other responsibilities towards the wider community. Where initiation involves circumcisions, the blood which is shed from the sexual organs has strong symbolic meaning. It binds together those who have been circumcised at the same occasion; it links them mystically with the departed members of the community who are, so to speak, in the ground where they have been buried. Circumcision blood also establishes a special bond between people and land which is something of great importance for the identity of the community. Therefore, land—in the broad sense of the soil, the crops, the trees, the minerals and what lives on it—must be treated with great care, for it is sacred through the shedding of blood from the reproductive organs of life.

Initiation opens the gate to the next phase of life in the process of being human. That is marriage and procreation, which form the focus of existence. It is here where the departed, the living, and those yet to be born, all meet. Failure to participate in this central drama of life amounts to excommunication from human society, unless obvious and abnormal circumstances prevent the individual from participating. In marriage and procreation the community is born afresh, it is perpetuated, it is immortalized. Through marriage and procreation, the departed or the living dead are kept in memory, and death is kept some steps behind life. Marriage and procreation also widen the network of relationships in society, bringing together the relatives from both sides, with all the enrichment and obligations which accompany that sense of kinship.

Death is the last major phase in the life of the individual. While death obviously cuts off the individual from the physical community, it at the same time links him up with the invisible community of the departed. Usually elaborate funeral rites mark the death of a person, and in some societies these last over several months and years. They point to the belief that death does not terminate the existence of a person. The community which takes part in these rites shares in absorbing the sorrows and grief of the bereaved relatives, thus making them lighter to bear. The dead continue to exist in the hereafter, and people continue to have links with the departed members of the family, as we have earlier indicated. African people are very much aware of the spirit world, which they experience in a variety of ways, including dreams, visions of spirit beings, possession by spirit beings (of either departed members of the family or other spirits), or through divination and certain phenomena of nature.

MAN AND THE WORLD OF NATURE

While we have concentrated here on the life of man, it is important to point out that man, according to African Religion, also lives in the wider world of nature. The image of man would not be complete without his relation to nature. Man is, in a serious way, the priest of nature, the priest in the world of nature. He links nature to God and God to nature, since he has moral consciousness which other creatures in nature do not have. Man can personify nature in order to communicate with it, to solicit its help or even order it about for the sake of his own welfare. But man realizes that nature will not necessarily obey him blindly. Man must seek harmony with nature, in order to be sure to reap the full benefits from nature. African Religion recognizes clearly that, if man abuses nature, in return nature will strike back at him. In this case, man is not a master over nature to treat it as he wishes. Instead, man is the priest towards nature—soliciting its kindness and expressing respect towards it. Above and behind this personified nature is God, the Creator and keeper of all things. The following prayer is a concrete illustration of the wish and the need for harmony between man and nature. It puts man in an intensely religious relationship with nature and the world in which he lives. The prayer comes from the Didinga people in the Sudan. It is recited by the official keeper of the community's woods and forests. By means of personification, the prayer summons the earth to be kind, fertile, and generous to the people who dig, sow, and work on it: "Be fertile when they give little seeds to your keeping," says one of the lines in this prayer, in a beautiful expression of man's wish to be in harmony with the earth. In turn, man promises to show gratitude by slaughtering goats to redden the bosom of the earth. The prayer runs on, pleading with the trees, the rivers and waters as though they were intelligent realities.

Recited by "the Warden of the Forest," in the presence of God, the living, the departed, and the whole earth, it runs:

O Earth, wherever it be my people dig, be kindly to them. Be fertile when they give the little seeds to your keeping. Let your generous warmth nourish them and your abundant moisture germinate them. Let them swell and sprout, drawing life from you, and burgeon under your fostering care:

and soon we shall redden your bosom with the blood of goats slain in your honour, and offer you the first fruits of your munificence, first fruits of millet and oil of sesame, of gourds and cucumbers and deep-mashed melons.

O trees of the forest and glade, fall easily under the axe. Be gentle to my people. Let no harm come to them. Break no limb in your anger. Crush no one in your displeasure. Be obedient to the woodman's wishes and fall as he would have you fall, not perversely or stubbornly, but as his axe directs. Submit yourselves freely to my people, as this tree has submitted itself to me. The axe rings, it bites into the tough wood. The tree totters and falls. Before the lightning the tree falls headlong, precipitate, knowing neither direction nor guidance. But the woodman guides the tree where he wills and lays it to rest gently and with deliberation. Fall, O trees of the forest and glade, even as this tree was fallen, hurting no one, obedient, observant of my will.

O rivers and streams, where the woodman has laid bare the earth, where he has hewn away the little bushes and torn out encumbering grass, there let your waters overflow. Bring down the leafy mould from the forest and the fertilizing silt from the mountains. When the rains swell your banks, spread out your waters and lay your rich treasures on our gardens.

Conspire together, O earth and rivers: conspire together O earth and rivers and forests. Be gentle and give us plenty from your teeming plenty. For it is I, Lomingamoi of the clan Idots, who speaks, Keeper of the clan lands, Warden of the Forest.[7]

These are but a few aspects of man as portrayed in African Religion. Man is created and lives as a religious being, having a relationship with god and with nature. Man exists in society; the individual is related to others in horizontal and vertical directions. Man is also a moral being, with responsibilities to his fellow men and to nature at large. God, through nature, creates the individual in the mother's womb. But the individual is also further created by society, which integrates him into the wider social world and enables him to help perpetuate society. The political, economic, cultural, and scientific activities of man are all developments within the religious framework of the image of man. Man belongs to both the physical world and the spiritual world, to the visible as well as to the invisible worlds. These two worlds interact constantly. Man plays a role in this interaction, since he belongs to both worlds in a special way which no other creatures are privileged to enjoy.

NOTES

1. Wole Soyinka, ed., *Poems of Black Africa* (London: Heinemann, 1975), pp. 57ff. (Line 4 from the end reads "But *then* death. . . ." I have changed it here, to read "But *when* death," which makes better grammatical sense and conforms to other lines of similar construction in the story.)

2. John S. Mbiti, *The Prayers of African Religion* (London: SPCK, 1975; New York: Orbis Books, 1976), p. 143.

3. John S. Mbiti, *Concepts of God in Africa* (London: SPCK, 1970), p. 60.

4. Mbiti, *Prayers,* p. 145.

5. J. Omosade Awolalu, *Yoruba Beliefs and Sacrifices* (London: Longmans, 1979), p. 61.

6. H. Callaway, *The Religious System of the Amazulu* (London: Folklore Society of Great Britain, 1870), pp. 57ff.

7. Mbiti, *Prayers,* pp. 69f.

5
KWESI A. DICKSON

African Traditional Religion: Monotheism or Polytheism?

In *African Traditional Religion: A Definition*,[1] E. B. Idowu examines a number of terms used to describe African religions (idolatry, fetishism, animism) and concludes, "down the ages, peoples have worshipped without being preoccupied with finding names for their religions. It is the outsider, the observer, the investigator, the curious, the detractor or the busybody, who first supplied labels."[2] But almost as if Idowu had not intended to close the debate regarding labels, he himself endorses the use of monotheism as a descriptive term for African traditional religion. I would like to draw attention away from labels like monotheism and polytheism, because they distort our understanding of African religions. Yet the use of such terms is quite understandable. They are commonly used in Western religious literature.

From the Western point of view, polytheism, which involves the belief in more than one god, has often been considered the most appropriate term for African religions. There is undeniably a multiplicity of gods in the African pantheon (their number varies from one people to another), and this element first caught the attention of Western observers who, often with some justification, saw a god behind every bush. Among many African peoples, there is also the tradition that God once lived with human beings but then removed himself to the heavens to avoid being inconvenienced by some careless person's inconsiderate behavior. By doing so, God apparently left the governance of this world to a variety of gods and goddesses. Regular acts of worship at the shrines of the individual deities seemed, to Western observers, to rule out the real existence of one God in African religion.

The idea that African religions were polytheistic also fit Western preconceptions about the supposedly "primitive" nature of African society. Because a long tradition of Western scholarship, which includes such influential thinkers as David Hume and Jean-Jacques Rousseau, has regarded polytheism as the "most ancient religion of mankind," it was generally associated with "primitiveness" and considered to antedate monotheism.[3] This hypothesis coincided with the underlying assumptions of one branch which equated Christianity with Westernism and relegated all other religions to a subordinate position as the work of the devil. A noted exponent of the developmental approach was the German scholar Ernst Troeltsch, but aspects of it are also evident in the all too common practice of categorizing religions as major or minor, higher or lower, and Karl Marx's misleading idea that "primitive man's" religion was necessarily a nature religion.[4]

Western discussions about the plurality of gods in African religion have, however, been the subject of much comment by African writers who view this approach as misleading. For example, Idowu approvingly cites Paul Tillich, who defined polytheism as "a qualitative and not a quantitative concept. It is not a belief in a plurality of gods but rather the lack of a unifying and transcending ultimate which determines its character."[5] Using this definition as the basis for his argument, Idowu contends that African religion is not polytheistic because there is a "unifying and transcending ultimate" in the African pantheon; and this, he says, distinguishes it from the divine hierarchy of the Greeks who viewed their gods as belonging to the same rank and file. Although Idowu admits that the gods "can be treated, for practical purposes, almost as ends in themselves," he points out that there is a "unitary control of the created order by Deity," and for this reason, African gods (divinities or deities) do not have the stature and independence which would make them "resting places" rather than the "halfway houses" that they are.[6] According to him, the African system of divinely created order tends to reflect sociological patterns, each divinity being like a minister in charge of an administrative unit. In addition, they are intermediaries between God and man, having become the "conventional channels through which man believes that he should normally approach Deity."[7]

But if African divinities can be interpreted in this manner, why do its practitioners tend to look upon them as ends in themselves? Idowu blames this development on the priests, who have presumably vested these gods with boundless powers, making them appear to be ends in themselves and enabling them to mediate more effectively between Deity and man. Hence, Idowu concludes that African religion is essentially monotheistic, however qualified that term might be. Like the Ghanaian scholar, J. B. Danquah, who hypothesizes that the Akan knew God and God alone (worship of the divinities emerging later as a corrupting influence), Idowu is avowedly partial to Wilhelm Schmidt's theory of *Urmonotheismus*, or primitive monotheism.

Idowu's exposition draws attention to the importance of God in traditional African religions and helps explain the reality of that God—a reality that had been called into question by many Western observers, for even though the formal worship of God is not conspicuous, the spiritual force which God represents is clearly present in the world of man. However, arguments against polytheism seem to underemphasize certain fundamental strands in African systems of belief. For example, when Idowu contends that the world of spirits is patterned upon human social structures, he is suggesting that this relationship demonstrates how all worship is ultimately intended for God. But does the analogy really hold? In traditional societies, the chief might well be in control of most affairs, but not all matters are brought to his attention; subordinate powers make decisions without consulting him, and these decisions can be final and irrevocable. Therefore, in some situations at least, these lesser powers enjoy a certain autonomy, which is recognized by the community.

According to Idowu, it would be misleading to say that the gods were created; it would be more appropriate to say that they "came into being in the nature of things with regard to the divine ordering of the universe," and this is supposedly the reason why "all Akan divinities are called sons of Onyame."[8] But it must be pointed out that terms describing familial relationships are often used metaphorically. The Asante refer to the Earth Goddess as the "wife" of God (Onyame), but such an expression is undoubtedly meant to be understood in a figurative sense. Such terms must always be understood within the context of African languages, not the European languages into which they have been translated. For example, the Akan use the phrase "sons of God," but they do not use it for all the divinities. In particular, they use it when referring to the water divinities Tano, Bea, Bosomtwe (all three are rivers), and Bosompo (the sea). The God name Nyame (or Onyame, Nyankopan) can also be used in the sense of rain, so that "it is raining" can be expressed as *Nyame rota* (God is falling), because in Akan thought, God is associated with the sky, even though he is not, strictly speaking, a Sky God. Indeed, one of the Asante attributes of God is *Amosu*, giver of rain. Rain "gives" streams, rivers, and seas their fullness. Thus, the descriptive phrase "sons of God" makes clear the close link between God and the water deities, which in turn serve as intermediaries between God and man.

Two other expressions are used by the Akan to describe the divinities: *abrafoa* (executioners) and *akyeame* (linguists).[9] Medicine cults are often described as *abrafoa*, for they are believed to "execute" God's judgments on offenders, bringing about destruction and death. Such divinities are similar to ministers with delegated powers, but like the phrase "sons of Onyame," the expression *abrafoa* cannot be used indiscriminately for all divinities. The term *akyeame* also has a very specific referent. In traditional Akan life, the linguist serves the chief by making his judgments, views, and pronouncements known to the community; he may even act for the chief in his absence. When gods are referred to as *akyeame*, it would seem to indicate that they are intermediaries between God and man; but the designation *akyeame* does not necessarily mean that the gods have a permanent and immutable role as linguists. It simply means that they would play the linguist's role as a consequence of having been empowered to do so at a specific time; in other words, the designation has a situational reference. In all cases, it is necessary to situate ritual verbalizations within the African language context in order to comprehend their true meaning.

Like terms, prayers reveal the nature of the attitudes Africans adopt toward the spirit powers. Whether in formal worship where practitioners present their petitions or in informal situations where ejaculatory expressions are uttered to counter developments that pose a threat to the individual's or the community's well-being, prayer plays a conspicuous role in the African's religious life. In many Akan prayers, for example, God, the Earth Goddess, and several lesser divinities are invoked by the worshipper or ritual specialist, even though the petitions are addressed specifically to one of the divinities, as in the following excerpt from a "Thanksgiving Prayer for Safe Delivery at Ntoa-bea Shrine—Aburi":

> Tweduampan Kwame, Friday Earth, come and drink;
> River Densu, drink; Nsakye, drink; Akrama, drink.
> . . . .
> Saturday River Dum! Saturday River Dum!
> Saturday River Dum!
> Come and drink, deity Ntoa, my lord.
> Female Ntoa and male Ntoa, when we call one we call all.
> It is Akua Makaa who, with due respect,
> Has safely delivered without harm.
> She says today she is coming to thank you,
> And ask for life and abundant health;
> She requires you to get help from above for the child.
> She holds in her hands gin, sheep and chicken;
> With due respect, she is coming to perform her duty
> . . . .
> The child was named after you deity Ntoa;
> Therefore she is called Ntoabea.
> I beseech you,
> Any evil person who with evil eye looks at this child
> Or entertains evil thoughts against her,
> Let him be accursed.[10]

In this prayer, a mother expresses her gratitude for a safe delivery to Ntoa, one of the divinities, and supplicates "life and abundant health" for the child. The ceremony takes place at the shrine of Ntoa, who is addressed several times in the prayer, but other spirit powers like God ("Tweduampan Kwame") and Earth Goddess (Friday Earth) are also invoked. In fact, the petitioner specifically asks Ntoa "to get help from above for the child." Ntoa obviously belongs to the spirit world, but the phrase "help from above" suggests that, although "each category of (spirit) beings has its appointed functions in relation to the world of observable happenings,"[11] its power to fulfill that function can be intensified by support from a superior force. God too is invoked in this prayer, but there is reason to believe that he is the only possible source of relief. In essence, the invocation of the spirit powers is an acknowledgement of the petitioner's dependency upon the spirit world, and this acknowledgement sets the scene for petitions which may then be addressed to a particular deity.

Sometimes, however, prayers contain direct references to a line of communication leading from the petitioner through a deity to God. The following prayer is a petition to Tano, one of the water deities described by the Asante as "sons of God":

> Grandsire Twereduampan! Thursday Earth goddess!
> Grandsire River Tano, here is your fowl.
> One of your sons is journeying to the underworld
> To stay with the Supreme Being and the Ancestors.
> As custom demands,
> The corpse must be sent to his home town,
> To rest peacefully with Mother Earth;
> Hence the corpse must cross you (River Tano).
> We beg you, let him be carried home in safety.
> Let Twereduampan hear that he is proceeding to him.
> We are only begging you!
> To the health of us all.

The line "Let Twereduampan hear that he is proceeding to him" illustrates Tano's position in relation to God, for it suggests that informing God the corpse is on the way contributes to assuring its safe arrival: Tano could not but provide a safe passage, because the destination of the corpse is God. In this prayer, a petition is being made through a divinity to God.

But there is no justification for reading the same relationship into all prayers, for prayers exist in which there is no mention of superior powers. In such cases, the worshipper addresses his petitions to a specific divinity, in the belief that the divinity above has the power to grant petitions. If a deity is considered responsible for a particular calamity, that deity is thought to have the power to undo whatever evil chain of events has been set in motion by the calamity. For example the following prayer is addressed to Antoa Nyamaa, a stream deity:

> Antoa Nyamaa ee! Come and receive drink.
> With your leave, your granddaughter Adwoa Atta has fallen sick,
> And has now learnt that you are responsible for her sickness;
> That is to say, you have "got" her.
> River Nyamaa, she is a child; forgive her.
> She brings you sheep and gin to remove the disaster.
> Receive, and in your mercy
> Remove the sickness from her.
> Here are your eggs, and this is your mashed yam.
> By your grace, let her recover quickly.

There is no hint in these lines that the petitioner is consciously seeking to reach beyond Antoa Nyamaa to God; and if there is no specific mention of such an intention, it would be highly inappropriate for the observer to create one on hypothetical grounds.

By this time, it should be clear that terms like monotheism and polytheism confuse and possibly even distort the true nature of African traditional belief. To describe African religion as polytheistic would be justifiable, if one considered only the fact that it accommodates more than a single deity. Yet such a description draws attention away from the high regard Africans have for God, a regard which could easily justify characterizing African religion as qualifiedly monotheistic. It seems best, however, to allow traditional practices and expressions to speak for themselves, instructing us in a far more profound way than any labels ever could.

NOTES

1. E. B. Idowu, *African Traditional Religion: A Definition* (Mary Knoll, N. Y.: Orbis Books, 1973).

2. *Ibid.*, p. 136.

3. See Raffaele Pettazzoni, *Essays on the History of Religions*, trans. H. J. Rose (Leiden: E. J. Brill, 1954), pp. 1-2.

4. See Ernst Troeltsch, *The Absoluteness of Christianity and the History of Religions* (Atlanta: John Knox Press, 1971). The third edition of the original German was published in 1929. See also John Hick, *God and the Universe of Faiths* (London: Macmillan, 1973), p. 120; and Hans Küng, *On Being a Christian* (New York: Pocket Books, 1978), p. 92.

5. Idowu, *op. cit.*, p. 66.
6. *Ibid.*, p. 135.
7. *Ibid.*, p. 171.
8. *Ibid.*, p. 169.
9. K. K. A. Anti, "Relationship Between the Supreme Being and the Lesser Gods of the Akan" (Unpublished M.A. thesis, University of Ghana, 1978).
10. This prayer and the two which follow are quoted with slight modifications from Anti, "Relationship Between the Supreme Being and the Lesser Gods of the Akan," Appendices 3, 5, and 19.
11. R. Horton, "African Traditional Thought and Western Science, 1," *Africa* 37 (January 1967): 52.

6

LÉOPOLD SÉDAR SENGHOR
Translated by *RICHARD BJORNSON*

The Revolution of 1889 and Leo Frobenius

It was in 1936. Several years earlier a handful of young, black students—Africans and West Indians—had launched the *Négritude* movement in the middle of the Latin Quarter in Paris. We had no lack of arguments with which to attract our fellow Africans and Negroes of the diaspora to the Renaissance of Black Culture. There were jazz, blues, and dance, but above all there was Negro art, the expressive force of which had struck Picasso and artists from the Paris School—Tristan Tzara and certain surrealist poets—like an illumination. Yet we began to seek other even more striking arguments after we encountered Leo Frobenius.

His interest piqued by a review he read in the journal *Les Cahiers du Sud*, Aimé Césaire bought one of Frobenius' major works, *Histoire de la civilisation africaine*. It was a translation, published by Emmanuel Gallimard, of *Kulturgeschichte Afrikas*. After having read it, Césaire passed it on to me, and I still have that copy with his name on it in my library. To understand the joy which took hold of us as we read this book, it is necessary to go back in time—to the instruction given in all the "white man's schools," public or private, in the colonies.

FROM RATIONALISM TO POSITIVISM

I know of no better way to illustrate the nature of this instruction than by describing my own case as an example of it.

After my primary education in a Catholic mission school, I entered the Libermann Secondary School and Seminary at Dakar, where I took four years of classical studies, including French, Latin, and Greek as well as mathematics. The father director was an excellent teacher, but he thought (and told us) that we had no civilization. For that reason, we had to assimilate, slowly and by stages, the essence of European civilization, of which France, naturally, offered the best model—a model that can be reduced to the spirit of method and organization or, *ad libitum*, the clarity of conception and expression which Descartes epitomizes. Nevertheless, all my French instructors, from the Libermann Secondary School and Seminary to the Sorbonne, taught me to respect the genius of the Germans.

They also taught us to distrust the imagination and particularly the emotions: everything that distracted or beguiled rational thought, like imagery and rhythm, not to mention melody, were only fitting in poetry. Later, they held up Paul Valéry's prose as the ideal model for us to follow.

I said "later." Actually, in thinking back, not without sadness, to the "kingdom of childhood," to the Senegalese village where I grew up in the full joyfulness of life until the age of seven, I dared to challenge (to the father director's face) the idea that we were totally without civilization. As a matter of fact, I remembered the King of Sine paying a visit to my father, a large landowner, when we were still "under French protectorate"; I remembered the nobility of the gestures, the polite elegance of the words, and the generosity of the gifts which were exchanged. Above all, I remembered the young girls' polyphonic singing during the evening celebrations and the dances of the athletes, graceful black men whose movements were an expression of beauty. From the kingdom of childhood, I retained three essential elements of the Negro-African aesthetic, which had affixed its seal to much of twentieth-century aesthetics: the symbolic image; the melody of forms and movements, sounds and colors; and, finally, the rhythm of asymmetrical parallelisms.

At the end of the third year, the father director, convinced that I was an opponent of "Indo-European" civilization (or Albo-European, as I prefer to call it), expelled me kindly and with politeness from the Catholic secondary school seminary. During the course of my last year at the lycée, a public secondary school which would later become the Van Vollenhoven Lycée, I began to be initiated into the essence of European thought—its rationalism.

Despite the Revolution of 1889, which I will write about later, René Descartes continued to reign supreme in the philosophy class. At the end of the Renaissance, as we were taught, he broke with medieval scholastic tradition, reestablished links with science and Greco-Latin philosophy, and thereby gave form to the modern temper of mind. He was the creator of modern European rationalism, the one who renounced Greco-Latin mythology and Judeo-Christian theology to teach us that reason is in harmony with the reality of the world, enabling us to comprehend nature and to exercise our influence upon it.

Of course, other seventeenth- and eighteenth-century philosophers would critique, modify, nuance, or embellish Cartesian doctrine. I am thinking above all of the Germans—Gottfried Wilhelm Leibniz's intellectual rationalism, Immanuel Kant's symbiotic rationalism, and G. W. F. Hegel's dialectical rationalism. Nonetheless, all of them, including the English empiricism of John Locke and the experimentalist versions of it propounded by the two Bacons, Roger and Francis, would more or less share the Cartesian idealism and the philosophy of the *cogito*. Indeed, all who believe in a "genetic" harmony between reason and world share this rationalism.

The Nordic peoples, especially the Germans, would be the first to react against Cartesianism, and to do it coherently and consistently. I have already mentioned the English empiricists. In actuality, the Renaissance barely touched them. To restrict myself to Germany, what emerged and developed during the sixteenth century was not a renaissance but a mystical baroque soul, or, better yet, a contradictory baroque man unable to choose between intuition and understanding.

This deeply rooted movement of the German soul will return in the middle of the eighteenth century, at the very moment when the "Classics of Weimar," including Johann Wolfgang von Goethe, reign triumphant. This is the first wave of the Romantic movement with writers like the Schlegel brothers August Wilhelm and Friedrich, and Novalis, Joseph van Görres and the Grimm brothers, Jacob Ludwig Karl and Wilhelm. These are enemies of reason. That is why they reject the idea of progress and preach a return to collective intuitions, to what I would call an *Ur-Deutschland*, if I were to adopt Leo Frobenius' manner of speaking.

This is the current of thought to which the philosopher Johann Gottlieb Fichte belongs after his *Discourse to the German Nation*. Fichte sets out to overcome the contradiction, which he discovered in Kant, between rational knowledge (the photographic imaging of nature, as we might say today) and the freedom of the self. He conjectures a unity of the finite self and the non-self, or absolute—a unity which is mediated by the word. Before Hegel, Fichte is the one who rediscovers the dialectic which the Greeks had inherited from the Egyptians, that is, from the Africans. I will return to this point when I come to Frobenius.

The Germans linger in the Romantic era, while the French, who came to it late, abandon it rather quickly. In actuality, Cartesianism (at least its rationalism) persisted in France with the "encyclopédistes" and their "Dictionnaire *raisonné* des sciences, des arts, et des métiers," the publication of which began in 1851. (I emphasize the word "raisonné.") Their acknowledged goal had been to place religion, politics, and ethics under the control of discursive reason.

In any case, the Romantic movement only lasted for several decades in France. Victor Hugo published the "Preface" to his *Cromwell* in 1827, and Auguste Comte published his first "Cours de philosophie positive" in 1826. Actually, until the Revolution of 1889 and during the greatest part of what one French writer called "the stupid nineteenth century," positivism held sway in France along with its literary corollary, rationalism. And, as is well known, this new movement did not remain without influence in Europe—an influence which made itself felt in Germany under the colors of a certain "realism."

Positivism is a reinforcement of Cartesian rationalism and at the same time a degradation of it. Descartes' mathematical idealism, which included intuition as well as other elements, was replaced by the experimental method and the search for facts: "significant little facts," as Hippolyte Taine called them. In short, with the advent of positivism and naturalism, the intuitive soul fled and the spirit became mired in matter.

AT LAST, FROBENIUS ARRIVES

Yet, positivism and other naturalisms barely tinged the German spirit, as it manifested itself in Germany and Austria. Transcending the idealism of Kant's German successors, Arthur Schopenhauer's pessimistic theory of will-to-live heralded the arrival of Friedrich Nietzsche.

In the middle of the positivistic nineteenth century, Nietzsche had the merit of doing a Germanic rereading of the Greeks from the pre-Socratics to Aristotle. I suspect that he felt the need to pause in reading Aristotle's *Nichomachean Ethics,* and, in particular, to reflect upon the following phrase: "Now there are, in the soul, three dominant elements which determine truth and action: sensation (*aisthésis*), mind (*noûs*), and desire (*orexis*)." Before him, Descartes had already noticed this sentence, for in his *Meditations,* he tells us that the three essential faculties of man are "thinking," "desiring," and "feeling." According to Descartes, *noûs* almost solely applies to discursive reason (*dianoia*) and intuitive reason (pro-aisthésis or *théôria*). Starting from this Aristotelian point of view and a pessimistic Schopenhaurian foundation, Nietzsche constructed his theory of the Superman. For him, the crucial goal, the destiny of man, was not to seek the truth, but life or, more exactly, a sense of life. In this period of general decadence, the true problem is that of values which might lend their meaning, and their spice, to life. It is a matter of burying timeworn values of decadence (those of the Greeks, Jews, and Christians as well as those of modern humanism and the Revolution of 1789) in order to encourage new values of freedom to grow, values nourished in the symbiosis of feeling and intuition, discursive reason and will.

In contrast, on the other side of the Rhine in France, other forces, born from the decline of positivism and the triumph of the symbolist movement, were preparing the Revolution of 1889. If I refer to the Revolution of 1889, it is of course by analogy with the French Revolution of 1789. To be sure, this revolution came forth from the rationalism of the encyclopédistes. 1889 is also the year in which Henri Bergson published his *Essai sur les données immédiates de la conscience.* He too spoke out, not exactly against rationalism, but against its intellectualist deviation and especially against materialistic positivism. He too had reread the famous Aristotelian sentence, giving to the word *noûs* its true meaning of symbiosis between discursive reason and intuition, although he emphasizes feeling and intuition. By means of his philosophy, he advocates "a conscious and considered return to the givens of intuition." Taking his stand on the values of life and freedom,

Bergson, like Nietzsche, invites us to cultivate man's creative potential.

It is a curious coincidence that, during the years when Bergson was writing his *Essai*, Arthur Rimbaud, a Frenchman from the North and a poet, was discovering the values of *Négritude*. After having sung the joy of the senses in his earliest verses, the poet becomes a visionary in *A Season in Hell*, turns his back on blind positivism, and celebrates the discoveries of his new art: "Yes, my eyes are closed to your light. I am an animal, a Negro. But I can be saved. You are Negro imposters. . . . I enter the true kingdom of the children of Ham. . . . I invented the color of vowels. . . . I ordered the form and movement of each consonant and, with *instinctive rhymes*, I flattered myself upon having invented a poetic word accessible, at one time or another, to all the senses. I held back the translation." (The emphasis is mine.) Here in very few words is defined the esthetics of Negro Art, which would, once again, place its mark on twentieth-century world esthetics and the German expressionism which emerged from it. It is not an accident. But all this deserves an explanation, and Leo Frobenius will give it to us.

This German ethnologist will transform ethnology by returning it to its true vocation as philosophy of ethnology and as sociology, its principal offshoot. Before Paul Rivet, my former professor at the Institute for Ethnology in Paris (who had in my opinion been influenced by Frobenius), he was the one who insisted upon three major facts of ethnography:

1. the existence of cultural areas everywhere in the world,
2. the unity of Negro culture on all continents, and
3. affinities between Teutonic peoples, especially Nordics and Negroes.

But before proceeding further, I would like to say a word about sociology.

In his *Structural Anthropology*, Claude Lévi Strauss defines sociology as "social philosophy;" and with a reference to the Anglo-Saxons, he sees it as "a totality of positivistic research bearing on the organization and functioning of the most complex societies." And he is quite right in emphasizing the positivism which marked sociology in its early days. If we move from England to France, we can see that Emile Durkheim, taking his inspiration from Auguste Comte, in turn regards sociology as a science of mechanistic facts. That is, sociology was born mired in a swamp. It is at that moment that Leo Frobenius arrived. He was armed with a new vision, opposed to that of positivistic ethnologists and sociologists. As a matter of fact, their method *par excellence* is the accumulation of facts, the perpetual accumulation of facts stripped of their values. Above all, when it is a question of studying non-European peoples, even if they are from the Mediterranean basin, what prevails is eurocentrism (if not albinocentrism)—that is, the factual, amaterialistic, bookkeeping, intellectualist point of view.

Frobenius' essential contribution is, first of all, a global perspective. It is not a matter of tabulating facts one-by-one but of seeing them as a totality in which they act upon each other. Turning his back upon discursive reason, he then advocates having recourse to feeling—to intuition—as a means of gaining insight into values, not facts or quantities. For only intuition can go beyond the material and penetrate to the realm of values, which are the signs, or better, the active agents of life. In addition to the ideas of Nietzsche, we can recognize here those of Bergson and Rimbaud. A new philosophy is involved—a philosophy that advocates poetry, which, in the etymological sense of its Greek root, was simultaneously vision and action. In short, if Frobenius invented a new research tool or, in more precise terms, resurrected an old method, he did it in an attempt to accomplish the ambitious work to which he dedicated his entire life: the creation of a new civilization by reconciling all peoples of the earth in a universal dialogue, as Pierre Teilhard de Chardin later expressed it. In a word, Frobenius is asking people to actively engage the faculties which are called feeling, intuition, and discursive reason and to do it in this order, which reflects their relative importance. Furthermore, as Cheikh Anta Diop remarked in his works on African history and civilization, this dialectic, which places greater emphasis on the soul than on the mind, comes to us from Egypt, where the Greeks went to learn it. As the eyewitness Herodotus tells us, this was an African Egypt, the inhabitants of which had "black skin and woolly hair." And it is precisely to this Africa, to this diverse unity, that Leo Frobenius applies his method, as we shall now see.

But before concluding this part of my essay, I would like to point out that this method is the same one employed by the Marxist anthropologist Maurice Godelier. "This method," he explains in an interview published in the *Monde Dimanche* of February 14, 1982, "is participant observation. That is, a prolonged immersion in the social relationships of the local area, a descent to the bottom of the well."

FROBENIUS' METHOD

Frobenius, who consciously chose Africa as the principal object of his studies (we will later see why he did so), begins by criticizing the method of the positivistic ethnologists and sociologists. In studying non-European peoples, or Third World peoples as we say today, these investigators refuse to abandon their own self-constructs, that is, their mechanistic European logic which pays attention only to "material facts" elevated to the status of "objective realities." In contrast, Frobenius proposes to go beyond quantifiable data in an attempt to grasp their qualities, their meaning: that which Frobenius calls their *Sinngabe*. It is this global perspective upon phenomena, upon appearances, which we previously mentioned. It consists of abandoning ourselves once again to feeling. Only this feeling, this emotive faculty, can, in conjunction with vision (which Frobenius calls *Gemüt*), lead us to intuition, to a deeper vision of genuine realities, to *Tiefenschau*.

Precisely because many Third World peoples are men of feeling and intuition, it is necessary to use this deeper vision to know and describe them. This is certainly true of Africans. However, before speaking about African civilization, I would like to say a word about what the German philosopher calls *Kulturmorphologie*, or "morphology of cultures." But what is *Kultur*? For Frobenius, "civilization" is not a "collection of facts shared by a society or a group of societies," as the positivist sociologists believed, but more of a spiritual state, a "style" common to a people or a group of people. As the spirit of a civilization, this style is designated by Frobenius with the word *Kultur*, just as the French or English might employ the word "culture."

Using this definition as a point of departure, Frobenius set forth his *Morphology of Cultures*. He begins by insisting upon the unity of human civilization—a unity which transcends the diversity of its many forms. But he goes further: he declares that all civilizations developed genetically by passing through the same stages of infancy, adolescence, and maturity. The most important and fertile stage is that of infancy, during which feeling and intuitive reason are most active. It is essentially a stage of art and, in more general terms, of creativity. During the second stage, discursive reason and will develop. They are the faculties which, working together, organize and verify sensations and intuitions. It is at this time that the adolescent separates himself from his *Lebensraum*, his environment, to discover his self and to promote it as a person. Then, bringing together his sensations, his intuitions, and his factual knowledge, he arranges them in an order which is not ideal but ideational, to borrow a term from Maurice Godelier, the Marxist anthropologist. At this point, after having achieved equilibrium among the four essential faculties as well as between itself and its world, an adolescent people can devote itself to the generic human activity, which is to create: from implements necessary for survival on the animal level to the most eleborate and beautiful works of art. Maturity, Frobenius' third stage, is characterized by the fact that discursive reason takes precedence over intuitive reason, practical application over creation, and the exploitation of life over the living of life. This is the age of decadence.

Basing his further argument on this psychology of peoples, Frobenius elaborates in his *Morphology of Cultures*. Before proceeding any further, however, it is necessary to state explicitly that, for the German ethnologist and philosopher (who is a consistent anti-racist), there are neither primitive peoples nor primitive races: all have passed through the stage of infancy. But some have retained the creative spirit of adolescence, whereas others have renounced it to mire themselves in the short-term pragmatism of adulthood.

In articulating this theory for his own enlightenment, Frobenius made Africa the principal object of his ethnographic research and his philosophical reflections. In the paragraph of the first chapter entitled "The Reality of the Interior World" from his *Destiny of Civilizations*, he defines *Hamitic civilization* and *Ethiopean civilization* by opposing their respective cultures. The first extends across North Africa, including the Sahara; and the second, across equatorial and tropical Africa—practically speaking across all of black Africa with the exception of the Hottentots, the Bushmen, and the Pygmies, who participate in the former.

The determining factor in Ethiopean civilization is the plant and, in more general terms, agricultural life and the family farm. Its social base is the patriarchy, which comprises all the descendants, for approximately four generations, from a common ancestor. Within this context, there is no private property: the land, the herds, and the working implements belong to the community. "The unity of the family" is, as the ethnologist explains, the central fact, and it extends to dead ancestors.

In contrast, the determining factor in Hamitic civilization is the animal, domestic or otherwise, and, in a more general sense, the raising of cattle and the nomadic life. "The economy," in fact, "oscillates between hunting and nomadic life." In this civilization, property is privately owned, a practice motivated by an ancient personalization of individuals in the bosom of the family. Here the familial structure is the matriarchy, where the clan embraces all the descendants of a female ancestor.

In these forms and under the influence of geographical and historical phenomena, the essential characteristic of both civilizations is a certain culture, a certain spirit appropriate to each and which Frobenius discusses under the term *Paideuma*. He defines this word in the following way: "a psychological notion which designates the spiritual structure of a people to the extent that it is manifested in cultural behavior." By analyzing each of these civilizations in light of geographical factors, prehistory-history, the facts of social relationships, and specifically art and literature, the German philosopher concluded that Ethiopean civilization could be characterized as "mystical" and Hamitic civilization as "magical."

What interested the founders of the *Négritude* movement during the 1930s was not only the definition of Ethiopean culture as belonging to Negroes, but above all the idea of Paideuma as applied to our own twentieth century. It has not been sufficiently noted that Frobenius insists upon culture, not race. For example, the Hottentots, the Bushmen, and the Pygmies are racially closer to the Negroes than to the Arabo-Berbers; however, he places them among the latter. And he puts the Germans, along with the Negro-

Africans, into Ethiopean civilization, whereas the French, the English, and the Americans are placed into Hamitic civilization. Curiously enough, a new science, ethnic "characterology" (a word which does not appear in Paul Robert's six-volume dictionary of 1958) has come along to confirm Leo Frobenius' analysis. As a matter of fact, in his famous work entitled *Le Caractérologie ethnique*, Professor Paul Griéger recognizes emotivity as a characteristic shared by the two ethnotypes of "fluctuants" and "introverts." The only difference is that the introverts, represented primarily by the Germans, have a slow reaction to emotional stimulus, whereas that of the fluctuants, of which the major representatives are Negroes, is rapid.

From the perspective of twentieth-century humanism, few pages have convinced me as thoroughly as those in Frobenius' *Destiny of Civilizations*. On the one hand, there is the magical spirit of the Hamites in "French rationalism, English realism, and North-American materialism"; on the other, there is German and Negro-African mysticism. In the first case, it is a question of distrusting intuitions and allowing one's self to be guided by analytical, logical thinking in order to gather the facts, the *Tatsachen*. Above all, it is a question of organizing and mechanizing the forces of production. The goal is not to contemplate the "other" and to communicate with it by losing one's self in it. Rather, it is to enjoy accumulated material wealth. Here one recognizes the materialistic civilization of the twentieth century—a civilization which has destroyed the celebrated equilibrium and despiritualized Euro-America by causing it to lose its *Gemüt*, its soul. In opposition, there is direct intuition, born in emotion and leading to a vision of realities, of *Wirklichkeiten*, which remain hidden behind the mechanically collected facts. And in its plenitude, this vision nourishes the gift of expression. From this point on, the principal concern is the "other": communicating with it, losing one's self in it while expressing it.

I would like to conclude by emphasizing that Leo Frobenius with his morphology of cultures presages Pierre Teilhard de Chardin and his vision of a "Civilization of the Universal." Moreover, he contended during his lifetime that the earliest civilization, like the earliest humans, appeared in Africa and that the black continent guided the progress of humanity up to and including the Upper Paleolithic.

On behalf of the German ethnologist and philosopher Frobenius, I should point out that the civilization of a given people can stop at one stage or another. Thus, Germany, having attained its maturity with "German mastery in the manipulation of facts" was in the process of returning to a "sense of the real, which always, ultimately, triumphs over bare facts." At least, he hoped so. In any case, after having ascertained that leadership in the world passed alternatively from Ethiopean civilization to Hamitic civilization (and vice-versa) during the long course of history, Frobenius in the *Destiny of Civilizations* advocated a cultural ecumenism which would maintain an equilibrium between feeling and will, soul and mind, as they are symbiotically reunited in the spirit. The Frenchman Teilhard de Chardin says much the same thing in works like *L'Energie humaine* and *L'Activation de l'energie* and, in general, in his theory of a "Civilization of the Universal."

This is a lesson which we would do well to contemplate after the Conference of Cancun at a moment when Euro-America and the Third World are preparing to initiate "global negotiations" under the auspices of the United Nations and within the framework of the North-South dialogue. In principle, it is a question of creating a New International Cultural Order. And, as I have emphasized for a number of years, there will be no New International Economic Order if a New Cultural Order is not established first. This is what Leo Frobenius and later Pierre Teilhard de Chardin were advocating: a new world of harmony and equilibrium, a world where each continent, each race, each nation, and, above all, each culture would contribute its own irreplaceable virtues.

7
V. Y. MUDIMBE

On the Question of an African Philosophy: The Case of French Speaking Africa

The notion of African philosophy is a recent paradigm.[1] At the beginning of the century one comes across expressions such as "primitive philosophy" or "philosophy of the savages" in most ethnographic and anthropological texts which refer to what nowadays is commonly called local or indigenous systems of thought. Today it is clear that the scientific discourse on Africa was then made up of ideological preconceptions and philosophical speculation on the chain of beings and its history, unproven evolutionary assumptions about cultures and human beings, and, finally, political considerations grounding the right to colonize. Within this intellectual mixture, African behavior, thinking, and weltanschauung were qualified as a preliminary step towards a more progressive human capacity. And with a *bel ensemble*, missionaries, anthropologists, and colonizers expounded means and techniques of changing the African context and transforming it according to both Western and Christian standards. An excellent sign of this period is Stefano Kaoze, a central African Roman Catholic priest, who in 1907-1911, when he was still a seminarian, published a long article on Bantu psychology in which he opposes the weaknesses of his own traditional system to the conquering force of Western philosophy and weltanshauung.

The notion of African philosophy has been ambiguous since it was first used in the 1910s, because of the pervasiveness of primitivist ideologies which mark the conditions of its possibility and imply references to prelogism in thinking, paganism in belief, and primitiveness in regard to the weltanschauung. Furthermore, there is a more general reason for this ambiguity, and it depends on the particular status of philosophy and its meanings. As a discipline, philosophy defines itself as essentially a critical, explicit, autocritical discourse focusing on human experience, its signs and symbols. Indeed, one can also understand philosophy in a wider sense and consider commentaries on a way of life and even the very way of life as a philosophy. In everyday life itself there is no problem of speaking about the philosophy of American businessmen, French policemen, Italian singers, or African musicians as long as one suspends any consideration of confusing implied particular modalities of behaving with philosophy as a critical and explicit discourse. The expression "African philosophy" often assumes this wide understanding. As such it covers and designates the particularity of a weltanschauung and commentaries bearing upon it. On the other hand, it seems clear that this wide usage of the notion of philosophy cannot be confused with the critical and personal works of African professionals of philosophy.

The present essay represents an attempt to mark the limits existing between the two understandings of philosophy in francophone Africa and to indicate the points of their complementarity from a critical perspective. I choose to deal with explicit commentaries and discourses on philosophy, not with things, nor with social formations and their sets of values. Yet I have every reason to believe that explicit discourses as well as practical wisdom and traditional sets of values might, under some conditions, participate in the same philosophical effort. On the other hand, in speaking of African philosophy, I am aware of the discreet insistence of metaphors and epistemological traces called upon, as in the case of less controverted signs such as African astronomy, African geology, or even African philology, which for everybody simply means the rigorous practice of a discipline within a geographical framework that is *African per accidens*.

When one runs through the chronological repertory of works of African philosophy,[2] one fact strikes the eye immediately: the large number of books of philosophy published in Central Africa, mainly in Zaire. This quantity of publication is due to the influence of Catholic missionaries during the colonial era. According to the terms of the 1906 Convention between the Holy See and the Congo Free State, an elaborate structure of religious education was developed, leading to major seminaries where candidates for the priesthood were introduced to Thomist philosophy before they undertook studies in theology. As a consequence the first Africans in this century to publish works claiming to be philosophical were churchmen: Alexis Kagame, Andre Makarakiza, F. M. Lufuluabo, and Vincent Mulago. Spiritually they are disciples of Placide Tempels; they often refer to and use his *Bantu Philosophy* (1945). Their status and the special order of their mission have prepared them to receive sympathetically the basic hypotheses of Tempels as well as the way he advocated them. This submission to one perspective has, however, never meant a mere repetition of Tempels' ideas, as shown by Kagame's reservation and the widening of his investigation from *La Philosophie bantu-rwandaise de l'être* (1956) to *La Philosophie bantu comparée* (1976).

Placide F. Tempels, a Belgian missionary in Central Africa from 1933 to 1962, offered his *Bantu Philosophy* to colonialists of good faith as a possible aid to the building of a Christian Bantu civilization. Tempels had lived more than ten years among the Luba Katanga people, sharing their language and cultural background, when he decided to publish a resumé of his experience. Rather than the philosophical treatise, his *Bantu Philosophy* could be understood as, simultaneously, an indication of religious insight, the expression of a cultural doubt about the supposed backwardness of Africans, and a political manifesto of a new policy for promoting civilization and Christianity. But this complexity is not what is commonly discussed when specialists speak of Tempels' philosophy.

It must be remembered that *Bantu Philosophy* is based on very simple premises. First, in all cultures, life and death determine human behavior; or, presented differently, all human behavior depends upon a system of general principles. Secondly, if Bantu are human beings, there is reason to seek the fundamentals of their beliefs and behavior or their basic philosophical system. From this position, Tempels, according to E. Possoz, attempts "a true estimate of indigenous peoples," rejecting "the misunderstanding and fanaticism of the ethnology of the past and of the former attitude of aversion entertained with regard to them."[3]

This "discovery" of Bantu philosophy, wrote Tempels, is so disconcerting a revelation that we are tempted at first sight to believe that we are looking at a mirage. In fact, the universally accepted picture of primitive man, of the savage, of the proto-man living before the full blossoming of intelligence, vanishes beyond hope of recovery before this testimony.[4]

The polemical argument which arose from this perspective tended to redefine the European Christian mission towards Africa. Taking upon himself the responsibility of reinterpreting the highest European conscience, Tempels could defy the then current policies of both Christianization and colonization in a chapter significantly entitled "Bantu Philosophy and our Mission to Civilize."

This is the result of a complex intellectual change. During the 1930s, the fundamental assumptions of colonization and Christian conversion had not yet been questioned. But some trends in French and German anthropology associated with scholars like M. Griaule and P. W. Schmidt were beginning to develop more sophisticated cultural taxonomies. With them, there emerges a new type of discourse which, apart from following Leo Frobenius and Maurice Delafosse's form of curiosity, insists on the originality of different cultures, thus, methodologically, implying the possibility of a typology of otherness.[5]

The most surprising fact is that an epistemological split had appeared within the anthropological field. This revolution has, until now, hardly been analyzed. On the one side, despite changes in methodology associated with the culturalist and functionalist schools, professional anthropology continued to maintain an evolutionary perspective with all its implications. On the other side, we have a new orientation of what I would like to call missionary anthropology. During Schmidt's time, with the foundation of the Vienna School, the new development was an original trend within the professional field. Rapidly, however, contributions from missionaries at work in Africa shifted from anthropological postulates to strictly philosophical considerations. This shift is, for instance, already discernible in *La Religion des primitifs* (1909) by A. Le Roy as well as in Colles' study on the Baluba (1913). During the 1930s and 1940s it is widely observable in almost all missionary studies on African religions and traditions. N. De Claene, A. De Clercq, G. Hulstaert, P. Schumascher, G. Van

Bulck, G. Van den Bosch, R. F. Van den Eynde, J. Van Wing, B. Zuure are, among others, representative of this new trend.

Contrary to the evaluations often made by modern anthropologists, their works are in general good, valuable, and interesting ethnography. Most of them tend to follow the norms of the Vienna School, the German or the French tradition in anthropology. As a rule, missionaries' scholarly contributions carefully describe a given African group or feature taken as a totality. Some of them, sharing or following the philosophy of *Anthropos* and, particularly, the aims of P. W. Schmidt's *Ursprung der Gottesidee* (1933-1949),[6] are inclined to arrive at synthetic conclusions from data provided by limited studies, for example P. Schebesta's analysis on "Die religiöse Anschauungen Sud-Afrikas"[7] or C. Tastevin's generalizations on "Les Idées religieuses des africains."[8]

The revolution represented by this current rests, firstly, on its heuristic procedures and, secondly, on its apologetic objectives. As in Schmidt's enterprise, the aim is not only the scientific practice of ethnography per se; instead, ethnography is regarded as a means for the careful and patient study of a multitude of cultural particularities. Subsequently, the ethnographic method is supposed to allow us to discern a universal system which, if correctly described, would, in turn, account for all cultural particularities. From this viewpoint, even the smallest element may help, on the first level, in the description and understanding of the originality, the "soul" of a culture; moreover, on the second level, it could contribute to a pancultural system, reflecting a universal theory. Thus, one of the major assumptions of the method is the existence of a universal theory or philosophy that each human community expresses in its own way and according to its own needs. This philosophy would be always and everywhere particular in its cultural and historical manifestations, but universal in its essence. Its presence marks the difference between human societies and animal communities.

Many contributions on African religions published between the 1930s and World War II are largely supported by the above assumptions. During these years the missionary viewpoint in anthropology encountered French cultural relativism, itself a product of what Léopold Sédar Senghor nicely described as the "German crisis of French thought," meaning the revolution which, in philosophy as well as in social sciences, followed the impact of Friedrich Nietzsche, Karl Marx, and Sigmund Freud on French scholarship. In any case, it became acceptable to recognize some wisdom in Africans, and it was no longer considered absurd to write about African "morality," "philosophy," or "knowledge" as did, for instance, R. Allier in *The Mind of the Savage* (1929); V. Brelsford in *Primitive Philosophy* (1935) and *The Philosophy of the Savage* (1938); and, with particular brilliance, the French team working on Bambara and Dogon traditions, S. de Ganay, G. Dieterlen, M. Griaule, and M. Leiris. With his *Bantu Philosophy*, Tempels appears as one of the most remarkable among the theorists of this trend. His use of Thomistic philosophical categories in order to clarify ethnographic data might seem debatable, but at the time, it represented a sound answer to unsolved questions in the interpretation of African cultures and their future.[9]

Kagame drew out all the consequences of Tempels' method. Using Aristotelian concepts, he tried, with his *La Philosophie bantu-rwandaise de l'être* (1956), to demonstrate simultaneously that Bantu philosophy is a reflection of a perennial and universal philosophy and, at the same time, the vital expression of the soul of a community. From this viewpoint, he adds, "The term philosophy could have been replaced by that of metaphysics so that we could have used 'The Bantu Metaphysics of Being' as the title."[10] This statement is important, since it explicitly indicates the full significance of the epistemological revolution discussed above: philosophy is to be understood as metaphysics, and the discipline serves to describe an African theodicy considered as a reflected image of a universal theodicy. As everyone knows, theodicy is simply another name for natural religion.

Kagame's *La Philosophie bantu-rwandaise de l'être* is both a critical response to Tempels' interpretation of Bantu culture and a sustained attempt to organize in a precise framework the philosophy of a "pagan culture." For the classical philosophical question of "what is" he substituted another one related to vital force. Following Aristotle, he distinguished, more rigorously than Tempels, four categories of being—*umuntu* "the human being," *ikintu* "a thing," *ahantu* "somewhere," and *ukuntu* "the manner," which includes seven of Aristotle's categories (quantity, quality, relation, action, emotion, position, possession) instrumental for his hierarchy of vital forces. The same process of transplanting Kinyarwanda categories into Aristotelian concepts—about the notions of existence, knowledge, and will, for instance—allowed him to describe the Bantu-Rwandais ontology, criteriology, psychology, cosmology, and ethics.

Most of Tempels' African disciples were more concerned about making philosophy agree with theology in order to promote a cultural integration of African thought with Christianity. Thus we have for example Jean Calvin Bahoken's *Clairières métaphysiques africaines* (1967), François-Marie Lufuluabo's *Perspective théologique bantoue et théologie scholastique* (1966), Célestin Mubengayi's *Initiation africaine et initiation chrétienne* (1966), and Mulago's *Un Visage africain du christianisme* (1965). Until the 1960s their major guides were still the Roman Pontiff's teachings (Benedict XV's *Maximum Illud* [1919], Pius XI's *Rerum Ecclesiae* [1926], Pius XII's *Evangelii Praecones* [1951]), which were based on the postulates that, in order to save Africans "sedentes in tenebris et in umbra mortis," it was necessary to establish an adapted Christianity, that is to naturalize the church and indigenize its teaching and liturgy. Gradually the policy shifted from an adaptation perspective insisting on the Africanization of external aspects of Christianity—for instance, the type of music and hymns used in liturgy—to a questioning of the content of Christianity. The new approach, the stepping-stone method, was based upon new premises. A major supposition would be that there are in African tradition and culture facts and beliefs, signs and symbols which are already a "praeparatio evangelica." Thus, the Good News might be preached on this basis, and Christianity would automatically take on a new form. The ideological implications of these schools are obvious in their vocabulary. The first uses an agricultural terminology (plant, transplant, sow the African field, bring the good seed, spread the good seed) which implies a *tabula rasa* or, at least, a waste land. The second approach seems to set a high value on construction vocabulary (establish, implement, build, construct the church), implying that its aim is a new organization of an existing system of beliefs.

All the African thinkers mentioned above use both approaches, sometimes emphasizing one, at other times combining them both in a new perspective. Divorced from an organic relationship with colonial Christianity, they contribute to a philosophy and a theology of the implantation of the church, which is critical to the dominant and pervasive theology of mission. This orientation, as already noted, was expressed in a dichotomy implying an evolution from paganism to Christianity and involving binary oppositions like Satan versus God and African primitiveness versus Western civilization. Hence, missionary objectives grew as a means of necessary metamorphoses: to substitute the health of Christian civilization for the illness of the African universe.

The new "discourse of method" promoted by Lufuluabo, Mulago, and others lists nationalist perspectives as indicating a reevaluation of pagan traditions and the generative possibilities of autonomous values. At first sight, it might appear as essentially a semantic revolution. The concept of pagan culture or, in current usage, of traditional culture tends to replace that of primitiveness used by some anthropologists. In an aggressive book, *Des Prêtres noirs s'interrogent* (1956), young black theologians put forward new sets of symbols and evaluated classical mediators. One year later, in 1957, the papal encyclical, Pius XII's *Fidei Donum*, seemed to approve of their primary desires: indigenization of the missionary philosophy of Christianization.

This religious commitment has created problems: either because one sees nostalgia for philosophical ethnocentrism based on platonico-aristotelico-thomism or Scotism, or because the usage these thinkers make of the term philosophy takes on a vulgar meaning, or because some critics have decided that these investigations depended on missiology and that the latter has nothing really to do with philosophy.[11] These critics forget that the epistemological perspective of theological research and of the semantic or hermeneutic questions it raises belongs to a philosophical view. Pushed further, the debate, if it is to be critical, should take up once again the preliminary question: What is African philosophy? And this presupposes other questions: on the one hand, the defining of philosophy and theology; on the other, the norms of possible cooperation between both disciplines.

Alongside the promoters of the concept of a philosophy helping in the inculturation of Christianity, other thinkers, such as T. Tshibangu, without pushing their Africanness, pose a question about the status of theology as a science or, at the crossroads of historical, philosophical, philological, and theological methods, produce works of exegesis of a high level. For example, the investigations of Joseph Ntedika on the evolution of the doctrine of St. Augustine's purgatory and on the Latin patristic heritage; the book of Jean Kinyongo on the origin of the meaning of the name of Yahweh; the analysis, provided by Dosithée Atal, of the structures and the meaning of the Johannic hymn; and the study by Laurent P. Mosengwo on the notion of *nomos* in the Pentateuch. Several more recent books are very close to the usual idea and technique of philosophical work; for example, Alphonse Pene Elungu's on Nicholas de Malebranche, Alphonse Ngindu's on Lucien Laberthonière, and that of Octave Ugirashebuja (1977) on Martin Heidegger.[12]

When the debate on African philosophy was intensifying in West Africa—precisely between 1956 (the date of the publication of Kagame's first philosophical text) and 1965 (the date of Frantz Crahay's article in *Diogène* in which the conditions for the existence of a Bantu philosophy are put forward) the dominant trend was in the traditional vein, except for the works of Senghor and the writings properly called Marxist. Works that are of a philosophical nature are limited in number. Moreover, these are, in general, articles. Before 1965, we could hardly count ten significant works with an explicit philosophical ambition. They included Ferdinand N'Sougan Agblemagnon's stimulating work on time in Ewe culture, his analysis of the concept of person, tradition, and culture in Africa and his research on metaphysics and ethics in the evolution of Black Africa;[13] Meinrad Hebga's defence of African logic, which inadvisedly implies that the relativity of modes of thinking can be founded on the basis of philosophical implications from the existence of non-Euclidian geometries;[14] Maurice Memel Fote's report on animist civilization prepared for a 1962 colloquium on religions held in Paris and his 1965 article on perpetual peace in the practical philosophy of Africans;[15] and Engelbert Mveng's *L'Art d'afrique noire* (1965), an essay in religious aesthetics.

Suddenly, from 1968 on, vigorous texts appear in Western Africa, proposing a rigorous usage of the concept and practice of philosophy. A critical school begins with the publication, in a 1968 issue of *Présence Africaine*, of Fabien Eboussi-Boulaga's essay against Tempels' *Bantu Philosophy*.[16] Its members, like Paulin Hountondji and Marcien Towa, overlap very widely or join the path marked out by F. Crahay's position.[17] They give the name ethnophilosophy to the investigation which, after Tempels and Kagame, speaks of describing and restoring traditional African philosophies. The impact of this criticism, as well as its significance, modify philosophy considerably from the 1970s onwards. Two external characters indicate this clearly: first, the center of African philosophical thought shifts from Central Africa to West Africa; then, methodologically exacting investigations and essays begin to come from Benin, Cameroon, Ivory Coast, and Senegal, and philosophical reflection tends to take on a resolutely secular outlook. Another noteworthy fact is the eviction, albeit temporary, of churchmen. In fact, starting with 1970, the Catholic School of Theology in Kinshasa takes a new breath of life and is now one of the most lively and dynamic centers of research in African philosophy and theology. It publishes three regular journals (*Les Cahiers des Religions Africaines, La Revue Africaine de Théologie*, and the *Bulletin of African Theology of the Ecumenical Association of African Theologians*), has launched three series of publications ("Les Recherches Philosophiques Africaines," "Les Recherches Théologiques Africaines," and the "Bibliothèque du Centre d'Etudes des Religions Africaines"), and organizes each year two international seminars, one in theology and the other in philosophy.

In their panorama of contemporary African philosophy, Oleko Nkombe and Alfons J. Smet, two members of Kinshasa School, have produced a classification of African philosophers.[18] They describe the internal structure of African philosophy in the form of a totality with vertices formed by the following schools:

1. the ideological current: reaction to theories and prejudices which, in the past, supported the slave trade and later justified colonization;
2. the trend recognizing traditional African philosophy: reaction to the myth of the "primitive mentality" of Africans which, through hermeneutical restoration, speaks of asserting the existence, solidity, and coherence of traditional African philosophies;
3. the critical school: reaction to theses or projects of the two preceding trends; it questions their validity and philosophical relevance;
4. the synthetic current: the assumption of preceding trends and the orientation of the data collected towards a hermeneutical, functional philosophy or a search for new problematics.

As operative as it may appear at first sight, this classification remains perplexing: it elevates a working hypothesis to a thesis. In fact, on the level of external structure, African philosophy is defined as implying two kinds of knowledge—Western and African—these being in a relationship of sub-contrariety, without one knowing exactly and clearly what is designated; but the value of his manner of inclusive disjunction seems questionable.

In the elementary logic of propositions, in the immediate inferences or reasoning which are supported by a single premise and lead immediately to a conclusion, a relation of sub-contrariety exists when two propositions can both be true at the same time but may not be false at the same time. Hence, there are three possible inferences: if the premise or first proposition is false, the conclusion can only be true; if, on the contrary, the premise is true, the conclusion is uncertain, since it could be true or false.

For example, in each of the following three types of reasoning, propositions are in relation of sub-contrariety.

1. An inference dear to certain anthropologists at the beginning of this century:
   Some Africans are not human beings (False).
   Some Africans are human beings (True).
2. A geometry teacher could harass or amuse his students by playing on the following reasoning:
   Some quadrilaterals do not have five sides (True).
   Some quadrilaterals have five sides (False).
3. A father, sooner or later, introduces his children to the following evidence:
   Some people are black (True).
   Some people are not black (True).

In order fully to understand the relationship of sub-contrariety in the model presented to us, we must note two things. First, the authors set an implication between, on the one hand, African wisdom and European knowledge and, on the other, this very knowledge and African wisdom. In other words, they establish the fact that African thinkers and Africanists draw from European knowledge their models of analysis, interpretation, and speculation; on the basis of this observation they conclude that "it is inconceivable to seek to understand African philosophy today, outside the relationship which unites it to European knowledge."[19] From the point of view of content, however, they believe that all African philosophical currents preoccupy themselves with the problems which concern the Africa of today. Between European knowledge and African wisdom would therefore exist, according to the authors, a relationship of sub-contrariety, because such categories are compatible with each other. The authors write, "We think that in spite of the differences existing between African wisdom and European knowledge, a common denominator can be found."[20]

The second point is that the authors state the resemblance between this relationship and inclusive disjunction. In logic, this is commonly called strict disjunction. It is a two-argument operation which produces a true result in three cases: when the two arguments are both true and when either argument is true. This is all fine, and even extremely provocative. But this very abstract model poses some problems of which the most immediate and perhaps the most important are contained in the arguments themselves: What are they and what exactly do they mean? I fear in fact that, in spite of the apparent clarity, European knowledge and African wisdom are, as expressions, opaque and thus insufficient to demonstrate support for a process of computation of propositions and analysis of propositional variables. Moreover, Nkombe and Smet insist on certain intellectual filiations. For example, they note the influence of Aristotle and the scholastics on Tempels and Kagame, that of Hegel on Eboussi-Boulaga and Towa, and that of Marx and Louis Althusser on Stanislas Adotévi and Hountondji. One could agree that it is one thing to observe and analyze intellectual or spiritual genealogies and quite a different one to generalize and speak of inclusive disjunction between European knowledge and African wisdom.

Whatever the case may be, if one accepts that, internally, African philosophy could be represented as a lozenge of sub-contrariety with the four trends as its vertices, one must assume that tension would be identical between vertices and would allow the latter, and hence the form of the lozenge, to be maintained. But is this obvious? Doesn't the trend toward the recognition of an African philosophy tend to be reconciled with the ideological school and the synthetic to fuse with the critical? One could graphically represent the result as a wavy line, like a snake with the tail representing the first two trends and the head the remaining two. In case the image of the tail might appear pejorative, let us suggest the image of a snake with two heads. This might express better the tensions between the principal orientations of African philosophy. On the one side, there are investigations on cosmologies and mores—Tempels and his disciples' perspective; on the other, there are the more modern trends that emphasize the critical virtues of philosophy.

To be clearer, it seems to me that, on the one hand, investigations to restore traditional African philosophy (the second trend) are complementary to the ideological school—eminently theoretical—of which they are concrete expressions. On the other hand, the critical trend—the third school—should be considered as an indispensable stepping-stone or, more precisely, as the first essential thing without which the fourth orientation—the quest for syntheses, hermeneutic or functional philosophy—would have no meaning, at least as a rigorous philosophical project. Let us therefore propose a representation which is, at the same time, less complex and more eloquent, one which symbolizes the unity of African philosophy. Let A and B (Fig. 1) be two groups in proportion to partial inclusion: the first would unite the works with a strong

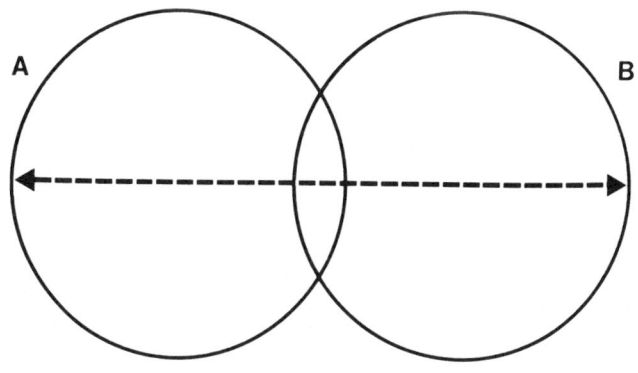

Figure 1

ideological bias (in the widest sense of the qualifier); that is, it would take up again Nkombe and Smet's terminology of the ideological trend and the school promoting a traditional African philosophy; the second would comprise productions with a philosophical bent in the strict sense, that is, works coming from critical perspectives. And let us admit, by virtue of hypothesis, that at the intersection of the groups, there exist African works which, by their aim or because they possess certain characteristics, can be considered as belonging to either of the two groups. For the second phase, in each of the two groups, it would, in principle, be possible equally to raise some smaller groups in proportion to partial inclusion. This, for purely schematic reasons, we will have the following representation: in A: A_1 and A_2; in B: B_1 and B_2 (Fig. 2).

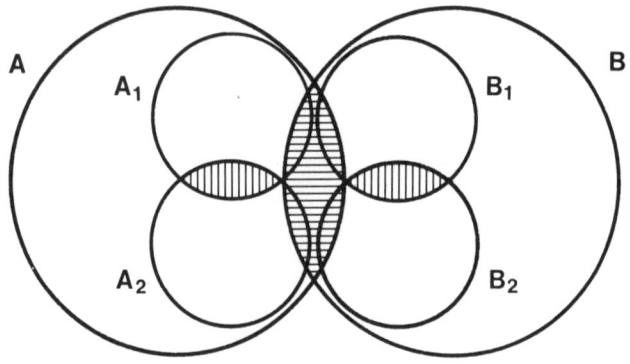

Figure 2

Now, if we trace a theoretical line (Fig. 1) which, from the center of the intersection of A and B, would run horizontally to the left and to the right, we propose that, on the left, the line indicates a decreasing application of philosophical principles and, on the right, an increasing application of the same. In other words, we will say: on the left, the further one gets from the intersection of A and B, the more the works can be qualified as philosophical in only the broadest sense. In the other direction, the more the line penetrates into B, the more it involves philosophical works in the strict sense, approaching more or less the philosophical ideal—to refer to the definition proposed not long ago by F. Crahay—an analytical, explicit, critical, and autocritical reflection.[21]

This representation could, in theory, be applied to the corpus of any non-African cultural tradition. In any case, it solves, in a simple way, the question of the definition of African philosophy. In order to establish a wide acceptance, Marcel Tshiamalenga for example—against Crahay, Hountondji and Towa—invoked realism in the definition of philosophy.[22] And, in view of relativizing the rigor of the ideal concept of the discipline, he asked, subversively, if Immanuel Kant was radically critical and autocritical? What was autocritical in G. W. F. Hegel, Arthur Schopenhauer, Sören Aabye Kierkegaard, Albert Camus, Gabriel Marcel? Finally he asked what was analytical in the pre-Socratic philosophers? Such questions are not easily answered. Our diagram simply indicates that one must openly understand and accept African philosophy as being a corpus of texts and discourses with a philosophical bent, in the strict and wide sense. One can, if necessary, occasionally circumscribe a more restrained field of philosophical exercise in the strict sense, in view of precise objectives. How can one illustrate this diagram in a concrete way? Let us follow the process of the increasing complexity of philosophical needs in African thought by considering the contents of Groups A and B.

In Group A, let us characterize two subgroups. The first comprises works arising from the need to express and to render faithfully the unity and the coherence of traditional philosophies, African systems (weltanschauungen) supposedly neither marked nor influenced by Western contributions. The second unites the works qualified by an explicit intention to separate and to analyze present constraints of African society, marking the present and future situation while remaining true to African ideals. In the first subgroup, the text produced could be called ethnophilosophical; in the second, ideologicophilosophical. Let it be understood that the two qualifiers are not, in any way, pejorative; they must be understood simply as classifying devices, allowing a differentiation by class in terms of the content of the works, of their methods and aims.[23]

In the ethnophilosophical subgroup, three classes may be clearly distinguished. The first is that of ethnographic description and ethnological exegesis. Of this, Western Africanists have provided numerous models, either strictly descriptive or in the form of anthropological analysis and interpretation. As an example of this class, we will cite two cases, namely, the works of Delafosse and Griaule. Numerous Africans have written works which belong to this group: essay writers like A. Diagne and M. Sidibe, both of whom published in the *Bulletin du Comité d'Etudes Historiques et Scientifiques de l'AOF* (1916-1938); Paul Hazoumé who produced *Doguicimi* in 1935; or, to go back to the 1910s, S. Kaoze, who wrote an article on "The Psychology of the Bantu." One may wonder whether or not this kind of work should be excluded from a classification of philosophical works and instead be relegated to the field of anthropology. Reasons for doing this are not wanting. But perhaps they should be held provisionally in abeyance until the field of African philosophy is clarified. In fact, how can one understand the purport of Ahmadou H. Ba's investigations or those of Fu-Kiau if one takes away their explicit philosophical ambition? They proclaim the reality of African tradition as a canon of truth and knowledge.[24] They believe that there is an African tradition in itself and consider themselves as the interpreters of this particular experience.[25] Yet in stating that Africans have their own distinct mode of being, they insist that this singularity is the condition of universality: if there were no particular individuals and traditions, there could not be real universals. This same orientation is true of Boubou Hama's reflection on the encounter of Africa and Europe. His aim is to account for the African originative experience vis-a-vis Western interpretative systems.[26] And a book like that of Tulu Kia Mpasu Buakasa on sorcery and witchcraft in the Kongo country is also affirmed as an explicit revealing trait of an unthought element of an African tradition.[27]

Two other classes of ethnophilosophical works are made up of those in which the authors attempt to restore the dignity of African culture either ontologically or hermeneutically. Ontological restitution, as Tshiamalenga calls it,[28] is undertaken by some of Tempels' successors, such as Kagame and Lufuluabo, who construct an African philosophy by finding in African culture the equivalents of Aristotelian or Thomistic categories, thanks to which they claim they can reveal implicit African systems of thought. The third class is characterized by efforts towards hermeneutical restitution. The authors identify a structured philosophy by sorting through the contents of extant ethnographic studies and collections of myths, stories, prayers, and ritual formulas. Examples are provided by E. N. C. Mujynya's studies of the status of man in the Bantu universe; examples include Mulago's study on Bantu religion and G. de Souza's on the concept of life among the Fon.[29] Insofar as these restitutions are concerned, the problem lies in the value of the translation which is operated from an original to a speculative discourse and authorizes the latter to be presented as a faithful mirror of an implicit philosophy. The step taken would be perfectly philosophical, if, first, it clearly started by a demonstration of an explicit character of the thought expressed by the traditional texts. These, it will be agreed, are neither silent nor chaotic.[30] Then, relying heavily on them, it would be philosophical if it offered a translation granted to the norms of hermeneutical readings. Alas, even when well started, this step often short-circuits the creative jump assumed by any translation and, satisfied by its initial movement, returns lazily to its point of departure to organize the supposed thought reflected by some fragments of initial texts.

It goes without saying that the distinctions established between the three classes of ethnophilosophical texts are theoretical. These classes do communicate, for the very reason that their intersections are inhabited. Hence, by way of illustration, J. C. Bahoken's study on the philosophy and religion of the Bantu of South Cameroon is linked at the same time to the hypotheses of ethnological exegesis and to the projects of ontologizing restitution.[31] In another noteworthy case V. Mulago, whose important study on the complementarity of Christianity and Africanity, *Un Visage africain du christianisme* (1965), situated in the wake of ontologizing restitution, has recently produced an investigation on traditional Bantu religion which is perfectly well inscribed in the trend of hermeneutic restitution.[32]

The second subgroup, that of works which are ideological in nature, unites works, the texts of which are defined as being ideologicophilosophical. Ideology is to be understood here in its strict sense, a body of ideas clearly structured and influential in the thinking and and, possibly, the behavior of the members of a given community. It presents the values contained in expressions like "a working class ideology," "a political ideology," or "an ideology of commitment." The joining of the terms ideology and philosophy, however, poses a problem: the first, by definition, generally establishes itself as active, militant, and practical; the second, as essentially speculative and contemplative. In my opinion, this problem expresses the very ambiguity of this subgroup, of which certain works—if not all—are equivocal. In any case, the best conceived and the most elaborate depend as much on the play of opposites customary to ideological militantism as on the efforts and abstract operations of philosophical speculation.

From then on, it would be superficial to dissociate clear and distinct classes. Let us be satisfied with noting prominent currents and then indicating rapidly the authors whose works are, in the main, philosophical.

A common denominator in different trends would be Black African nationalism. This is found in the pan-Africanism illustrated in particular by Cheikh Anta Diop, Patrice Lumumba, and Kwame Nkrumah. The same passion for the continent characterizes Senghor's or Julius Nyerere's African socialism. But, contrary to its nonreligious origins, the socialist ideology in these projects has been spiritualistic and community oriented.

The movement of *Négritude* or African humanism put forward by Senghor for forty years is more speculative.[33] Numerous commentators have explored it: sympathetically, in the case of Alioune Sene and Thomas Melone, or with violence, as in Towa's 1971 critique of Senghor.[34] In spite of the criticism to which it has been subjected, *Négritude* still inspires the quest for an African personality and its cultural values either through contrasted reflections, as Jean-Marie Abanda Ndengue has tried to show in Cameroon, or as a reflector, as in the book which I. Kimoni has devoted to Negro-African literature and to the questions bearing on the culture which brought it about,[35] or again as an exemplary place of fascinating norms for the transgression of the iron law imposed by the same. Thus, with Alfonse Nguvulu in his research on humanism and, unassumingly, in Kinyongo's meditation on "the evident Being,"[36] we are spellbound by its authenticity. The ideology of the same name, despite the 1967 specifications of Mabika Kalanda, who wished to question all values, whether African or not, and despite Senghor's efforts to promote it through *Négritude*, is nevertheless on its way out.[37] Only with great difficulty can one put such a mystification side by side with Eboussi-Boulaga's investigations of African authenticity and philosophy. The Cameroonian philosopher has preferred serious reflection on the processes and conflicts of being an African today to easy ideological militantism.[38] Finally, we have the last trend in ideological investigation with, for example, Kwame Nkrumah's *Consciencism* (1964) and Marxist theorists who, promoting African development, militate for strict loyalty to Marxist rules.[39]

Now that we have made a general survey of classes and trends of ethnophilosophical and ideologicophilosophical works, should we not recall that these systems are complementary? Or that there exists (to take up again the classification of groups used above) an intersection between these two subgroups, since we have proposed from the beginning, the following hypothesis: because of the aims of their contents, these works originate in the same group.

Two facts, one internal to the corpus and the other external, confirm this complementarity. On the internal side, the reflections on African humanism and the ideologies of *Négritude* or authenticity all generally draw their material from an ethnographic context, and they are often inspired by anthropological exegeses. We could, for example, imagine Senghor without Frobenius or Delafosse. But *Négritude* cannot be understood outside of ethnological discourse. Another example of a different nature is that of pan-Africanist ideology. If this ideology cannot be confused with trends of restoring traditional African philosophies, it nevertheless resembles them. Like them, it is motivated by negation. The projects of philosophical restitution deny the negation given to African culture until recently; pan-Africanism opposes the negation of African societies imposed first during the slave trade and later during the colonization and balkanization of the continent. That said, I do not believe that here would be the place to question the validity and the relevance of this compensatory negation. On the external side, it is interesting to note some syntheses of the ethnophilosophical and ideologicophilosophical elements. The virtuosity of J. Jahn's *Muntu* (1961) is well known. The book integrates the categories of Kagame's Rwandese-Bantu philosophy with Senghorian concepts in order to present a new African culture. According to Jahn, African tradition as well as neo-African culture is a matter of choice: Africans have "a perfect right to declare authentic, correct and true those components of their past which they believe to be so."[40] The argument which is close to that of African traditionalists is interesting. It means that people invent their version of history or culture, and from this viewpoint history or culture is nothing more than a symbol. Outside Catholic Church circles, little is known of Dominique Nothomb's undertaking which, being inspired by the same sources, establishes African humanism with regard to indigenous stepping-stones toward Christianity.[41] From a strictly philosophical point of view, one could, as Crahay did for Jahn, criticize these syntheses for being based on texts of uncertain philosophical status. That done, one can see that these syntheses attest to the skillful use of the complementarity existing between ethnophilosophical and ideologicophilosophical texts.

We must now note some ideologicophilosophical texts, most particularly the essays of Nkrumah and Senghor. They are different from other texts of the same group because of their explicit, autocritical, and rigorously organized discourse on specific languages and conditions. Let us take, for instance, *Nation et voie africaine du socialisme* (1961) or *Pour une relecture africaine de Marx et d'Engels* (1976) by Senghor. Both of them expand the philosophical dimensions of reading and of understanding the needs of the development of black Africa. Both rely on an ideological horizon, but one can easily concede that the depth of patience and reflection which supports these texts, as well as their critical perspective, places them in a strictly philosophical field. If we refer to Figure 1, we might say that this space is in Group B, which consists of works of a strictly philosophical bent.

In Group B, the works tend to correspond or, more precisely, respond to Crahay's ideal definition of philosophy used above: "an explicit, analytical, radically critical and autocritical as well as systematic reflection, bearing on experience, on its human conditions and the meanings and values which it reveals."[42] It is, however, clear that all the texts of the group cannot, in the same way or to the same degree, manifest the conditions required by this ideal definition of philosophy. For a vivid illustration, let us take our horizontal line running across groups A and B from one end to another. If the theoretical function of the full realization of all the philosophical conditions required by the definition is a given point on a horizontal line, this point is found on the extreme right of the line. The field of philosophy in the strict sense would be on this line, between two limits: on the left, in A, on the border of the relation of partial inclusion existing between A and B; on the right, the extreme point of B, beyond which there can no longer be any elements which are members of B. The works of African philosophy, in the strict sense, would therefore be displayed along the line and would be included between the two limits noted. By the manner in which they realize the presuppositions of philosophical work, some texts would be more or less close to the philosophical ideal situated, as we have seen, at an extreme point on the border of B. In the other direction, some other works, because of their proximity to the ethnophilosophical and ideologicophilosophical productions, would be more or less near the point of limit in A: stated in a different way, a place on the arc which, in A, demarcates the zone of inclusion of B. Nevertheless, realism would urge us to consider this border as not well defined. Instead of supposing a clear division, we would have to make provision for a relatively free zone to allow movement from the field of philosophy in the strict sense to that of philosophy in a wider sense. And, if one can accept comparisons, this intermediate region would be similar to the isoglossal zones which philologists recognize in the drawing of geographical borders separating two linguistic communities that are spatially close to each other.

How is African philosophy in the strict sense presented? As a new field, it is difficult to establish an organization for it as clear as that of the works of philosophy in the wider sense.[43] To begin with, because of the criterion of increasing complexity of philosophical needs, the easiest way would be to take note of its high points in chronological order: (1) a philosophical reflection on the conditions of the possibility of African philosophy, (2) a reflection on the significance of Western science, (3) a reflection on philosophy as a critical auxiliary to the process of African development, and finally (4) philosophical hermeneutics.

The first African text which seriously invites critical reflection on the foundation of an African philosophy is that of F. Eboussi-Boulaga, "Le Bantu Problématique" (1968).[43] A long article published by *Présence Africaine*, it is built on two startling premises. The first is a comment by Albert Gérard concerning a statement made by the Congress of Black Writers and Artists held in Rome: "By declaring that the philosophical effort of traditional Africa has always been reflected through vital attitudes and has never had purely conceptual ends, the Committee on Philosophy created by the Congress of Rome recognizes in fact that African thinking has not gone beyond the preconceptual stage."[44] The second involves a major problem with the schema of Tempels' *Bantu Philosophy*: the presupposition that an ontology can be derived from behavior and customs, not as a symbol of human language but as a sort of observable being. From these two positions, Eboussi-Boulaga is going to hunt down the meaning, trace the limits of "this beautiful argumentation from the outside" operated by Tempels, and end with the need for philosophical thinking of another kind. Towa expands the question by insisting that we go back to the analysis of ethnophilosophical assumptions and to the necessity of promoting an essentially critical step. He thinks that to bring to light a genuine Negro-African philosophy would securely establish the fact that our ancestors philosophized, without at the same time absolving us from philosophizing.[45] However, it is surely Paulin J. Hountondji who, with his book pointedly entitled *Sur la philosophie africaine* (1977), draws all the conclusions for a critical African philosophy. He pleads for an African philosophy which would be fully a philosophy; therefore, like any philosophy, in one sense, it is a metaphilosophy, evolving through thought and critical reflection on its own history and its own sociohistorical conditioning.[46]

The second point, that of a critical reflection on the significance of Western science, derives from the criticism of anthropology and extends to the human sciences.[47] This reflection has recently been used with particular success in the field of psychopathology with Ibrahim I. D. Sow's book on a dynamic African psychiatry (1977);

in it the author seeks to closely define an African model that is psychopathological and culturally regional.[48] Works of this type seemed unduly critical to some, and one could reproach them for overcrowding the scientific horizon with reiterative challenges which merely show impotence and sterility of thought, rather than dynamic creativity. In actuality, up to now, criticism has tended to focus mainly on works discussing the possible conditions for African philosophy. Often unfair, it too quickly discredited new currents by aspiring to show, on the one hand, an exacting philosophical maturity and, on the other, a challenge to compromise and to an ideological complacency that promotes mystification in African studies. At least these discussions are good indications of the creative power of African self-criticism.[49]

We may suppose that these trends favor the most prolific orientations in contemporary work: the search for a philosophy which could become a critical aid to development and for a philosophical hermeneutics. The first, illustrated by N. Atangana, E. Njoh-Mouelle, and P. E. Elungu,[50] was well covered in two seminars organized by Zairean philosophers: one, at Lubumbashi University, in 1976, on the theme of "The Place of Philosophy in the Human and Cultural Development of Zaire and Africa"; the other in Kinshasa, in 1977, on "Philosophy and Liberation." With his book on the crisis on Muntu (1977), Eboussi-Boulaga elevated the debate to a higher level of complexity, especially by raising questions about the psychological maturity, the linguistic tools, and the usefulness of new critical outlooks. At the same time, in the 1970s, hermeneutical research was born. Avoiding the dead end into which works of restitution inspired by Tempels have led, the new generation was inspired by Hans Gadamer and Paul Ricoeur to read and interpret African tradition; for example, Tshiamalenga with his research on the *ntu* vision of man and the philosophy of sin in the Luba tradition.[51] The same is true of such stimulating works as those by Prosper I. Laleye, Oleko Nkombe, and Oscar Bimwenyi.[52]

In conclusion, we must once again note that some African thinkers philosophize quietly, far from the insistent and noisy arguments concerning Africanness or *Négritude*. They brave the thought of Saint Augustine, Malebranche, Heidegger, Laberthonière, Althusser,

Ricoeur, Gadamer, or Henri Bergson.[53] This African philosophy (which is now thought, sought, defined, and affirmed by itself) is diverse and multiple. Limitations do exist to the outline we have proposed. First, African philosophy cannot yet be thought of in the past, as is, for example, the case with the German philosophy of the eighteenth century. Recent and new, African philosophy exists in the present and, rightly or wrongly, promises itself a fine future. Second, my presentation is only one possible view of this philosophy. One could very easily give another picture of it which, for example, might take into account three major variables: the type of philosophical reflectors, the objective of philosophical systems, and the meaning of the concept of philosophy. One example would be Tempels and Kagame versus Towa and Hountondji. On the one hand, Aristotle and Thomas Aquinas are reflectors of a philosophical practice; on the other, one finds Hegel, Marx, and Althusser. Tempels dreamed of an African Christian civilization; Hountondji believes that Africa's salvation should come from a Marxist lesson, at any rate that it is conditioned by the advocacy of science. Tempels thought that philosophy was a means of vital communication; according to Hountondji, philosophy can only be metaphilosophy. This incredible dialogue seems highly amusing as long as nobody introduces another variable: the possibility of challenging and questioning the epistemological field that allows it and accounts for its persistence.

In all events, one might observe that the trends I have presented could also, from the viewpoint of their methodological presuppositions, be classified into three main groups: first, the domain of anthropological philosophy which, initiated by Tempels and his disciples, has developed into theories of cultural contrasts (Laleye, Mulago, and Sow) as well as into hermeneutics and linguistic philosophy (Kinyongo, Nkombe, Tshiamalenga, and in general the school of Kinshasa); second, the domain of speculative and critical philosophy, which in a radical manner opposes both the silent sectarianism of anthropology and the methodological laziness of ethnophilosophy, defining itself as a field of metaphilosophy and promoting questions on the being of African philosophy (Eboussi-Boulaga, Elungu, Hountondji, and Towa), while allowing strong debates on relationships existing between philosophy, cultures, and epistemological frameworks (Adotevi, Sow, and Pathé Diagne); and third, the domain of Marxist projects with its various charter programs, which both emphasize the universality of its methodology and specify intellectual, materialist practices as instruments for a political power that would organize African social formations according to socialist rationality.

In this essay, I have preferred to understand Kagame and Mulago as philosophers in the same way as Hountondji or Eboussi-Boulaga are because, in my sense, all of them are part of a history of African philosophy in the making. A historical process may well do without the distinctions on the strict or wide use of a discipline and may only retain corrections, complementary acts, and successive "goings beyond" in the image of the model recently offered by E. Fleischman with his Jewish criticism of Christianity.[54] And this criticism, let it be said in passing, was not, except in a few cases, made by professional philosophers. That is to say that the interference, in my analysis, of distinctions between philosophy in the strict sense and philosophy in the wider sense means that it allows a possible classification and a question: What is philosophy? And, more immediately, how can it be understood in Africa?

Attempts have been made to give answers to these questions in particular works, from which I have discussed some of the most representative ones. Answers are also given in a number of journals and good periodicals.[55] Departments of philosophy in the majority of French speaking African universities (Benin, Cameroon, Congo, Gabon, Ivory Coast, Senegal, Togo, Zaire) produce much ongoing research. Professional and scholarly associations are being formed; they include *L'Association des Professeurs de Philosophie* (Ouagadougou), *Le Conseil Inter-Africain de Philosophie* (Cotonou), *La Société Africaine de Philosophie* (Dakar), and *La Société Zaïroise de Philosophie* (Lubumbashi). We must finally note the important role played by the journal *Présence Africaine* and the African Society of Culture. They originally divided up the areas of research in this domain and continue to provide outlets for African thought.

APPENDIX A: TEMPELS' PHILOSOPHICAL SCHOOL

1. Jean-Calvin Bahoken, Cameroonian Protestant minister. Ph.D. (Strasbourg University, France). Major work: *Clairières Métaphysiques Africaines* (Paris: Présence Africaine, 1967).
2. Alexis Kagame, Rwandese Roman Catholic Priest. Ph.D. (Gregorian University, Rome, Italy). Major philosophical works: *La Philosophie bantu-rwandaise de l'être* (Brussels: Académie Royale des Sciences Coloniales, 1956); *La Philosophie bantu comparée* (Paris: Présence Africaine, 1976).
3. François-Marie Lufuluabo-Mizeka, Zairean Roman Catholic Priest, Member of the Franciscan Order. Ph.D. (Rome, Italy). Major works: *Vers une théodicée bantoue* (Tournai: Casterman, 1962); *La Notion luba Bantoue de l'être* (Tournai: Casterman, 1964).
4. Andre Makarakiza, Roman Catholic Archbishop of Kitega (Burundi). Ph.D. (Rome, Italy). Major work: *La Dialectique des Barundi* (Brussels: Académie Royale des Sciences Coloniales, 1959).
5. Celestin Mubengayi-Lwakale, Zairean Roman Catholic Priest. Member of the Community of Immaculate Blessed Mary (CIMC). Ph.D. (Rome, Italy). Major publication: *Initiation africaine et initiation chrétienne* (Léopoldville: Centre d'Etudes Pastorales, 1966).
6. Vincent Mulago gwa Cikala Musharhamina, Zairean Roman Catholic Priest. Ph.D. (Rome, Italy). Major works: *Un Visage africain du christianisme* (Paris: Présence Africaine, 1965); *La Religion traditionnelle des Bantu et leur vision du monde* (Kinshasa: Presses Universitaires du Zaïre, 1973).
7. Edmond Mujynya Nimisi Chiri. Zairean Professor of Philosophy and Politician. Ph.D. (Fribourg, Switzerland). Major publication: *Le Muntu dans l'univers des Bantu* (Lubumbushi: Presses Universitaires du Zaïre, 1972).

APPENDIX B: MILESTONES IN AFRICAN PHILOSOPHY

1887 E. W. Blyden, *Christianity, Islam and the Negro Race* (Rpt. Edinburgh: Edinburgh University Press, 1967).

1899 L. Frobenius, *Die Geschichte des afrikanischen kultur* (Leipzig).

1907-1911 S. Kaoze, *La Psychologie des Bantus et quelques lettres*. (Reprod. anastatique par A. J. Smet, Kinshasa: Faculté de Théologie Catholique).

1933-1949	W. Schmidt, *Die Ursprung der Gottesidee* (Munster: Aschendorff).
1945	P. Tempels, *La Philosophie Bantoue* (Elisabethville: Lovania; New edition, Paris: Présence Africaine, 1949; English version, 1959).
1948	M. Griaule, *Die d'eau: entretiens avec Ogotemmêli* (Paris: Ed. du Chêne, 1948; English version, London: Oxford University Press, 1965).
1948	J. P. Sartre, "Orphée noir," in *Les Temps Modernes*, 4, pp. 577-606.
1954	Chiekh A. Diop, *Nations nègres et culture* (Paris: Présence Africaine).
1956	A. Kagame, *La Philosophie Bantu-Rwandaise de l'être* (Brussels: Académie Royale des Sciences Coloniales).
1958	Jahneitz Jahn, *Muntu, Umrisse der neoafrikanschen Kultur* (Köln: E. Diedericks).
1962	Léopold S. Senghor, *Pierre Teilhard de Chardin et la politique africaine* (Paris: Seuil).
1964	Kwame Nkrumah, *Consciencism. Philosophy and Ideology for Decolonization with Particular Reference to the African Revolution* (London: Heinemann).
1965	Frantz Crahay, "Le 'Décollage' conceptuel: Conditions d'une Philosophie Bantoue, in *Diogène*, 52, pp. 61-84.
1968	Fabien Eboussi-Boulaga, "Le Bantou problématique," in *Présence Africaine*, 66, pp. 4-40.
1975	Alfons J. Smet, ed., *Philosophie Africaine*, 2 vols. (Kinshasa: Presses Universitaires du Zaïre).
1977	F. Eboussi-Boulaga, *La Crise du Muntu* (Paris: Présence Africaine).
1977	P. Hountondji, *Sur la philosophie africaine* (Paris: Maspero; English version, Bloomington: Indiana University Press, 1983).
1980	Alfons J. Smet, *Histoire de la philosophie africaine contemporaine* (Kinshasa: Faculté de Théologie Catholique).

NOTES

1. This paper was originally prepared for the 25th annual meeting of the African Studies Association in November 1982. It provides me with a welcome opportunity to express my appreciation to Denyse de Saivre and Moses Musonda who have aided in shaping it. I owe a tremendous debt of gratitude to Janet and Wyatt MacGaffey for their reading of the manuscript and stylistic suggestions, and to Shirley J. Averill for the typing. It is, however, clear that none of them shares responsibility for the content of this paper. An earlier version of this article was published in *African Studies Review*, 26 (1983): 133-154.

2. A. J. Smet, "Bibliographie sélective de la philosophie Africaine," in *Mélanges de Philosophie Africaine* (Kinshasa: Faculté de Théologie Catholique, 1978), pp. 181-262; and V. Y. Mudimbe, "La pensée africaine contemporaine, 1954-1980. Répertoire chronologique des Ouvrages de Langue Francaise," in *Recherche, Pédagogie et Culture* 56, 9 (1982):68-73.

3. Placide Tempels, *Bantu Philosophy* (Paris: Présence Africaine, 1945), p. 14.

4. *Ibid.*, pp. 167-68.

5. See, for example, L. Frobenius, *Geschichte des afrikanischen Kultur* (Leipzig: 1899); M. Delafosse, *L'Ame nègre* (Paris: Payot, 1922); M. Delafosse, *Les Nègres* (Paris: Rieder, 1927); M. Griaule, *Dieu d'Eau. Entretiens avec Ogotemmêli* (Paris: Chêne, 1948); M. Griaule "Philosophie et Religion des Noirs," in *Présence Africaine*, 8-9, (1950): 307-12; M. Griaule, "Le Savoir des Dogon," in *Journal de la Société des Africanistes*, 22 (1952): 27-42. About Schmidt, see the following note.

6. P. W. Schmidt, *Die Ursprung der Gottesidee. Eine historisch-kritische und positive Studie II Teil: Die Religionen der Urvölker*, bd. IV of *Die Religione der Urvölker Afrikas* (Münster: Aschendorff, 1933); P. W. Schmidt, *Ursprung der Gottesidee*, bd. VI of *Endsynthese der Religionen der Urvölker Amerikas, Asiens, Australiens, Afrikas* (Münster: Aschendorff, 1935); P. W. Schmidt, *Ursprung der Gottesidee*, bd. VII of *Die afrikanischen Hirtenvölker: Hamiten und Hamitoiden*; bd. VIII of *Die afrikanischen Hirtenvölker: Niloten und Synthese mit Hamiten und Hamitoiden* (Münster: Aschendorff, 1940-1949).

7. P. Schebesta, "Die religiöse Anschauungen Süd-Afrikas," in *Anthropos*, 18-19 (1923): 114-24.

8. C. Tastevin, "Les Idées religieuses des africains," in *Géographie*, 62 (1934): 243-70.

9. One could say that *Bantu Philosophy* bears witness to a peculiar moment of Tempels' personal development and his encounter with the "other." The adventure ended in the constitution of a syncretic Christian community. At any rate, as W. DeCraemer put it, "One cannot blame him

[Tempels] for not having been familiar with a revigorated, dynamic, and existence-oriented Existentialism that did not influence Catholic thought until after World War II." W. DeCraemer, *The Jamaa and the Church. A Bantu Catholic Movement in Zaïre* (Oxford: Clarendon Press, 1977), p. 29.

10. A. Kagame, *La Philosophie bantu-rwandaise de l'être* (Brussels: Académie Royale des Sciences Coloniales, 1956), p. 8.

11. See Nt. Tshiamalenga, "Qu'est-ce que le philosophie africaine?" in *La Philosophie Africaine* (Kinshasa: Faculté de Théologie Catholique, 1977).

12. For a more systematic analysis and complete references, see V. Y. Mudimbe, *Visage de la philosophie et de la théologie contemporaine au Zaïre* (Brussels: Cedaf, 1981).

13. F. N. Ablegmagnon, "Du 'Temps' dans la culture ewé," in *Présence Africaine*, 14-15 (1957): 222-32; F. N. Ablegmagnon, "Personne, tradition et culture," in *Aspects de la culture noire* (Paris: Fayard, 1958), pp. 22-30; F. N. Ablegmagnon, "L'Afrique noire: la métaphysique, l'ethique, l'évolution actuelle," in *Comprendre*, 21-22 (1960): 74-82; F. N. Ablegmagnon, "Totalités et systèmes dans les sociétés d'afrique noire," in *Présence Africaine*, 41 (1962) 13-22.

14. M. Hebga, "Plaidoyer pour les logiques de l'afrique noire," in *Aspects de la culture noire* (Paris: Fayard, 1958), pp. 104-16.

15. M. Memel-Fote, "Rapport sur la civilisation animiste," in *Colloque sur la contributions les Religions* (Paris, 1962), pp. 31-58; H. Memel-Forte, "De la paix perpétuelle dans la philosophie pratique des Africains," in *Présence Africaine*, 55 (1965) 15-31.

16. F. Eboussi-Boulaga, "Le Bantou problématique," in *Présence Africaine*, 66 (1968): 4-40.

17. F. Crahay, "Le 'Décollage' conceptuel: conditions d'une philosophie bantoue," in *Diogène*, 52 (1965): 61-84.

18. O. Nkombe and A. J. Smet, "Panorama de la philosophie africaine contemporaine," in *Mélanges de philosophie africaine* (Kinshasa: Fac. de Théologie Catholique, 1978), pp. 263-82. In spite of the criticism which we direct to Nkombe and Smet, our debt to them is important. Their sketch plan was very helpful to us in our first organization of the "disorder" of African philosophy.

19. *Ibid.*, p. 264.

20. *Ibid.*, p. 266.

21. Crahay, *op. cit.*, p. 63.

22. Tshiamalenga, *op cit.*, p. 44.

23. Towa and Hountondji have popularized the term ethnophilosophy, which, in a negative manner, designates works that are philosophical in a wide sense. I am using the term in its etymological value: *ethnos-*

philosophia or weltanschauung of a community. One could relate this meaning to the first uses of the word in the 1950s.

24. A. H. Ba, *Aspects de la civilisation africaine* (Paris: Présence Africaine, 1972); A. Fu-Kiau, *Le mukongo et le monde qui l'entourait* (Kinshasa: Office National de la Recherche Scientifique, 1969).

25. The concept of African tradition is an interesting problem that I shall not address here. Let us say that it signifies a theoretical construct made of pan-African symbols. Whatever they are, these symbols could be understood as being in essence metaphors or, more precisely, metonyms in which the sign of one thing stands for another.

26. B. Hama, *Kotia-Nima*, t.1. *Recontre avec l'Europe*; t.2. *Recontre avec l'Europe*; t.3. *Dialogue avec l'Occident* (Paris: Présence Africaine, 1969); and B. Hama, *Le Retard de l'Afrique, essai philosophique* (Paris: Présence Africaine, 1972).

27. T. K. M. Buakasa, *L'Impensé du discours. Kindoki et Nkisi en pays Kongo du Zaïre* (Kinshasa: Presses Universitaires du Zaïre, 1973).

28. Tshiamalenga, *op. cit.*, p. 38.

29. E. N. C. Mujynya, *L'Homme dans l'univers des Bantu* (Lubumbashi: Presses Universitaires du Zaïre, 1972); V. Mulago, *Un Visage africain du christianisme* (Paris: Présence Africaine, 1965); and G. de Souza, *La Conception de "vie" chez les Fons* (Cotonou: Edit. du Bénin, 1975).

30. J. Kinyongo, "Essai sur la fondation épistémologique d'une philosophie herméneutique en Afrique: le cas de la discursivité," *Présence Africaine*, 109 (1979): 12-16.

31. J. C. Bahoken, *Clairières métaphysiques Africaines. Essai sur la philosophie et la religion chez les Bantu du Sud-Cameroun* (Paris: Présence Africaine, 1967).

32. See note 30.

33. Léopold Sédar Senghor, *Liberté I: négritude et humanisme* (Paris: Seuil, 1964).

34. Alioune Sene, *Sur le chemin de la négritude* (Cairo: Impr. Catholique de Beyrouth, 1966); Thomas Melone, *De la négritude dans la littérature négro-africaine* (Paris: Présence Africaine, 1962); and Marcien Towa, *Léopold Sédar Senghor: négritude ou servitude* (Yaoundé: CLE, 1971).

35. J. M. Abanda Ndengue, *De la négritude au négrisme* (Yaoundé: CLE, 1970); and I. Kimoni, *Destin de la littérature négro-africaine ou problématique d'une culture* (Kinshasa: Presses Universitaires du Zaïre, 1975).

36. A. Nguvulu, *L'Humanisme négro-africain face au développement* (Kinshasa: Okapi, 1971); and J. Kinyongo, *L'Etre manifesté. Méditation philosophique sur l'affirmation de soi, la participation et l'authenticité au Zaïre* (Lubumbashi: Synthèse, 1973).

37. M. Kalanda, *La Remise en question: Base de la décolonisation mentale* (Brussels: Remarques Africaines, 1967); and Léopold Sédar Senghor, "Authenticité et négritude," in *Zaïre-Afrique*, 102 (1976): 81-86; and Léopold Sédar Senghor, *Liberté III: négritude et civilisation de l'universel* (Paris: Seuil, 1977).
38. F. Eboussi-Boulaga, *La Crise du Muntu* (Paris: Présence Africaine, 1977).
39. See, for example, A. A. Dieng, *Hegel, Marx, Engels et les problèmes de l'Afrique noire* (Dakar: Sankoré, 1978).
40. J. Jahn, *Muntu. An Outline of the New African Culture* (New York: Grove Press, 1961), p. 17.
41. D. Nothomb, *Un humanisme africain* (Brussels: Lumen Vitae, 1965).
42. F. Crahay, "Le 'Decollage' conceptuel: Conditions d'une philosophie Bantoue." *Diogène*, 52, pp. 61-84.
43. See, for example, A. J. Smet, "Histoire de la philosophie africaine: Problèmes et méthode," in *La Philosophie africaine* (Kinshasa: Fac. de Théologie Catholique, 1977), pp. 47-68; A. J. Smet, *Histoire de la philosophie africaine* (Kinshasa: Fac. de Théologie Catholique, 1980); H. Maurier, *Philosophie de l'Afrique noire* (St. Augustin bei Bonn: Verlag des Anthropos-Instituts, 1976); A. A. Dieng, *Contribution à l'etude des problèmes philosophiques en Afrique noire* (Paris: Nubia, 1983).
44. Eboussi-Boulaga, "Le Bantou Problematique" in *Présence Africaine*, 66 (1968):6.
45. Marcien Towa, *Essai sur la problématique philosophique dans l'Afrique actuelle* (Yaoundé: CLE, 1971).
46. P. J. Hountondji, *Sur la philosophie africaine. Critique de l'ethnophilosophie* (Paris: Maspero, 1977). See also P. J. Hountondji, "Distances," in *Recherche, Pédagogie et Culture*, 49, 9 (1980):27-33; and P. J. Hountondji, "Que peut la philosophie?" in *Présence Africaine*, 119 (1981):47-71.
47. See, for example, S. Adotévi, *Négritude et négrologues* (Paris: Plon, 1972); V. Y. Mudimbe, *L'Autre face du royaume: Une: introduction à la critique des lignages en folie* (Lausanne: L'Age d'Homme, 1974): V. Y. Mudimbe, *L'Odeur du père* (Paris: Présence Africaine, 1982); B. Ngoma, "La Récusation de la Philosophie par la Société Africaine," in *Mélanges de Philosophie Africaine* (Kinshasa: Fac. de Théologie Catholique, 1978), pp. 85-100.
48. I. E. D. Sow, *Psychiatrie dynamique Africaine* (Paris: Payot, 1977).
49. See, for example, Dieng, *op cit.*
50. N. Atangana, *Travail et développement* (Yaoundé: CLE, 1971); E. Njoh-Mouelle, *De la médiocrité à l'excellence* (Yaoundé: CLE, 1970); E. Njoh-Mouelle, *Jalons. Recherches d'une mentalité neuve* (Yaoundé: CLE, 1970); E. Njoh-Mouelle, *Jalons II l'Africanisme aujourd'hui* (Yaoundé:

CLE, 1975); P. E. Elungu, "Authenticité et culture," in *Revue Zaïroise de Psychologie et de Pédagogie*, 2, 1 (1973): 71-74; P. E. Elungu, "La Philosophie, condition du développement en Afrique aujourd'hui?" in *Présence Africaine*, 103 (1977): 3-18; P. E. Elungu, "La Philosophie africaine hier et aujourd'hui," in *Mélanges de philosophie africaine* (Kinshasa: Faculté de Théologie Catholique, 1978), pp. 9-32.

51. Nt. Tshiamalenga, "La Vision ntu de l'Homme: Essai de philosophie linguistique et anthropologique," in *Cahiers des Religions Africaines*, 7 (1973): 176-99; Nt. Tshiamalenga, "La Philosophie de la faute dans la tradition luba," in *Cahiers des Religions Africaines*, 8 (1974): 167-86; Nt. Tshiamalenga, "Langues Bantu et philosophie: Le Cas du Ciluba," in *La Philosophie africaine* (Kinshasa: Fac. de Théologie Catholique, 1977), pp. 147-58.

52. P. I. Laleye, *Pour une anthropologie repensée* (Paris: La Pensée Universelle, 1977); O. Nkombe, "Méthode et point de départ en philosophie Africaine: authenticité et libération," in *La Philosophie africaine* (Kinshasa: Fac. de Théologie Catholique, 1977), pp. 69-87; O. Nkombe, "Essai de sémiotique formelle: Les rapports différentiels," in *Mélanges de philosophie Africaine* (Kinshasa: Faculté de Théologie Catholique, 1978), pp. 131-48; O. Nkombe, *Métaphore et métonymie dans les symboles parémiologiques: L'Intersubjectivité dans les proverbes tetela* (Kinshasa: Fac. de Théologie Catholique, 1979); O. Nkombe, "La Métaphysique vive et la métaphysique morte," in *Combats Pour un Christianisme Africain* (Kinshasa: Faculté de Théologie Catholique, 1981), pp. 149-58; O. Bimwenyi-Kweshi, *Discours théologique Africain* (Paris: Présence Africaine, 1980).

53. For example, see P. E. Elungu, *Etendue et Connaissance dans la philosophie de Malebranche* (Paris: Vrin, 1973); A. M. Ngindu, *Le Problème de la connaissance religieuse d'après Lucien Laberthonière* (Kinshasa: Faculté de Théologie Catholique, 1978); J. Ntedika, *L'Evolution de la doctrine du purgatoire chez S. Augustin* (Paris: Etudes Augustiniennes, 1966); O. Ugirasheguja, *Dialogue entre la poésie et la pensée dans l'oeuvre de Heidegger* (Brussels: Lumen Vitae, 1977).

54. E. Fleischman, *Le Christianisme 'mis à nu'* (Paris: Plon, 1970).

55. The following journals come out regularly: *Bulletin de la Société Africaine de Philosophie* (Dakar), *Les Cahiers du Département de Philosophie* (Yaoundé), *Les Cahiers des Religions Africaines* (Kinshasa), *Les Recherches Philosophiques Africaines* (Kinshasa), *La Revue Ivoirienne de Philosophie et de Culture* (Abidjan), and *Psychopathologie Africaine* (Dakar). There are also some which come out irregularly: *Les Archives de Philosophie Africaine* (Lubumbashi), *Les Cahiers Philosophiques Africains* (Lubumbashi), and *Conséquence* (Cotonou).

8   ABIOLA IRELE

Contemporary Thought in French Speaking Africa

In the introductory pages of his short book *Feuerbach and the End of German Philosophy*, Friedrich Engels provides an interesting testimony as to the impact which *The Essence of Christianity* had upon his and Karl Marx's generation of German intellectuals. Engels' testimony not only throws light on a significant moment in the development of the ideological system to which he made such an important contribution but also, in broader terms, illustrates the correlation between the political and social conditions of a historical period and the movement of ideas which it reflects. In the particular instance of mid-nineteenth century Germany, and with specific reference to the development of Marxism as a system of thought, Engels' testimony points to the realization among the young German intellectuals about the lack of a real correspondence between the idealism of established German philosophy, in particular its Hegelian brand, and the social and economic transformations that were then taking place. Feuerbach was thus an important stage in the reaction against Hegel of which Marx's dialectical materialism was to be, in one particular direction, a culmination. The full import of this reaction came then to be a profound transformation of the mental universe which would ultimately lead to a significant revolution of thought.[1]

    I want to suggest in this essay that a comparable development in the realm of thought is taking place in Africa today, a development which, will, I believe, have implications for the way in which we as Africans perceive ourselves and our position in the modern world—for the way in which we not only conceive our collective historical being but also our possibilities within the historical process as it unfolds in our own time.

Put quite simply, this development involves a complete rethinking of the tenets and assumptions that have gone into the formation of African attitudes and found an articulation in the prevailing intellectual reaction to the colonial experience. The terms in which the investigation of the African experience has so far been carried on are being questioned and revised, and the set of problems perceived by an earlier generation of African and black intellectuals is now being supplanted by a new set of problems, raised by the younger generation. In other words, there is beginning to be a redefinition of what one might call the "African problematic," and this redefinition appears to be related to the changed realities of the contemporary African situation in the post-colonial era. A new perception of African problems is thus emerging, affecting as a consequence the mental processes which were implied in the emergence of the nationalist consciousness.

This development is most evident in the way the movement of ideas has been proceeding among French speaking African intellectuals. The clearest indication is provided here by the steady buildup of the reaction against the *Négritude* movement and the ideas it propagated, especially through the writings of Léopold Sédar Senghor. I propose therefore to examine this phenomenon, placing it in a perspective that sees it as an evolution, not so much in historical terms but rather as a process—a dialectic, if one prefers—having a certain coherence which derives from an immediate relation to the course of a general African experience.

When one considers the broad movement and the main points of emphasis in modern African thought,[2] it seems clear that it has so far been dominated by a single problem: that of identity. By this, I mean that, for generations of African intellectuals urged by the very pressures of the colonial experience to engage their intelligence upon the fact of this experience and to consider its implications for themselves and their fellow Africans, the central theme of their reflection has been that of self-definition in terms of being Africans. The intellectual response to European conquest and domination took the form of a long and sustained effort on the part of the Westernized elite to situate themselves anew in relation to their cultural and spiritual antecedents as defined by their African environment and to apprehend in themselves an essential African nature, supposedly obscured by the cultural and spiritual impositions of the dominant European civilization, but retaining a profound correspondence with their original sources of being.

Though often posed in these abstract terms, the problem of identity as perceived by these intellectuals was of course bound up with the historical encounter between Africa and Europe in terms of its concrete effects upon every African involved in this encounter. In particular, it was not divorced from the social interests of the rising African bourgeoisie. As the example of the Gold Coast intellectuals clearly indicates, cultural nationalism subserved immediate political and economic ambitions and provided a rationale for them.[3] But it is also important to consider that the prominence which African intellectuals have regularly given to the problem of identity has been a function of their cultural and psychological situation as a class. The African intellectual is indeed an individual at the meeting point of two cultures. It is probably safe to say that the successive generations of intellectuals who came to maturity within the colonial system experienced the contradictions of the system most directly as an intense psychological and moral tension, a tension they interpreted as a form of spiritual alienation. They tended therefore to subsume all the other concrete issues that made the objective reality of their situation—the political, social, and economic issues of colonial dependence—under the single problem of recovering a unified consciousness of the self.

We find the most vivid dramatization of this issue in Cheikh Hamidou Kane's novel, *L'Aventure Ambiguë*, whose hero, Samba Diallo, is the prototype in modern African literature of the Westernized African torn between two worlds and the conflict of values which each represents. In Kane's novel, the trauma of European conquest in the various areas of life and expression within an African social formation is perceived ultimately in sole relation to a disruption in the hero's being and consciousness; thus, his existential plight represents the thematic focus, the significant structural level of the novel.[4] The example illustrates the way in which the affective coloration of the intellectual reaction to colonialism conditions, as it were, an idealist orientation in African thinking, which comes to provide the terms of a whole discourse around the issue of identity.

There was of course an objective dimension to the African intellectual's preoccupation with the problem of identity. Colonial domination was not only a political fact but represented as well the imposition of global constraint upon the colonized society; it also effected a general reordering of life, producing social and cultural tensions that were reflected in the consciousness of the individual, and through the interpenetration of minds, in a collective cultural malaise. The so-called messianic movements in Africa as elsewhere attest to the comprehensive nature of cultural resistance by the colonized. They define the more restricted form of reaction among the intellectuals, and it appears, in sociological terms, to be an articulated form of counteracculturation.

But if the quest for an original integrity of being came to dominate African thinking, it was not only because it fulfilled a psychological need but also because it served to answer the system of rationalizations by which Western ideologues sought to justify European domination of other races.[5] We know that the cultural argument was a prominent and even central one in the imperialist ideology. It was directly from this argument that the implication was drawn as to the natural inferiority of the African and by extension of the entire black race, and this supposedly made its members fit to be subjugated. The myth of inferiority could not but provoke an anxiety in the African intellectual who encountered it at every turn as part of the process of his intellectual formation within the colonial educational system and indeed as a regular feature of his colonial experience. More than this, the myth could not but induce in him a process of self-exploration, touching upon the quality not only of his individual mental dispositions but also of the entire cultural and spiritual inheritance in his African background. The implication here is that the terms of reference for African self-reflection were determined by the fact of its opposition to the ideology of imperialism. What has been called modern African philosophy starts as a polemical form of thought, a counterthesis, placed in historical and logical relation to the scheme of ideas and representations by which the colonial system was sustained.

The sociological significance of modern African thought, in its preoccupation with the problem of identity as the intellectual focus of a whole movement of counteracculturation, is thus complemented by its ideological significance as the elaboration of a whole system of countervalues. In its restatement of a formulation regarding the nature of the African—and of the black race in general—proposed by the racial ideology which went with European domination, the intellectual reaction of the African came to involve a comprehensive reassessment of the African universe in both its objective historical dimensions and in its inner spiritual qualities. The bent of this enterprise was clearly to give a new and positive significance to a world that had been devalued in real terms as a result of the Western negative appraisal of that world and of the race associated with it.

It has been necessary to recall these elements that define the framework of development of modern African thought in order to place the *Négritude* movement in its proper historical perspective. The special significance of *Négritude* resides first of all in the fact that it is the culmination of the process of self-reflection implied in the intellectual reaction to colonial domination and, secondly, in the particular quality of its formulation of what I've called the African problematic, that is, of a long-standing question about the place and role of the African in a world dominated by the West. The special significance to which I've called attention implies a progression in that the theory of *Négritude* gathers up into a focussed articulation the various strands of the process of African self-exploration, then ties them up into a unifying concept of African and black identity. To place this progression in a clear light, it is enough, I believe, to indicate the way in which Edward Wilmot Blyden's notion of the "African personality" is given complex elaboration in Senghor's *Négritude* and transformed into a fully fledged theory of African being.[6]

In considering *Négritude* itself, we need to distinguish between two acceptations of the term. In its first and general sense, the term refers to the phenomenon of black awakening, as a global response to the collective situation. Associated with this sense is Jean-Paul Sartre's definition of *Négritude* as "an affective attitude to the world,"[7] that is, a subjective disposition expressive of the black man's total apprehension of his peculiar situation. Sartre not only related the black man's apprehension to the historical conditions of his existence as a member of an oppressed race, but basing his analysis on the character of the black poetry in French which was the immediate occasion of his definition, he went on to give an active significance to the black *prise de conscience*, seeing in this the passage from an unreflected to a reflected mode of experience. It indicates therefore a collective revolutionary project destined to transform the conditions of the black man's existence and thus, ironically, to eliminate the need for a self-directed consciousness on the part of the black subject himself. We might say that Sartre's definition situates *Négritude* in a relative perspective and is intended to accord it a universalizing purpose.

The other sense of the term emerges from Senghor's formulation of *Négritude* as a concept and can be considered a special case, a restricted sense within the general one. In effect, for Senghor, the term in its proper reference designates an attribute of the black man, specific to the race in its timeless constitution as a distinct branch of humanity. Senghor insists on the distinction between "subjective *Négritude*," which corresponds to Sartre's definition, and "objective *Négritude*," which denotes an African mode of life and values and the fundamental adherence of the black man's basic personality to this reality. *Négritude* in this sense seeks to grasp the singular wholeness of the varied "patterns of culture"[8] that characterize African societies as well as their derivations in the New World—that is, an underlying principle which may be said to define a common spirit of African civilization.[9] Along this range of references, the term points ultimately to the conception of a unique racial endowment of the black man.

There is a clear divergence between Sartre's historical conception of *Négritude* and the ethnic conception which emerges from Senghor's formulation. The point of remarking upon this divergence is to emphasize the motivation behind Senghor's thinking; it appears to be the need to differentiate the black man, to present him in his original bond with a determining structure of African civilization. The salient points of this theory are too well known to require exposition here, but we may remark upon three aspects which contribute to its coherence and give it significance.

To begin with, Senghor's *Négritude* rests upon a theory of culture. The observation already advanced in regard to Senghor's conception of the term indicates that the concept of *Négritude* is grounded in a firm correlation between race and culture. This is not to say that *Négritude* is a racial theory in the sense that it is an exclusive vision of a race and the way of life associated with it. There is, however, an explicit postulation of an intimate relationship between the biological constitution of the black race and the cultural works it has produced in history. For Senghor, culture has a racial character to the extent that culture is the effect of a total response by man to his environment, a response that involves his total being, including his organic constitution. The distinctive features of the various forms of African cultural expression derive from a long process of adjustment by man to the natural milieu of Africa; they represent a structure of equilibrium between the physical determinations of the environment and the human pressures, immediate and spiritual, upon the environment. The process of adjustment to the milieu left its impress on the African in such a way as to determine a racial character in all black men.[10] Senghor has often had recourse to certain notions of character study to distinguish the black race from the other races, to explain the observable differences between human groupings in terms not merely of their external aspects but of the common internal dispositions which they express and which affect modes of living. Whatever this approach is worth, the point remains that Senghor's theory of *Négritude* is predicated on the idea of a lively reciprocity between racial character as conditioned by an original formative milieu and the different cultural forms to be found in the world.

Senghor's purpose becomes all the more evident when we consider the second aspect of his theory, the fact that it involves an epistemology. One of the key ideas in Senghor's system is that of emotion, which he virtually erects into a category of knowledge and attributes to the African as a cardinal principle of his racial disposition. Senghor has devoted considerable attention to what he calls the "physiopsychology of the African."[11] He has sought to clarify what, in the very organic constitution of the African, makes for a distinct tonality in his comportment, in his manner of being. By identifying this element as a particular quality of emotion, Senghor postulates a distinct African mode of apprehension to which the neuroorganic equipment of the race (as shaped over the ages) predisposes the black man: a mode of "affective participation" by the black subject in the object of his experience.

It is easy to recognize here the influence of Lucien Lévy-Bruhl, but once again, the point of remarking upon this influence is to note Senghor's method of dealing with the French anthropologist's idea of "primitive mentality" by hardly assuming it on his own account while giving it a different connotation and even significance. For Senghor, each people, race, and civilization has its own manner of envisaging the world, and each manner is as valid ultimately as another. The African manner is rooted in the values of emotion rather than in the logical categories historically developed in the tradition of European rationalism, and it is as valid in its own terms as the European, hence his well-known dictum: "Emotion is African as Reason is Hellenic."[12]

The physiopsychology of the African, the result of his timeless insertion within a certain milieu and his organic adaptation to that milieu, thus conditions a distinctive mode of apprehension. That mode itself finds objective expression not only in characteristic cultural forms but also in the superstructural sphere of collective life in the realm of thought and values. The emotive disposition of the African, for example, appears as the principal factor in the pronounced mystical outlook of man in the African world, an intense religiosity that expresses a total grasp of life in the universe. At the imaginative and spiritual level of collective expression, this outlook receives an elaboration in those mythical representations and symbolic schemes which define a structure of being and consciousness. In proposing this view of African life, which also has implications for his interpretation of traditional forms of social organization in Africa, Senghor gives to his theory of *Négritude* the dimension of a cosmology.

For reasons which will become apparent later, it is important to draw attention to the contribution made by Father Placide Tempels' exposition of the so-called Bantu philosophy to the architecture of Senghor's theory. As is well known, Tempels extracted a coherent worldview from the mores of the Baluba (in present day Zaire) and attached this label to it. The crux of this philosophy is an ontology in which being is conceived not as a static notion but as a "vital force" and in which the universe is seen as an interrelation of forces within the whole realm of existence. According to this primordial scheme, everything that can be thought to exist is endowed with vital force and contingent upon certain factors that may intervene in the course of existence.[13]

It is not surprising that Tempels' theory features prominently in Senghor's *Négritude*, into which "Bantu philosophy" is integrated in such a way as to demonstrate a distinctive African form of spirituality. The attraction of Tempels' work resides not only in its apparent vindication of the African claim to an elevated system of thought but also in its providing a conceptual framework for this African mode of thought. The vitalist emphasis of Bantu philosophy ties in very well with the epistemology implicit in Senghor's *Négritude*, and its postulation of a hierarchy of forces attributes to the African a comprehensive world view which presupposes characteristic structures of mental projection. In his assimilation of Bantu philosophy into a general scheme of ideas concerning the nature of the African, Senghor's purpose is to present through *Négritude* an independent African system of thought, a distinctive African humanism.

In the preindependence period, *Négritude* was the dominant ideology in francophone Africa. Thanks to the personality of Senghor, it has maintained an ideological presence in the postindependence period, and the attacks that continue to be directed against it attest to its ongoing importance. The peculiar force of *Négritude* stems from the fact that it formed so comprehensive a system of ideas that, in one way or another, it responded to African interests in the colonial situation and thus came to serve as a significant ideological reference—in both a positive and a negative sense—for the intellectual activity of French speaking black intellectuals. We may even go further to observe that *Négritude* was the most complete expression of the African state of mind in relation to the colonial experience. The political and cultural aspects of nationalism in Africa must be taken together, in their intimate association, to achieve a full appreciation of the nationalist phenomenon itself, because the drive for political autonomy reflected the growth and consolidation of a confident awareness of the self. The specific contribution of *Négritude* to this development was to articulate, in the form of an all-encompassing concept of black identity, the sense of the African's separate cultural and spiritual inheritance.

Senghor's method, as we have seen, consisted in seeking a validation of this concept by reference to an "objective *Négritude*" of the African's collective cultural expression, as documented in the ethnographic literature devoted to African societies. Senghor's example inspired a line of development in French African intellectual activity that came to have important consequences for its subsequent direction. This line of development involved what amounts to an entire school of scholars, who, in the wake of Tempels, devoted their attention to the investigation and elucidation of traditional thought systems in an effort to derive from them a distinctive African philosophy.

The most notable effort in this connection was perhaps that of Alexis Kagame, who sought to follow up Tempels' work by verifying within his native Rwanda culture the Belgian missionary's theory of Bantu ontology. In his book, *La Philosophie Bantu-Rwandaise de l'être*, published in 1956, Kagame adopted an original approach to the question. It consisted of analysing the Rwanda language in an effort to demonstrate the existence among its users of a different and more precise intelligence of the notion of being than the one that had been suggested by Tempels. Kagame pointed out that this notion was rendered in the abstract by the radical *ntu* and in its manifestations or modalities by four terms derived from it: *Umuntu*, which designated man, a being endowed with intelligence; *Ikintu*, anything without intelligence; *Ahantu*, space-time; and *Ukuntu*, modality, such as quantity, quality, and relation.[14] Kagame maintains that for the user of the language, these terms prescribe a universal order and correspond to the world. More, they represent not only an order of essences but also an order of concepts and thus provide an image of the mental structure which the language itself determines in its users. The ontology of the Rwanda is thus present in the grammatical structure and the semantic field proposed to them by their language; it has an effect on thought processes comparable to that of classical Greek on the pioneers of Western philosophy and in particular on Aristotle. Kagame goes on to claim that the Rwanda conception of the world based on this ontology is explicit, having found expression in the oral tradition of the people and constituting an effective factor of their indigenous forms of social organization and total cultural life. In a subsequent work, *La Philosophie Bantu Comparée*, Kagame recognizes the cultural unity of the area covered by the Bantu family of languages, not only in terms of their common use of classifiers but also in what he describes as "the mental organization of the symbol of ideas, the categorization of beings and whatever else exists, the conception of the world of the existence of what lies beyond."[15]

Kagame's exploration of the Bantu worldview takes him well beyond Tempels, whose theory of "vital force" he refutes; but he does appear to remain within the same perspective, for he too wants to establish the reality of a distinctive African mode of thought and existence. Quite apart from the theoretical merits of the case he makes, the ideological import of his point of view cannot be missed. It becomes even more manifest in the work of other francophone African scholars concerned with Bantu philosophy as a specific problem or as part of a general construction of an authentic African system equivalent to that of Western philosophy.[16] All this effort came in the wake of *Négritude* and reflects its spirit, its attempt to give a conceptual form to an immediately felt sense of African identity.

The same spirit animates the work of Cheikh Anta Diop, the foremost representative of another group of scholars whose activity runs parallel to that of the philosophers. This group may be described as the historical school of the *Négritude* movement. It may come as a surprise to see Cheikh Anta Diop associated in this way with Senghor, but the rapprochement is justified by the fact that his work takes its place and meaning from the same context of cultural nationalism as that in which *Négritude* was born; Diop occasionally even employs some of the latter's conceptual terms. In a more fundamental way, Diop's work addresses itself to the same problem of African identity which preoccupied writers in the *Négritude* tradition.

Diop has called his method "historical sociology," but no neat label can be attached to his approach, which involves a vast erudition and has its foundations in the natural sciences and the humanities. The range of his scholarship is evident in his first work, *Nations Nègres et culture*, which can be said to have attained the status of a classic in black intellectual circles.[17] It is easy to explain the success of this book, for it contains the most overt and vigorous challenge to the cultural argument of the imperialist ideology; its firm nationalist stand is still able to elicit a deep African response even today. As is well known, the primary objective of the book is to demonstrate the Negro origins of ancient Egyptian civilization and thus to refute the argument that the black race had produced no great world civilization; however, the discussion extends beyond an argument for this thesis to a demonstration of the continuity between ancient Egyptian civilization and the contemporary cultures of black Africa.

A full exposition of Diop's thesis cannot be undertaken here, but it is not without interest to chart the lines of his thinking for an understanding of its mechanisms and its course. It is essential in this respect to stress the fact that Diop's presentation of his thesis was in fact the intervention of an African in a debate, that had long been going on in Western scholarly circles, about the racial character of the ancient Egyptians. His contribution was motivated by a dissatisfaction with the point of view espoused by European scholars who seemed (to him) to have gone deliberately against the evidence in classifying the Egyptians among the white races. Diop attributes this point of view to the effect of racial prejudice against the black race and credits it with producing a falsification of history. An element of racial indignation thus permeates Diop's discussion, lending to his work a strong polemical tone which may not be thought compatible with objective scholarship, but which, under the circumstances, was necessitated by the force of the established ideas with which he was contending. Nevertheless, Diop does raise important issues of historical method in his ruthless assault upon the prevailing ideas, showing up the system of rationalizations by which they were constructed. The least that can be said is that *Nations nègres et culture* succeeds in reopening the whole question about the racial origin of ancient Egyptian civilization.

In two subsequent works, *Anteriorité des civilisations négres* and *Parenté génétique de l'Egyptien pharaonique et des langues négro-africaines*,[18] both of which must be seen as complementary to the first work, Diop further develops his arguments for considering ancient Egyptian civilization as essentially a creation of the black race; he does this by marshalling an array of evidence drawn from a formidably diverse range of special fields: archaeology, paleontology, physical anthropology, oesteology, classical European studies, historical and comparative linguistics, as well as the central field of Egyptology itself. It is impossible to judge the value of the evidence, internal and external, without some specialized knowledge in this vast area of scholarship. It is possible to note, however, that his examination of ancient Egyptian institutions and thought provides him with a cultural argument for postulating an essential affinity between the forms of social organization and the cosmology of the ancient Egyptians and those that appear to characterize the traditional African world. In this respect, he comes closest to Senghor, both in his vision of the African world as a unified whole and in his acquiescence with the theory of Tempels as regards the vitalist conception of the world. The cultural argument leads Diop to the following categorical affirmation:

The identity of Egyptian culture and black culture could not be more evident. It is by reason of this essential identity of genius, culture and race that all black men can today legitimately link their culture to ancient Egypt and build a modern culture on that basis. It is a dynamic, modern contact with Egyptian antiquity that will enable Negroes to discover more and more each day the intimate relationship between all Blacks on the continent and the mother valley of the Nile. It is by means of this dynamic contact that the Negro will arrive at the profound conviction that these temples, these forests of columns, these bas-reliefs, these mathematics, this medicine, all this science, are indeed the works of his ancestors and that it incumbs upon him to recognize himself completely in them.[19]

For all the ideological flavor of this statement, it would be a limited view of Diop's purpose to see in this passage merely a simple reversal of established Western prejudices against the African and the black race. It is certainly true that Diop appears here at pains to demonstrate that Africans have had a past of great technical and intellectual achievement. Elsewhere, he makes the point that Western civilization owes an original debt to Africa through the direct influence of ancient Egypt on its early formation in classical Greece. But the real thrust of Diop's affirmation lies in another direction. The cultural argument is accessory to a much wider project: it serves to establish ancient Egyptian civilization as a retrospective reference and primordial model of African existence and endeavor. Diop's purpose is not merely to refute the theory of black inferiority by presenting the African in the image of technical man, *homo faber*, but more significantly to provide a broader perspective upon African collective experience and identity, this identity being defined not as an intangible entity of his racial being but as an effective presence in the world. In this perspective, the colonial experience itself is reduced to a mere interlude in a historical process that stretches back to an original time during the emergence of the race and forward to a creative future of new fulfillment.

Indeed, Diop can be said to have constructed a general model of history, stated in geosociological and ethnic terms, within which his particular conception of African development finds its place and meaning. In his book, *L'Unité culturelle de l'Afrique noire*, he reacts against the evolutionist view of human experience which, in the hands of Western scholars, almost invariably ascribes a superior position to the white race and to Western forms of cultural expression. Diop proceeds to a vast demarcation of the prehistoric and ancient world between the northern and southern races, using as a basis their different kinship structures. Thus, he associates the patriarchal system with the southern, arguing that the opposition is the effect of a primitive differentiation between the nomadic life of the former and the sedentary life of the latter. Diop develops this opposition throughout the full range of social institutions and value systems which he sees as characteristic of each race in its original determination. He arrives at the conclusion that the course of human history can be explained by the interaction, often marked by conflict, between the aggressive disposition and pessimistic world outlook of the northern races, conditioned by their prolonged nomadism, and the more peaceful inclinations and optimistic approach to the universe of the southern races, due to their much earlier sedentarization—in terms, that is, of the opposition between the divergent historical personalities incarnated in the two races.[20]

Few scholars would, I imagine, want to commit themselves to this ethnic conception of history, but it is essential to point out that in its actual exposition in Diop's book, it is not merely an opposition between North and South that is postulated, but in fact a relation; the manifestations in history of the two races are seen as two distinct currents, two related directions of a single universal historical process. As against the unilateral conception of Hegel and those Western scholars who have derived their philosophy of history from him, Diop proposes an all-embracing perspective to view the course of human development: a perspective that throws a new light upon Africa, grasped as an indivisible whole and upon its contribution to that development. As he says, "Historical science itself cannot shed all the light one might expect it to cast upon the past until it integrates the black component of humanity, in proportion to the role it has actually played in history, into its synthesis."[21]

We may conclude then that two clear moments emerge in the unfolding of Diop's ideological project. The first consists in the effort to establish a historical and cultural connection between ancient Egypt and black Africa, in such a way as to give historical depth and resonance to the contemporary African consciousness. The second derives from the will to place the African continent and the black race firmly within the movement of universal history, to project the vision of a universal history in which Africa is profoundly involved.

The two currents I have tried to distinguish as the "philosophical" and the "historical" within the general movement of cultural nationalism among French speaking African intellectuals can be said to complement each other admirably, despite their divergence on certain points. Their common acceptance of a global reality of African identity, in whatever terms this is defined, and their common insistence upon its distinctive quality can be said to resolve their divergent points of view within a common vision of African existence. Both Senghor and Diop proceed by attaching a positive value to the objective difference between African and European civilizations at the moment of their historical confrontation; they take up, each in his own way, the ideological gauntlet thrown down by European racism and ethnocentrism. The differences between them appear, therefore, largely a matter of detail, or, more correctly, of perspective, affecting areas of emphasis in each writer's effort to give body to his idea of Africa—to think through the vicissitudes of a disturbing history to a fundamental vision of African integrity.

The two currents represented by Senghor and Diop thus bear upon the same African problematic that had been created by the colonial experience. It would be a simplification to say that the reaction against the trend of intellectual and ideological activity which they both represent arose immediately with the passing of the colonial era, but there can be no doubt that it has developed in amplitude largely as a function of the consequent change in attitudes and by direct reference to the new social and political realities of the post-colonial situation in Africa. The workings of the process leading to this development can be seen in the way the objections to *Négritude* have converged to define a new perspective upon African problems at the present moment.

The objections to *Négritude* have tended to focus not only on its explicit theoretical terms but also on what are taken to be the practical political and social implications of the theory. This double trend was established in the essay entitled "La Négritude: Réalité ou mystification?" published in 1956 by an African student, Albert Franklin, whose vigorous criticism anticipated practically all the arguments that were later developed against Senghor's theory by his adversaries.[22] Directing his critique specifically at Sartre's "Orhpée noir," Franklin attacked the French philosopher's apparent endorsement of the image, offered in *Négritude* poetry, of the black man as a nonrational being, disposed to mystic communion with nature rather than to a technical mastery of it. Franklin observed that such an image had no basis in reality, and even if it did, it would not imply a fixed essence of African man but was to be seen rather as an indication of the low state of technical development in traditional African society—a state which could be transcended, giving way to a scientific and rational approach to the universe.

This argument has turned out to be the dominant line of attack on Senghor's theory; it was first given a detailed elaboration by Stanislas Adotévi in his book, *Négritude et négrologues*, which contains the most comprehensive critique of *Négritude* so far published. Adotévi places himself on a resolutely sociological plane from which to view the theory. In this way he comes to reject what he regards as its static conception of African cultural reality, resulting from an abstract schema that is out of touch with the diversified forms of concrete life in the various African societies:

> It presupposes a fixed essence of blackness that cannot be affected by the passage of time. In addition to this immutability is the idea of a specific nature that can not be confirmed in terms of sociological determinants, historical fluctuations, or geographical realities. It makes black men everywhere and at all times into similar beings.[23]

It is not only Senghor's unified conception of African and black cultural expression that is called into question here but also the correlation between race and culture on which it is founded, along with the biological underpinnings that are woven into the structure of his theory. Adotévi specifically attacks this "biologism," which appears to him to be so embedded in the ideological presuppositions of European racism as to be no more than a restatement of them in terms which amount to an acquiescence with their negation of the black man.

As can be seen from the turn which Adotévi's critique finally takes, the political objection to *Négritude* is accompanied by a certain radical stance which does duty in the post-colonial context for the political nationalism of an earlier period and generation. It is in this context that Frantz Fanon came to impinge so directly and so decisively on the development of African thought. It is impossible to doubt that this influence has been dominant in the accentuation of radical thought in post-colonial Africa generally and especially in the radical tone of an opposition to *Négritude* by which a significant section of the younger generation of French African intellectuals can be recognized.

When one considers the effect of Fanon's thought on the ideological temper of this generation, there is no little irony in the fact that the point of departure for his entire reflection was *Négritude*—with the important qualification that it was the profound impression made upon him by the particular manifestation of its spirit in Aimé Césaire's work that impelled him to this reflection. Césaire's brand of *Négritude* involves no elaborate theory of blackness in a total and aggressive response to centuries of denigration and humiliation. The intense symbolism of aggression, which is the hallmark of Césaire's poetry, not only gives expression to this affirmation in an extraordinary burst of poetic energy but it also offers a peculiar complexity of imagery which results from the transformation of a deep structure of consciousness. Césaire's poetic expression thus becomes quite literally an affect: it involves a drama of consciousness, a sloughing off process by which the complex of negative associations through which the black subject has been forced to perceive himself is overturned and transformed into a mode of mental liberation and, ultimately, of self-acceptance.[24]

This cursory examination of Césaire's poetry has been essential for a placing of Fanon's development, because the psychological and moral ferment of Césaire's consciousness, as revealed in his poetry, is the hotbed in which Fanon's thought strikes its roots and issues. It is hardly an exaggeration to say that Césaire's poetry provides the essential ground plan for Fanon's reflection, which can be regarded as a transposition (into ideological propositions) of the psychological processes and wider implications at work in Césaire's poetry. It is indeed the general application of his understanding of these issues to the situation of the black man that forms the subject of his first work, *Peau noire, masques blancs*.[25] The book is a reflection upon the black subject's experience of himself and of the world, as conditioned by his situation. It is, in a sense, a phenomenology of black existence. In simple psychological terms, Fanon investigates the way in which the introjection of social values is disturbed in the case of the black subject placed within a sociopsychological field dominated by the white paradigm. The conflict between the external fact of his blackness and his internalization of a highly valorized symbolism of whiteness creates a distortion of his self-image and installs within him a profound neurosis, with repercussions upon his total mode of being. *Peau noire, masques blancs* contains a diagnosis of the black condition that is certainly more pertinent to the Afro-American and Caribbean experience than to the African, but it has a general relevance in that Fanon offers a psychological (one might even say clinical) explanation for the sense of alienation suffered by the black man under white domination.

Fanon's active participation in the Algerian revolution widened his vision beyond the horizons of *Négritude* and provided a theater for the development of his ideas on a broader format. From the evidence of his testimony on the Algerian war of independence in *Sociologie d'une révolution*,[26] the Algerian insurrection was for him as much a political act, founded upon the moral requirements of an oppressed nation, as an occasion for the colonized natives to effect a reconstruction of their collective personality. The demands of the war, as Fanon recounts it, led to a profound inner transformation of the Algerians themselves—in the general mobilization of the physical and psychic energies of an entire people, old values inappropriate to the situation were swept away, new values created, presaging a new social order. The revolution thus took on the significance of an immense process of collective metamorphosis.

The pronounced psychological bias of Fanon's account of the Algerian revolution issues directly into the ethics of violence developed in the first chapter of his last book, *Les Damnés de la terre*.[27] It is essential to view his ideas on violence in their proper historical context as well as in the full perspective of the evolution of his thought. The mechanisms which Fanon brought to light in his analysis were first suggested to him by his reading of Césaire's poetry and later confirmed in the live context of the Algerian war. In this sense, he was doing no more than continuing the diagnosis of his first work, establishing a real correspondence between the symbolic projection and the physical exteriorization of the torment in the colonized subject's consciousness. His advocacy of violence against colonial domination appears therefore as a prescription, in the full medical sense of the word. His preoccupation with the psychiatric effects of colonial oppression, the distortions it creates within the colonized native, led him to see in the aggressive reaction against this oppression quite simply a therapeutic means of self-recreation for the colonized subject. Through the violence directed at his oppressor, the colonized subject remakes himself as a full human being, without any limiting qualifications to his human status and quality.

Fanon's ethics of violence has a pedigree within Western political thought, for Engels, George Sorel, and V. I. Lenin have all meditated upon the significance of violence in politics. But Fanon gives an original dimension to the question. In his view, the value of violence in the revolutionary situation lies not simply in ensuring the effectiveness of political action, not simply in being the "midwife of history," but in self-realization of the historical subject himself; it has to do with a vision of man creating his own identity in the effervescence of a progressive movement in history.

In its bearing upon *Négritude*, such a vision seems fully in accord with Sartre's emphasis upon the revolutionary significance of the movement, at least of the spirit of its poetic expression as exemplified by Césaire. Senghor's subsequent elaboration of the term into a concept of an African being informed by a living coherence of the traditional culture seems to have alienated Fanon. Indeed, Fanon displayed an insensitivity to the cultural thesis of African nationalism that may be imputed, not as might at first be thought to his West Indian background but rather to his cosmopolitanism. The Algerian experience seems indeed to have confirmed in him what looks like an aversion to traditional cultures to which he tended to attribute a factitious character, if not a retrograde significance. To Fanon's ingrained lack of sympathy for the cultural positions of *Négritude* was joined a political and ideological hostility directly related to his radical commitment. Fanon's sojourn in Ghana as FLN ambassador may well have strengthened this commitment, if it did not engender it. His observation of Kwame Nkrumah's Ghana opened his eyes and his mind to the contradictions inherent in the post-colonial situation, where a national bourgeoisie substitutes itself for the departed colonizer without undertaking an overhaul of the social structure to bring about greater social justice. The Ghanaian experience can be said to have inspired his critique of the new ruling class in Africa, for a crucial chapter of his last book displays a remarkable prescience on the subject. The point that is relevant here, however, is that his dim view of the African bourgeoisie led him to discount both its preindependence nationalism and the cultural affirmation that went with it. In the post-colonial situation, the cultural theories of the bourgeoisie amounted, for him to no more than a form of ideology, in the pejorative sense often given the word by Marx: a superstructural mask thrown over the class interests of the elites. Fanon's scant regard for this form of cultural expression emerges clearly from the following comment: "The substantiality of Negro-African culture is built around the people's struggle, not songs, poems, or folklore."[28]

Later in the same text, Fanon stresses his point with the converse of this statement: "One can hardly desire the spread of African culture unless one contributes concretely to that culture's conditions of existence—that is to say, to the liberation of the continent."[29]

Fanon's cultural ideas are linked to his radical critique of the new African bourgeoisie in such a way as to lead him to proffer a new and different conception of culture in the context of African development—a revolutionary conception which presents culture as the product of a collective enterprise involving the historical fortunes and destiny of the people. The significance of Fanon's cultural ideas attaches to the vision of a new, revolutionary humanism which he proposes, the mission he assigns to non-Western peoples "to create a new man." But it is easy to understand how his conception of culture and his wider projection into the

Third World does away with the traditional problematic of African thought, centered upon the issue of identity. Fanon transcends this issue and clears the path for a new direction of thought.

Fanon's work belongs to an established tradition of intellectual and ideological interest in black Africa on the part of New World Blacks, an interest which springs from the sense of a common historical predicament and which has created a pattern of reciprocal ideas and attitudes among black intellectuals on both sides of the Atlantic. His early preoccupation with the racial problem certainly arises from a sentiment of personal involvement, but his individual temperament and the peculiar inclination of his intellectual gifts made him respond to a new configuration of events, and that gave a new direction to his thinking. The result of Fanon's contribution was to leave the racial problem shorn of sentimentalities and the cultural issue raised along with it divested of the sublimities with which it had been adorned by his predecessors. The attitude he introduced into the debate on African problems, especially on the cultural question, amounts to a new realism; and the ideological spirit it has fostered now pervades the writings of that section of the francophone African intelligentsia which it is convenient to call the "new philosophers," represented notably by Marcien Towa and Paulin Hountondji.

The progression from the critique of *Négritude* to a new ideological position is clearly marked in the succession of three short books published by Towa. The first is a study of Senghor's poetry with the provocative title, *Léopold Sédar Senghor: Nègritude ou servitude*.[30] Towa's analytical approach is, however, seriously compromised by his literal reading of a form which works through allusion and suggestion, by his fastening upon immediate denotations and missing the tense harmony of the structure of connotations in the poetic text. This insensitive approach in Towa's study serves an ideological purpose—to discredit the poetry and the theory of *Négritude*, which is assumed to be its sole reference. Towa attempts to place both the poetry and the theory in a direct and unilateral correspondence with Senghor's biography and his actual options in the real world, but apart from the doubtful value of the procedure in literary criticism, his obvious hostility to Senghor betrays him into distortions and simplifications which bear no relation either to the deeper meanings of Senghor's poetry or even to the verifiable facts of his political career. There is an obvious forcing of the radical tone in Towa's first book, and it largely invalidates his demonstration.

Towa is on a more even keel in his second book, *Essai sur la problématique philosophique dans l'Afrique actuelle*,[31] in which he leaves poetry alone to deal exclusively with ideas; the result is a remarkably coherent work whose argument ends by forcing conviction. His critique of *Négritude* is directed here against what we have called the philosophical current of the movement, the effort deriving from the inspiration of Tempels' *Bantu Philosophy* and sustained by recourse to Western anthropology as a means of demonstrating the existence of a distinctively African mode of philosophical thinking. Towa recognizes that the aim of this effort was to rehabilitate the African by a revaluation of his part, but he objects to the claim that it constitutes a philosophical enterprise. The procedure adopted by the adepts of *Négritude* in its philosophical garb consists (for Towa) in simply enlarging the concept of philosophy itself in order to include African cultural and mental productions within it. Philosophy in this sense becomes coextensive with culture in the ordinary sociological meaning of the word, and African philosophy becomes no more than an unreflective presentation of certain forms of cultural expression associated with traditional Africa, placed in opposition to Western forms and to a more strongly articulated tradition of Western philosophy. For Towa, this procedure is illegitimate from a strict methodological point of view, since it creates a terminological confusion between philosophy in its nature and function, and cultural anthropology or ethnology considered as a discipline; hence, he dubs this current of thought "ethnophilosophy." He points out the way in which this confusion is fostered by the equivocal character of the procedure:

Ethnophilosophy objectively discusses beliefs, myths, rituals, and then suddenly transforms itself into a metaphysical profession of faith, without taking the trouble to either refute Western philosophy or present a rational justification for its adherence to African thought. (p. 31)

Beyond this terminological confusion, Towa discerns in the procedure of the ethnophilosophers an insufficient understanding of the objectives of philosophy, an inadequate grasp of its critical function in an open debate upon ideas and values. This leads him to a denunciation of what he regards as the dogmatic implications of appealing to the past to sanction African thought in the present. It is precisely here that the real direction of Towa's argument begins to emerge. The effort to resuscitate a heritage of values and a world view from the past is, he contends, irrelevant to present African preoccupations and aspirations: "An original African philosophy torn from the dark night of the past could not be, if it ever existed, but the expression of a situation that was itself in the past" (p. 35).

Elsewhere, Towa makes clear the sense he gives to this "relation to the world" by linking the cultural question with the problem of Africa's continued political and economic dependence upon Europe and with the general issue of the material underdevelopment of the continent. His critique of cultural nationalism in a situation of African weakness takes on the radical tone of Fanon: "Senghorian Negritude and the ethnophilosophy that seeks to extend its influence keep alive the illusion that Africa could contribute a 'spiritual supplement' to the European soul before European imperialism has been totally eliminated from Africa" (pp. 51-52).

Towa's echo of Fanon's cultural ideas gives them a new resonance by sounding them against a background of disillusionment with African independence and of a grim and lucid appraisal of the African situation, "For it is our deficiencies that now impose themselves upon our attention, not our wealth and our possibilities" (p. 39).

Towa's critique of *Négritude* and ethnophilosophy is thus bound up with an ideological and political position determined by a sombre awareness of contemporary realities in Africa, of the incapacity of cultural nationalism to effect a genuine transformation in the hoped for direction—of its irrelevance, in a word. The presiding idea in Towa's reflection develops with an implacable logic out of this awareness. The following passage, in which it is expressed, can be considered the most significant in the book:

The desire to be one's self immediately leads to the proud reappropriation of one's past, because the essence of self is no more than the culmination of its past; however, when the past is examined and scrutinized lucidly, dispassionately, it reveals that contemporary subjugation can be explained by reference to the origins of the essence of the self, that is to say in the past of the self and nowhere else. (p. 41)

Nothing can be more explicit than this statement of a new mode of self perception. Here Towa is reversing the whole trend of African intellectual effort in the modern age, breaking with its entire framework of presuppositions and valuations. From this negative appraisal of the effort to affirm a specifically African and spiritual identity, Towa proceeds to a reformulation of the African problematic in terms that are more directly related to the requirements of the moment: "Therefore, as a warrant of our humanity, we propose to replace the search for originality and difference with a search for the avenues and means to power as the ineluctable condition for the affirmation of our humanity and our freedom" (p. 53).

Towa's position here implies an entirely new program of African intellectual activity, one no longer centered upon the question of African identity but upon that of our potential in the modern world. As he puts it more succinctly elsewhere: "What we need to become, not what we uniquely are, should determine our questions" (p. 56).

The complementary aspect of Towa's call for a renunciation of the self as constituted by the African past represents an opening toward new perspectives of thought and action. If the spirit of the traditional past is inoperative in the present, and if it is understood that the immersion of traditional man in that spirit is responsible for our conquest and domination by Europe, then we should seek out the secret of the power which overwhelmed us and ascertain the direction from which it came. Towa finds this secret in the European practice of rationality, the key to the scientific and technological progress which enabled Europe to master the world of nature and dominate the other populations of the universe: "Due to its close affinity with science and technology, European philosophy seems to be the source of European power; for that reason, it will help us bring about the revolution of consciousness that underlies the construction of our own power" (p. 68).

Towa assigns then to Western philosophy a practical function which amounts to its serving as an agent of development for African people after their experience of colonial domination. He is careful to specify that his argument does not imply "a journey to Canossa" by African culture but rather a total reassessment within radical perspectives of the conditions of African life, including a critical interrogation of the past. The advocacy of Western rationalism appears therefore as a tactical move to ensure a firmer hold by the African on the territory of his total being, but it implies nonetheless a revolution of being in the same sense in which Fanon had preached it—a total act of self-regeneration.

The fact that Towa is a professor of philosophy is not without interest for an appreciation of his ideas as developed in this essay, for not only does it reflect a professional concern for a rigorous demarcation of the area of his discipline but indeed a passionate faith in the effective significance of philosophy within the context of real life. This becomes even more apparent in his latest book, *L'Idée d'une philosophie africaine*,[32] which represents a development on the preceding one on many points. The distinguishing theme of this book, however, is an effort to found the philosophical enterprise in Africa upon a tradition of critical thought within the continent itself.

Towa begins by developing, at greater length than in the earlier essay, his point that philosophy in its essential meaning is a critical activity, that the philosophical enterprise must be conducted as a reasoned mode of discourse rather than by reference to a general system of beliefs, ethical precepts, or symbolic constructions which, whatever their poetic force, do not contain within themselves any principle of verification. In order to oppose philosophy (considered as thought in its engagement with what he calls "the absolute") to myth and religion, Towa goes back to the distinction between wisdom derived from considered judgment and received opinion untested by reason. By proposing anew this classical dichotomy, Towa stresses the social significance of a philosophy that implies a liberation of minds and, as a consequence, of individuals in their social determinations.

He then argues for a consideration of the rational spirit manifest not only in ancient Egyptian thought—which, following Cheikh Anta Diop, he ascribes to Africa—but also in traditional folktales. The very fact that a major segment of these tales dramatizes social and moral conflicts gives them a critical function within the context of traditional life; hence, they become the mode of expression of an intelligence that constantly calls into question established values and institutions, including religious beliefs. Their philosophical value and status reside, therefore, in their function as a critical interrogation of the natural world and of social facts.

Against this background, Towa considers the general problem of the place and role of philosophy in Africa at the present time. He returns to his earlier preoccupation with philosophy as an agent of development. As he puts the matter, "The possibility for a philosophical renaissance in Africa is tied to its political and economic fate"(p. 51). Thus, projecting in schematic form a philosophy of history that derives its inspiration from Hegel, he relates the processes of thought itself to their objective manifestations and effects upon human life. Consequently, when he affirms that mind is activity, it becomes easy to understand his restatement of the correlation between philosophical activity—pure thought—and the logic of science and technological development, as well as his advocacy of Western rationalism as a means of accession to modernity.

In this book, as in the earlier work, Towa's preoccupation with the possibility of an African philosophy, with the problem of philosophy itself, is commanded by immediate concerns of a political and ideological order. As he says, "Philosophy is essentially a relation between a theory and the demands of social life" (p. 112). In the particular development that he gives to this proposition, it implies a radical calling into question of the present structures in our contemporary societies as determined by the values, options, and practice of the ruling classes.

Towa's thinking is obviously tributary to Fanon's, but it has an originality all its own both in his manner of carrying the latter's ideas to their logical limits, thereby giving explicit conceptual form to their implications, and in his effort to place these ideas on a sound philosophical foundation. The marked ideological orientation of this effort makes for certain theoretical weaknesses which will be touched upon in my conclusion. For the moment, it is useful to point out a contradiction between his earlier stand against the methods of the ethnophilosophers and the procedure, adopted in his latest book, of attaching a philosophical significance to traditional folktales, simply on the basis of their critical function. It is obvious that such a value can be given to any form of imaginative expression within any culture as long as it fulfills a similar function, without compelling a recognition of its status as a form of philosophical thinking in the restricted, technical sense suggested by his own definition. It does seem, therefore, that Towa is attempting to attenuate the cutting effect of his earlier position—which, it should be noted in passing, assumes the existence of a distinctive mode of African thought, even if it rejects both the method of its exposition in ethnophilosophy and the relevance of the mode and its exposition to present African concerns. We might say then that Towa is attempting to put back with the left hand what he took away earlier with the right, a procedure that can only be justified at the cost of special pleading.

When we turn to Paulin Hountondji, we find a position that is much more uncompromising. His ideas are developed in a series of journal articles, the earliest of which appeared in 1969. Some of these were included in a volume, *Libertés*, published in Cotonou in 1973; but a more complete selection was later collected, revised, and placed together in the volume entitled *Sur la "philosophie africaine"*, published in Paris in 1977.[33] Hountondji's work thus predates and overlaps with that of Towa: their ideas coincide on many points, but Hountondji's critique is more comprehensive and his whole manner more emphatic, hence the greater impact his work seems to have made in French African intellectual circles.

Hountondji's ideas proceed from the same ideological reaction against *Négritude* as Towa's, from the same standpoint which links ethnophilosophy with the movement of cultural nationalism (of which *Négritude* is the theoretical expression). But as his various references to the movement indicate, he refuses to concede any positive significance to the effort to rehabilitate African culture. For him, the relationship between this movement and the colonial ideology it is intended to combat, reveals a peculiar ambiguity, a pathetic correspondence between the terms of African affirmation and the opposite system of ideas or representations proposed by the colonial ideology in its image of Africa. Thus, he observes,

by desiring at all costs to compare ourselves to Europe . . . , we are still defining ourselves *in relation to* it; we make it our primary term of reference and ascribe the origin of our civilization's meaning to it. The nature of demonstration of this kind is to be essentially reversible: its terms can be reversed, transformed into their opposites, and cultural superiority can be transmuted into inferiority or vice versa, in the mythological space of an objectless comparison.[34]

The motivation of ethnophilosophy in its association with cultural nationalism renders its entire undertaking suspect: it accounts for the equivocation discernible in its procedures and formulations and compromises from the outset the very principle of its mode of discourse. This fundamental weakness affecting its conceptual framework becomes the object of Hountondji's critique, since the equivocal character of ethnophilosophy not only obscures its ideological motivation but has implications for a proper understanding of the nature and function of philosophy:

> Precisely for that reason, a political critique of ethnophilosophy could not possibly suffice; one must also provide a theoretical critique that transcends the changing practical effects of this discourse and attacks the concepts on which they are based, for in the final analysis the ambiguity of these concepts explains the reversibility of its effects.[35]

One might say then that Hountondji undertakes a "critique of ethnophilosophical reason" in its conceptual constitution, a critique directed primarily against its manifestations in the work of the African practitioners of ethnophilosophy but also intended to affect the framework of concepts elaborated by Western ethnology and the value systems they imply, both of which seem to him to have insidiously made their way into the African formulations.

Hountondji's main line of attack proceeds from the categorical stand he takes against the notion of collective philosophy. His objection to ethnophilosophy concerns what he sees as its fixed attachment to the reconstruction of African worldviews and systems of thought whose common character is that they can be opposed to European ones. The collective philosophy derived in this way from African forms of cultural expression is unconscious and unreflective, merely deduced by the outside observer and assumed to be immanent in a culture and to serve both as the underlying principle of the mental processes of all its members and as a normative reference for moral and social life. Hountondji objects to what he considers the reductionist penchant of the ethnophilosophers, who throw a veil of uniformity over processes that are in reality diverse and by so doing perpetuate the image of African societies as a spontaneous adhesion of all their members to a common system of ideas and norms.

In order to illustrate the unfruitfulness of the dominant perspective of the ethnophilosophers, Hountondji undertakes, in the first three essays of *Sur la "philosophie africaine,"* a critical exposition of the ideas and methods of Tempels and his African successors. In view of his recognition of the quality and usefulness of Kagame's work, his critique of Kagame is particularly significant, for it illuminates Hountondji's own conception of philosophy. While conceding the fact that Kagame's approach shows a greater analytical rigor than that of Tempels, whose ideas it is intended to verify and correct, Hountondji objects to the terms of Kagame's formulation of Rwanda ontology and to his general perspective upon the idea of a collective philosophy. In the departures made by Kagame from Aristotle's scheme, Hountondji discerns distortion of the Greek philosopher's method—a distortion which produces an equivocal result. Kagame's attempt to derive the categories of Rwanda ontology from the grammatical structure of the language appears to Hountondji to constitute a misrepresentation of Aristotle's method, for the latter's purpose is not so much to explore the structures of the Greek language as to go beyond their factitious character and found language itself upon a universal and necessary order. It ought to be said at once that this criticism itself demonstrates a misunderstanding of Kagame's purpose, which is precisely to show that Aristotle's categories cannot be universal, since they are formulated within a language quite differently structured from Rwanda and to demonstrate, from the insight and vantage point afforded by a non-Western language, a different mode of representation of reality which is not simply inherent in the structures of the Rwanda language but explicit in its larger transformations in the oral tradition.[36]

But it is on this point that Hountondji's objection finally rests: the fact that Kagame professes to reconstruct a philosophy from the oral traditions which provide him with what he calls "institutionalized documents." For Hountondji, such a method is illegitimate not only because, by employing it, Kagame subscribes to a myth of collective philosophy but especially because these institutionalized documents themselves are by their nature anything but philosophical texts. By drawing upon them, Kagame commits a "confusion of genres"; he is merely projecting upon them a philosophical significance which they do not and cannot have. The combination in Kagame's work of analytical scruple and a recourse to the oral tradition for his demonstration results in something of a paradox for Hountondji: "This same scientific rigor prohibits one from arbitrarily projecting a *philosophical discourse* behind the products of language, which are themselves presented as anything but philosophy" (p. 30).

Again, it is evident that Hountondji's idea of a philosophical text does not correspond with that of Kagame, whose specialized knowledge of the very elaborate forms of Rwanda literature permits him to draw out of them a mode of thought that employs an imaginative key to represent the world and express a human apprehension of it.[37]

This divergence of view between Kagame and Hountondji on the proper status of oral tradition in the practice of philosophy in Africa points to a more fundamental disagreement about the nature of philosophy itself. On the basis of Hountondji's critique of Kagame, it becomes evident that the former is at pains to hold ethnophilosophy to a rigorous conception of the discipline, if it is to qualify as philosophy. For Hountondji, in effect, the assumptions and formulations of ethnophilosophy are contrary to the spirit of philosophy, which entails a conscious and explicit mode of discourse: "No more than any other philosophy, African philosophy could hardly be a collective vision of the world. It can not exist as philosophy except in the form of a confrontation between individual thoughts, a discussion, a debate" (p. 48). This requirement excludes any possibility of considering a reconstruction of African systems of thought as philosophy, of creating a distinctive African philosophy merely by the repetitive recall of an unconscious and implicit collective worldview, without submitting the elements of this worldview to critical treatment. Hountondji maintains that it is not a vision of the world that makes for philosophy, but its description, its mode of presentation; not the content, but the form of discourse. At best, philosophy can bear an African label by reason only of the existence of a body of explicit texts produced by Africans who are conscious of working within a regional tradition and of being engaged in a discussion which maintains an essential connection with the international philosophical community.

In a sense, the discussion presently under way contributes to the constitution of African philosophy considered from this point of view. Hountondji even remarks that African philosophy already exists in this sense, and he includes within it the work of the African ethnophilosophers whom he criticizes; in his view, they are in reality doing no more than providing an individual interpretation of what they take to be an African vision of the world, with each interpretation producing different and often conflicting results: "Incontestably philosophical, their only weakness was to work out mythically, under the guise of a collective philosophy, the philosophical form of their own discourse" (p. 22).

Hountondji seems to be moving here towards a formal definition of philosophy. However, in the most substantial essay of his collection, "La Philosophie et ses révolutions," he attempts to validate his conception of philosophy as a particular form of debate by affirming that philosophy is not a system in the sense of a closed structure of ideas—however coherent or grandiose that structure may be, as in the case of Hegel—but by its very nature a perpetual movement, a chain of responses from one individual philosopher to another across the ages, a progression in which the future direction of the philosophical enterprise cannot be determined, since it must keep open the perspectives of human thought. This observation leads him to affirm that structurally, in its substance, philosophy is historical, drawing its life from the evolution of a continuing debate regulated by a single preoccupation with verification, on which point philosophy shares a common nature with science. Here are his own words on the question:

A philosophical or mathematical work can only be understood as a moment in a larger debate that sustains it and passes beyond it: it always refers to previous positions, either to refute them or to confirm and embellish them. It has no sense except in relation to that history—in relation to the terms of a debate which continually evolves and in which the only constant is an unvarying reference to the same object, to the same realm of experience, the definition of which is, moreover, determined during the course of that evolution. In short, scientific literature is historical through and through. (p. 100)

It has been necessary to quote this passage because it is surprising that, in expressing this point of view, Hountondji does not seem to have perceived its limitation. Even if we are to believe that history constitutes the essence of philosophy rather than serving simply as a contingent factor of its incarnation in Europe, there remains a difficulty. For when we roll back its process, by a kind of regressive method, we inevitably arrive at some point of departure in its evolution, and there we are left to wonder how this point, without an antecedent, can assume the character of philosophy. This difficulty is bypassed in Hountondji's discussion by his assimilation of philosophy into science, in contradistinction to mental projections of the imaginative kind. As we have seen in his critique of Kagame, Hountondji does not consider that the material with which ethnophilosophy operates—its sources and texts as provided by the oral tradition—belongs in the category of philosophical literature. The mere fact that they can and do frequently serve as vehicles of thought is not sufficient to class them within that category. The reason he adduces for his rejection is that philosophy forms part of scientific literature. As he says, "It shares the same life and evolves according to the same rhythm as mathematics, physics, chemistry, and linguistics" (p. 99).

Whatever one may think of this large claim for philosophy, it soon becomes plain that Hountondji is not using a metaphor, that his assimilation of philosophy to science is in fact a synonymy. For him, philosophy is in fact a second order of science in its empirical practice, nothing other than the form of its reflection: "Philosophical practice, or that particular form of theoretical practice that is commonly called philosophy, is inseparable from that other form of theoretical practice commonly called science" (p. 124).

The influence of Louis Althusser becomes apparent in the terminology and the turn of mind it suggests. In the immediate context of Hountondji's essay, it leads to his observation that no serious and meaningful philosophical enterprise can be undertaken in Africa without a comprehensive effort of scientific research and activity. "That which Africa needs first of all is not philosophy, but rather science," he declares (p. 124). And as part of the implication of his assimilation of philosophy to science, fundamental to all his thinking, is his restriction of the meaning of philosophy to theoretical analysis, which has for its corollary the exclusion of metaphysics and all kinds of pure speculation. It is important again to quote him fully on this:

That sort of philosophy, that sort of theoretical research rigorously constructed on the basis of science, leaves us miles away from the concerns around which the myth of a so-called traditional African "philosophy" crystallized and evolved. It leaves us far from metaphysical problems about the origin of the world, the sense of life, the meaning of death, man's destiny, the reality of the after-life, the existence of God, mythology and everything else in which philosophical musings habitually take delight. (p. 124)

The statement here represents a frontal attack upon ethnophilosophy from within the principles of philosophy itself. It is not only a definition of the proper domain of philosophy—a definition which is, at the very least, controversial—but more significantly a vehement call for the application of a rigorous scientific method in African philosophy. Certainly a note of impatience often emerges in Hountondji's writing; it might be considered the emotional overtone of his intellectual reaction to the formulations of ethnophilosophy. His inclusion of Kagame within the trend he is reacting against appears to reveal his lack of a sense for proper discrimination, and it unquestionably does an injustice to the quality of the Rwanda priest's work, although it ought perhaps to be seen as an attempt to deal with the movement as a whole by attacking an exceptional case which, by its very quality, endorses a general trend to facility.

Marcien Towa and Paulin Hountondji meet on the common ground not only of their opposition to ethnophilosophy but also on the ground of their radical commitment to modernization in Africa. Both see ethnophilosophy as an expression of cultural nationalism that, no longer relevant to the African situation, actually constitutes a fruitless diversion from urgent tasks. As stated earlier in connection with Towa, the pronounced ideological hue of the work of the new philosophers raises a number of issues around which a lively controversy has in fact already begun. It will not be possible here to describe the details of this controversy,[38] but by way of conclusion, it is not without interest to remark upon some of the implications and effects of the countermovement they represent.

To start with, the rather preemptory tone of both Towa and Hountondji makes it difficult to discern in their work a concern for the necessary discriminations required in a debate of this kind. It is evident that Towa's attack on ethnophilosophy, motivated by a disaffection towards Senghor, has a passionate character that necessarily affects all arguments *ad hominem*; it is significant that in his last book he displays what amounts to an ambiguous attitude in relation to his earlier position on the question of tradition. Moreover, in their insistence upon the need for Africa to adopt a modern scientific spirit, both Towa and Hountondji are flogging a dead horse; the point itself has never been in doubt with the adepts of cultural nationalism. They take for dogma what is rather a general premise of ethnophilosophy—the possibility of deriving a valid alternative view of human life and experience from the traditional background, what Willie Abraham (who is attacked by Hountondji) calls a "paradigm."[39] It is true of course that reference to tradition and the past eventually acquired a moral value with Senghor and that Cheikh Anta Diop gave it a didactic significance; nonetheless, it is obvious that its essential aim is to restore to the African a sense of historical initiative from which colonial ideology diverted him.

Particularly in this regard the new philosophers lay themselves open to criticism. The implication of their position is to leave to African thought and effort no possible perspective other than a Western one. Their linkage of Western ideas and values with modernity and development does not entail an assessment of the inadequacies of Western civilization in all its ramifications—political, social, economic, cultural, and spiritual. It is not made clear in their writings why the rejection of the African past should not imply, as well, an assessment of the Western model in its objective and practical significance, a consideration of why there ought to be a retreat from judgment in regard to it. Their position seems therefore to be partial, in both senses of the word, leading to a disquieting restriction of thought and implying a limitation of the African's sense of creativity.

One is, of course, aware that this result is far from the intentions of both writers, but it is evident from the terms and processes of their thinking, especially in the case of Hountondji, that their position arises from an inflexible adherence to conventional Western canons. Hountondji's ideas on language, for example, are limited by a strictly Western conception of speech acts, and even then they lag behind the contemporary findings of linguistics; as a result, he advances views that are actually quite inaccurate. Similarly, in his latest book, Towa focuses upon the present significance of European thought, but in presenting its history he omits important details about the actual process of its development. It seems then that both these representatives of the new generation of French African intellectuals have been so impressed by the Western achievement that they feel obliged to offer it as a model for African development.

But for all their limitations, the strength of their passion is not in doubt. They are moved to take a position against the prevailing spirit of cultural nationalism by their commitment to a progressive vision of Africa. As against the noble idea of the past, which animates cultural nationalism, they are struck by the picture of Africa's present weakness. The disillusionment occasioned by present experience induces in them an acute sense of realism, which runs counter to the romanticism of their elders. They are the counterparts, in the domain of thought, of the new breed of African fiction writers, who are also disinclined to accept a complacent view of Africa. And what the Ouologuems, the Kouroumas, and the Fantoures are dramatizing in their novels, Towa and Hountondji are expressing with a relentless logic present as explicit, clear ideas.

We may discern in the phenomenon they represent—in its opposition to earlier movements, ideas, and attitudes—something of a conflict of generations. However, the more meaningful interpretation is to see it as the conflict between a resolutely unsentimental awareness of African difference (and of the real disadvantages it entails in the modern world) and a nostalgic attachment to that difference—a conflict reminiscent of the one between the modernists and the Slavophiles in prerevolutionary Russia.

It ought to be stressed, however, that the position of the new philosophers carries with it absolutely no hint of an inferiority complex in relation to Europe; there is no suggestion of self-contempt in their work. If anything, it reflects a new self-confidence capable of sustaining a critical examination of the African background. There is an irony here, for the new philosophers owe their new confidence to the effort of their predecessors, against whom they have now turned; it is indisputably an inheritance from their elders. If the younger generation of African intellectuals is able to feel unperturbed by the image of the African and the black race presented by the colonial ideology, if that image no longer wounds their self-awareness, it is surely because the intellectual and ideological battles have already been fought for them. As a result of those battles, African independence has become a reality; their problem is no longer to justify that reality but to determine what to do with it.

Finally, it is undeniable that the debate they have initiated has renewed the whole movement of African intellectual activity and given a new sense of urgency to ideological preoccupations in the contemporary context. Cultural nationalism was essentially retrospective in character, even if it involved a vision of the future; the current trend on the other hand is markedly prospective in nature. *Nègritude* was and remains a limiting concept in the sense that it seeks to circumscribe an area of African being so as to mark it off from others, to define the frontiers of African identity and expression. The ambition of the new generation of French African intellectuals is precisely to extend those frontiers.

NOTES

1. For a full discussion, see Shlomo Avineri, *The Social and Political Thought of Karl Marx* (Cambridge: Cambridge University Press, 1968).

2. See Robert July, *The Origins of Modern African Thought* (London: Faber and Faber, 1968).

3. The point emerges clearly from several studies, notably D. Kimble, *A Political History of Ghana* (Oxford: Clarendon Press, 1963); and July, *op. cit.*

4. See Abiola Irele, "Faith and Exile—Cheikh Hamidou Kane and the Theme of Alienation," in *The African Experience in Literature and Ideology* (London: Heinemann, 1980).

5. G. W. F. Hegel's *Philosophy of History*, in its general reference to non-Western peoples and its particular bearing on Africa, provides the most important intellectual foundation for the colonial ideology. It was on this foundation that classical anthropology sought to rationalize European domination of other races by presenting them as inherently inferior to the white race. This ideological thrust of classical anthropology found its culmination in Lucien Lévy-Bruhl, *La Mentalité primitive* (Paris: Librairie Felix Alcan, 1922). For a general account of the relationship between anthropology and colonial ideology, see Gerard Leclerc, *Anthropologies et colonialisme* (Paris: Fayard, 1972).

6. Senghor made the acquaintance of Blyden's work only recently, as

he admits in his preface to Hollis Lynch, ed., *Selected Letters of Edward Wilmot Blyden* (Millwood, N. Y.: KTO, 1978); however, the progression of ideas suggested here is real, inscribed in the logic of the development of modern African thought from the mid-nineteenth to the mid-twentieth century.

7. Jean-Paul Sartre, "Orphée noir," in *Situations III* (Paris: Gallimard, 1948); English translation by Samuel Allen, *Black Orpheus* (Paris: Présence Africaine and Black Orpheus, 1962).

8. The title of a well-known book by Ruth Benedict.

9. Léopold Sédar Senghor, "L'Esprit de la civilisation ou les lois de la culture négro-africaine" in *Présence Africaine*, 8-10 (1956): 56ff.

10. Léopold Sédar Senghor, *Les Fondements de l'africanité* (Paris: Présence Africaine, 1967).

11. Léopold Sédar Senghor, "L'esthéthique négro-africaine," in *Liberté I* (Paris: Editions du Seuil, 1964).

12. *Ibid*. I have translated "négro" here as "African" rather than the literal "Negro" or "black" in order to stress the fact that, in this context, Senghor's formula refers to a fact of civilization and is not intended to suggest that the black man is congenitally inaccessible to intellection. On this point, see Léopold Sédar Senghor, "Pour une philosophie négro-africaine," in *Ethiopiques*, 23 (1980); 5-32.

13. Placide Tempels, *La Philosophie bantoue* (Paris: Présence Africaine, 1949).

14. Alexis Kagame, *La Philosphie Bantu-Rwandaise de l'être* (Brussels: Académie Royale des Sciences Coloniales, 1956). Kagame's ideas were later to be popularized in Janheinz Jahn, *Muntu* (London: Faber and Faber, 1961).

15. Alexis Kagame, *La Philosophie Bantu comparée* (Paris: Présence Africaine, 1976), p. 56.

16. For a selection of representative works exemplifying this current, see the list of references in Paulin Hountondji, *Sur "la philosophie africaine"* (Paris: Maspero, 1977).

17. Cheikh Anta Diop, *Nation négres et culture* (Paris: Editions Africaines, 1955); 3d ed. (Paris: Présence Africaine, 1979). References are to the latter edition.

18. Cheikh Anta Diop, *Antériorité des civilisations négres: Mythe ou réalité* (Paris: Présence Africaine, 1967); Cheik Anta Diop, *Parenté genétique de l'egyptien pharaonique et des langues Négro-africaines* (Dakar: Nouvelles Editions Africaines, 1979).

19. Diop, *Nations négres*, p. 212.

20. Cheikh Anta Diop, *L'Unité culturelle de l'Afrique noire* (Paris: Présence Africaine, 1959).

21. Diop, *Antériorité*, p. 11. See also Lancina Keita, "Two Philosophies

of African History: Hegel and Diop," in *Présence Africaine*, 91 (1974): 41-49.

22. Albert Franklin, "La Négritude: Réalité ou mystification," *Présence Africaine*, 14(1952): 287-303.

23. Stanislas Adotévi, *Négritude et négrologues* (Paris: Union Generale d'Editions, 1972), p. 45.

24. For a fuller discussion, see Abiola Irele, *Les Origines de le négritude à la Martinique: Sociologie de l'oeuvre poétique d'Aimé Césaire* (Unpublished doctoral thesis, University of Paris, 1966).

25. Frantz Fanon, *Peau noire, masques blancs* (Paris: Seuil, 1952).

26. Frantz Fanon, *Sociologie d'une révolution* (Paris: Maspero, 1966). First published in 1959 under the title *L'An v de la révolution algerienne*.

27. Frantz Fanon, *Les Damnés de la terre*, 3d ed. (Paris: Maspero, 1975).

28. Fanon, *Damnés*, p. 164.

29. *Ibid.*, p. 165.

30. Marcien Towa, *Léopold Sédar Senghor: Négritude ou servitude?* (Yaoundé: CLE, 1971). Page number of quotations are included in the text.

31. Marcien Towa, *Essai sur la problématique philosophique dans l'Afrique actuelle* (Yaoundé: CLE, 1971).

32. Marcien Towa, *L'Idée d'une philosophie africaine* (Yaoundé: CLE, 1979).

33. Paulin Hountondji, *Libertés* (Cotonou: Editions Renaissance, 1977); and Paulin Hountondji, *Sur la "philosophie africaine"* (Paris: Maspero, 1977).

34. Hountondji, *Libertés*, p. 36.

35. Hountondji, *Sur "la philosophie africaine,"* p. 241.

36. Kagame's approach to the question has been confirmed by the eminent French linguist, Emile Benveniste, in his essay "Catégories de pensée et catégories de langue," in *Problémes de linguistique generale* (Paris: Gallimard, 1966), pp. 63-74.

37. See Alexis Kagame, *La Poésie dynastique au Rwanda* (Brussels: Institut Royal Colonial Belge, 1951); and Andre Coupez and Thomas Kamanzi, eds., *Litterature de cour au Rwanda* (Oxford: Oxford University Press, 1970).

38. Hountondji's position has been challenged notably by Niamey Koffie, "L'Impensé de Towa et d'Hountondji," in Claude Summer, ed., *Philosophie africaine* (Addis-Ababa: N. P., 1980); and Olabiyi Yai, "Theorie et practique en philosophie africaine: Misére de la philosophie speculative," in *Présence Africaine*, 108 (1978): 65-91. An abridged English version of the last named article appeared in *Second Order*, 2, 2 (1977).

39. Willie Abraham, *The Mind of Africa* (London: Weidenfeld and Nicholson, 1962).

9   VICTOR T. LEVINE

Political-Cultural Schizophrenia in Francophone Africa

I

Need one apologize for using the term "schizophrenia"? It appears in this essay not to designate a psychopathological syndrome but specifically as a metaphor intended to encompass the complex interaction between some attitudes and behaviors which owe their origins to French political cultural traditions and those rooted in the African colonial experience. The conventions for the use of such a metaphor are well established and still observed; they derive mainly from the sociological-anthropolical-historical literature of cultural contact, "acculturation," cultural accommodation, and the like. Such propositions as emerge from the study of these phenomena are understandably open to challenge, since they rest on a variety of often dubious models and premises and on the analysis of what is largely circumstantial evidence. However, as there is no way to reduce the experience of individual and group culture contact to the level of scientific experimentation, we are left with untidy, imperfectly recorded words and deeds. No apologies then. The difficulties notwithstanding, in the study of members of the francophone African elite—the so-called *cadre* of the countries formerly under French domination—schizophrenia seems to suggest an evocative way of approaching some of the nuances of politically relevant cultural ambivalence.

II

If one were simply to regard the colonial situation through the eyes of a dialectician, then the origin and growth of nationalism in francophone Africa (as elsewhere on the continent) could be seen as the natural reaction to the colonial situation. Accordingly, nationalism becomes "an ideology of rejection," (*une idéologie de refus*), the logical, dialectical affirmation of an identity, for the submerged *sujet*, of the right to self-determination for those denied political rights.[1] There is much to such a formula since the first stirrings of nationalism in what became francophone Africa seemed to come in the form of open resistance to the imposition of French rule. The rebellion of Lat-Dior, the Damel of Cayor (in Senegal), the struggles of the Abomeyan kings against the French, the resistance of Al Hajj Ummar, Samori Touré, and the Bornouan Rabeh—all certainly can be said to represent early attempts to resist the encroachments of colonialism and to preserve authentic African political values. The examples of religion's protonationalist agitation in the French Congo and the resistance to forced labor and to the excesses of administrators in the Cameroons and the Congo help to bolster this thesis. This point of view receives further support from the literature of anti-colonial protest, from West Indian René Maran's *Batoula* (which in 1921 won the Prix Goncourt) and the writings of Mongo Beti and Ferdinand Oyono,[2] and from the post-World War II push for independence, accompanied by manifestos, declarations, and programs with highly specific anti-colonial content.

The dialectic formula of nationalism as rejection and anti-colonialism, appealing as it is, is nonetheless only partially valid as a description of what nationalists did and thought. What it overlooks, particularly in francophone Africa, is the political schizophrenia of many of the leading nationalists themselves, a condition evident in both their political language and their behavior as nationalists. To begin with, francophone African rejection of French colonial rule was usually conditional, partial, and, until very late in the decolonization process, hesitant. With the exception of a relatively small number of radical or revolutionary nationalists, the thesis of political independence from France had few advocates until 1957 or 1958, and even those then converted displayed little enthusiasm for the idea. The political rhetoric of local nationalist leaders was similar enough, but when Léopold Sédar Senghor, Philibert Tsiranana, Felix Houphouët-Boigny, Mamadou Konaté, or Barthélemy Boganda spoke of independence, what they meant was autonomy within some form of a French political community, not complete rejection of France and all that it had meant to them. Further, it must be stressed that almost from the earliest days of the political awakening in French speaking Africa, the dominant theme in political discourse was the quest for the fullest realization of the French political values as these were expressed in the French Revolution and in the colonial doctrines of assimilation. It was only after World War II that the assertion of an African identity mingled with the earlier theme, and even then it was expressed as a hope for integration rather than a demand for complete separation from France. To put it in other words, those Africans who were brought to articulate their discontent with the colonial situation came to do so within the framework of an all too familiar dilemma: they felt part French themselves, having learned the language and the basic ideas of their criticism from the French. But they were also irrevocably African and, as Africans, had tasted the bitter frustrations and the anger of the colonized. Thus, they could despise the French for the more repressive, cruel aspects of the French colonial system, but they could never fully bring themselves to reject a political and social culture whose language, ideas, and life style they had in varying degrees made their own. As a consequence, the language and ideas of francophone African nationalism expressed as much the nationalists' feelings of having been betrayed and rejected by France and the French as it reflected their own rejection of French colonialism as a system of political and economic domination.

Albert Memmi, one of the French theorists of anti-colonialism, explained the failure of French colonialism in just such terms: "It was the colonized who first sought assimilation, but it was the colonizer who refused to grant it."[3]

At first, among the *évolués* of French West Africa, the sense of betrayal was muted, and the promise of assimilation remained an article of faith among those expressing discontent with the political status quo. Here is Galandou Diouf, an important early Senegalese political figure, in 1915 proclaiming the need for political justice:

Forgetting their own and their ancestors' past, certain undesirable Frenchmen from the métropole would like to try keeping us under the yoke of slavery, despite all the liberties generously granted us by the great French Revolution. The French Republic, gentlemen, freed us, as it did you; if we were most recently slaves, you were among the first to be freed from bondage.[4]

Of all the francophone African intellectuals, it is Senghor who most clearly expresses the tense counterpoint between rejection of French colonialism and love of France. In his *Prière de paix* (1948), he clearly recognizes the evils of colonialism, yet he was forgiving.[5]

The examples could be multiplied indefinitely, but one more will suffice to make the argument. In 1938, Paul Hazoumé, the Dahomean ethnologist, writer, and later, nationalist politician, published *Doguicimi*, a historical novel that vividly recreates the court life of the Abomeyan kingdom conquered by the French in 1892. The book celebrates Dahomean tradition and the values of African life, and as such it falls within those themes of the nationalist argument that asserts the depth and richness of African life as against the cultural and political values of the West. Yet, Hazoumé ends the novel with an epilogue in which he argues that his heroine, Doguicimi, would have welcomed the arrival of the French, who "would have seemed to you [Doguicimi] to embody the qualities necessary to put an end to the incessant wars of the Dahomean kings, to the slave trade, and to human sacrifices that were ruining rather than enriching the country."[6] He suggests that Doguicimi would have rejoiced that the French, rather than the English, became the eventual occupiers of the country, because they brought "peace, liberty, and humanity." To be sure, Hazoumé was regarded by some of his younger intellectual contemporaries as overly francophilic, but the African-French ambiguity is visible in his novel, as it was in his political life. In 1915 Hazoumé had been coeditor (with Emile Zinsou Bodé) of a clandestine monthly, *Le Récadaire de Benhanzin*, which attacked an obnoxious French Governor, Charles Noufflard. Later, after 1945, Hazoumé became an influential member of the Indépendants d'Outre-Mer (IOM) group in the French parliament and an active participant in the Dahomean nationalist arena.[7]

Doudou Thiam, the former Senegalese foreign minister, not only argued that this internal conflict delayed the development of nationalism in francophone Africa but also marked it as a salient point of difference between francophone and anglophone African nationalism:

> In fact, nationalism, whose concrete form is the demand for independence, arose much earlier in English speaking African countries. This is because British colonial policy did not pass through the detour of assimilation. African political leaders in British territories knew, very early, that it would be a vain hope to seek to invade the House of Lords or the Commons. They knew that they could not recover their dignity or exercise their liberties except within the framework of independence; in contrast, French speaking Africans reasoned in terms of "French dignity," "French liberty," and "French equality." But it must be noted that, whatever the road taken, the results were the same in both cases.[8]

Thiam brings us back to nationalism in its more conventional forms, as assertions of the right of self-determination for dependent peoples. The end of the process was independence, pursued with visible reluctance in some cases, with enthusiasm in others, but independence nonetheless.

III

Independence, when it came to most francophone African territories in 1960, did not, however, resolve the political schizophrenia of the elite. In one respect, it was already too late. Despite the millenial aura surrounding the coming of independence, the event could neither grant members of the francophone elite a refurbished African identity nor surcease from the painful ambiguities of the cultural limbo into which the colonial situation had cast them. Whatever else the promise of assimilation may have meant to the French—to the cynical, a cheap way of gaining colonial auxiliaries, to the idealists, a way of affirming the best in the French democratic tradition—for the African it could not but represent the supreme compliment the conqueror pays the conquered: "Join me, and you will become like me!" To be French meant to be powerful, to be masterful, to be in control, and above all to dominate. Moreover, France did not make the same mistakes in West and Equatorial Africa that it made in North Africa and

Indochina—of offering mastery without also relinquishing control. Here, in black Africa, France negotiated independence with the elite it had created, thus reinforcing the seductive compliment of assimilation with the bonds of friendship. Independence thus meant not only gaining domination—by replacing the French as the ruling elite—but also the possibility of retaining the French cultural overlay which had made negotiated independence possible in the first place.[9] If the francophone African leaders had not been *interlocuteurs valables*, would the French even have considered negotiating with them?

It is sometimes forgotten, given the strident tone of much of the African nationalist literature, how easily independence was acquired—at least in most of francophone and anglophone Africa.[10] The proper dialogue could be conducted in the rhythms of the French legal and political language which many francophone leaders had learned in French parliaments, universities, and *grands écoles*. Then there were more or less hasty but easy adaptations of the Fifth Republic's constitution to fit the presidentialist preferences of most francophone leaders. And, of course, the most useful links with France could be maintained: commercial, cooperation, and defense agreements; French *cooperants, conseillers techniques* in ministries, schools, and the armed forces; preferential trade arrangements; inclusion in the franc monetary zone; generous financial and project aid for development; and finally, access to the little known but critical *compte d'opération* at the Bank of France, the guarantee that budgetary support would be available to those regimes chronically unable to cover their governmental expenses. And for those African leaders finding most favor in the highest French eyes, there was help in maintaining internal peace up to and including the possibility of French troops to quash attempted *coups d'état*; among the beneficiaries of this form of assistance have been presidents Ahmadou Ahidjo (1960-1965), Senghor (1962), Fructuoso Nchoma Onana Mba (1964), François Tombalbaye (1968-1972), Felix Malloum (1978-1979), and Albert Bernard Bongo (1981). In the central African republic, both Jean-Bedel Bokassa and David Dacko had French help in seizing power from each other: in 1966 when Bokassa overthrew Dacko and in 1979 when Dacko took over from Bokassa. In all, it was an overwhelmingly attractive package; only Guinea, which unilaterally declared its independence from France in 1958, failed to share in these benefits.

There were other returns as well, less visible, but significant nonetheless. There were vacations in Paris for the highest officials, scholarships in French universities and lycées for the children of the elite, and when de Gaulle's so-called French "Community" collapsed of inertia in the early sixties, a new cultural commonwealth—"*la francophonie*"—was created, dedicated to keeping green the garden of shared French cultural values and traditions. The annual meetings of what is now called the Conference of French and African Heads of State and Government also served to maintain the French tie. Every French leader from Charles de Gaulle to François Mitterand has used the occasion to assert his African policies and to preside over what (French President) Georges Pompidou once called "the Commonwealth of the French Spirit."

It is relatively easy to argue that all this represented a French neocolonialist design, meant to give the appearance of independence while permitting France to retain ultimate control over its former colonies.[11] The fact remains, however, that all these arrangements were consciously negotiated, agreed upon by both sides. To argue otherwise is to give too little credit to the Africans themselves; they were hardly duped or manipulated—the new bilateral links were seen as pragmatic, logical, and above all, desirable. It should be added that later, when some of the arrangements ceased to be useful, they were changed, renegotiated, or simply dropped.

In another sense, of course, assimilation ceased being a viable goal at independence. It could hardly be otherwise, since the new course had to involve a search for a new set of national myths to cover the bare bones of formal statehood. Yet the old myth retained a good deal of its potency, so much so that francophone intellectuals actively sought ways to recapture an African sense of identity, one which, if it could not altogether submerge the old myth, could at least give it an African face worthy of the elite's new status.

In francophone Africa, the search was catalyzed by the *Négritude* poet-politicians such as Aimé Césaire, Léopold Sédar Senghor, and their disciples, who sought to transform the nationalism of rejection (*l'idéologie de refus*) into a special ideology of Negro-black identity. They were not alone; the identity problem became very much of a constant issue among francophone intellectuals. For example, the stated purpose of the First Pan-African Cultural Festival (held at Algiers in 1969) was to examine and celebrate African culture. However, its hidden agenda was to disengage African culture from the cultural influences of the colonial past. The task proved no easy one, and the published proceedings of the conference are excellent testimony to the deep-seated cultural schizophrenia of the participants.[12]

Early in the conference there was a curiously epiphenomenal (but very French) debate about what to call the new African cultural synthesis, and this debate took place even before the content of African culture was examined. *Négritude* had its champions as well as its detractors, and some of the latter proposed "Africanity" or "Africanness" as an alternative formula. Stanislas Adotévi of Dahomey suggested "mélanisme,"[13] and Basile-Juléat Fouda of Cameroon distinguished Western (Occidental) from African cultures as a dichotomy between what he termed "Promethean" (technology producing) and "Apollonian" (inward turning, introspective) personalities.[14] The debate was interesting, but without lasting results. However, as interesting as the debate itself was the common basis of discourse: the participants from Algeria, Burundi, Cameroon, Congo, Ivory Coast, Dahomey, Upper Volta, Mali, Morocco, Mauretania, Niger, Rwanda, Senegal, Chad, and Tunisia all spoke perfect French. Their references to French authors, philosophers, and thinkers were twice as numerous as those to Marx and Lenin and three times as frequent as those to others, including Africans. The participants' cultural ambivalence was directly addressed by only one speaker, Fouda, but it was implicit in the papers and statements of the rest. Like it or not, the francophones could hardly avoid facing the problem, though most self-consciously sought to avoid doing so. The point, of course, is not that the search for a distinctly African cultural *mythos* is a foolish or vain pursuit; at least the political reasons for the search are clear enough. It is the fact of the mixture which is inescapable, and indeed, recognition of that fact may have subconsciously helped to launch the attempt to negate it by asserting an uncorrupted, primordial African cultural prototype.

Again and again the question of African identity has been raised at cultural congresses, in the novels, essays, and poetry of the francophone intellectuals, as well as in the pages of various journals (most of them published in Paris) devoted to discussions of African culture and politics. Among the better known are *Présence Africaine, L'Afrique Littéraire et Artistique, Ethiopiques, L'Esprit Créateur, Présence Francophone* (published in Canada), and *Abbia* (published in Cameroon). Perhaps the bluntest epitome of the elite's cultural dilemma was evoked in the pages of *Présence Africaine* in a 1970 article by Joseph Bipoun-Wum, "Elite et peuple dans l'Afrique d'aujourd'hui." Parts are worth quoting at length. At one point, Bipoun-Wum inquires into the origins of the African elite:

The African elite does not emanate from African society. . . . [It] was created to accomplish the colonial design, and it could not do so without leaving its own milieux, because colonialism . . . is the juxtaposition of two societies that are not only different and opposed, but also [mutually] impenetrable. The two societies could not penetrate each other because, by definition, the one [the colonial] had the role of crushing the other [the African]. And this elite—ie., us—emerged from that society which eventually became dominant, [but which nonetheless remained] spiritually crushed. Hence . . . the African elite must first obtain a certificate of authenticity [if it is to be a true elite]. . . . It is a euphemism now to speak of an African elite. Our role as an elite is not due to the internal evolution of our societies . . . rather, we are the direct fruit of colonization. We are first of all a western elite. . . . I say that fundamentally, if possible, we must become African again while remaining "civilized." But that will be difficult.[15]

Bipoun-Wum then goes on to argue that the African elite is above all a functional elite, designed to make colonialism work and then, later on, to man the post-colonial African state. By any set of criteria, it (the elite) does not measure up to the classical definition of an elite:

You will tell me that we are in a dominant position. From what point of view? Because we—and not our fathers—are entitled to wear a suit and tie? Because we have social prestige? . . . [Do we] offer African society . . . a model that can influence the masses? . . . [Do we] offer the African society of tomorrow a different conception of the better life? Not really. I think that we are basically no more an African elite than the Europeans among us. . . . The European elite has truly accomplished its task, and we now only follow the model it set for us.

For Bipoun-Wum the way out is "immersion in the masses," a "re-Africanization" of hearts and minds, but even he seems unconvinced by his own argument.

IV

Is the phenomenon described here unique to francophone Africa? In the larger sense, it obviously is not. The cultural hybrid, *l'homme quasi-déraciné*, is a generic type, more likely to be found, to be sure, among colonized peoples where the imperial power has sought—or consciously created—cultural converts. The conquering or dominant race, people, and/or society is a natural pole of attraction, and cultural cooptation is the surest, most time-tested method of dominating subordinate peoples and integrating them into the conqueror's system of rule. The Romans understood this, as did the Arabs, and latterly, in varying degrees, so did the European colonial powers. The British *Raj* in India could not have functioned without its corps of culturally coopted native auxiliaries, the Portuguese needed their *mestizos* and *assimilados* to help run their colonies, and the French empire could not have survived without its *assimilés* and *évolués*. No matter if the cooptative myth eventually—and usually—turned out to deliver far less equality than it promised: while the empire lasted, the myth worked more often than not. In French speaking Africa, at least, there was never any dearth of willing candidates for cultural conversion.

Yet there was a sharp difference—a difference in consequences—between the sub-Saharan and the North African *assimilés* and *évolués*. In French sub-Saharan Africa—*l'Afrique noire*—the *assimilés* and *évolués* were in fact coopted into the colonial system. The series of structural-constitutional colonial reforms derived from the French Constitutions of 1946 and 1958 were elaborated as much in collaboration with the African *évolué* elite, as by French legislators and lawyers. As a consequence, it was the members of the black African elite who stood for elections, organized political parties and trade unions, and became deputies and representatives in local African and French metropolitan legislatures. Their political parties tended to resemble French parties (in part because some were derivative of French ones); their legislative debates were echoes of those in the French National

Assembly; and even when colonial administrations were attacked, it was in the phraseology of French political rhetoric. I have elsewhere pointed out that the members of the francophone African political elite—the legislators, the deputies and senators of the Republic, the ministers of government—were formed by and within the colonial system and hence found it far easier, when the moment came, to negotiate independence rather than buy it with the currency of their own blood.[16] They may have at times sounded revolutionary, but their actions tended to belie their words. Even the few genuine revolutionaries, the leaders of francophone Africa's *marxisant* parties (Senegal's *Parti Africain de l'Indépendance*, Upper Volta's *Sawaba*, Cameroon's *Union des Populations du Cameroun*, for example) cast their language and actions in terms completely comprehensible to the French metropolitan Left.

The North African Maghrebian *assimilés* and *évolués*,[17] though formed in a similar mold, found it much more difficult—and in the case of Algeria, impossible—to effect the relatively peaceful political devolution available to the African *évolués* below the Sahara. Like their black brethren, the Maghrébins recognized the internal contradictions of the colonial system, but unlike the former, they found their political efforts checked with a degree of brutality relatively unknown elsewhere.[18] The difference, it need hardly be pointed out, was that French governments and indeed most French political opinion, tended to regard the French Maghreb and Algeria in particular with intimate, proprietary eyes. Algeria, even the French Left agreed, was destined to remain French forever; it was much easier to view sub-Saharan French Africa as another Indochina—distant and destined for association with France, but not intrinsically French. Moreover, and much more to the point, French North Africa was home to some 1,500,000 Frenchmen, the *pieds noirs*, many of whom could trace their families' presence in the area back to the 1830s. There was no way they could be overlooked: they were living witness to the French destiny of the Maghreb. They were true settlers; and the Maghreb colonies, true settler colonies of a people little given to dispersion outside its own borders. Not so in sub-Saharan Africa. The French could be found in the hundreds (very occasionally, in the low thousands, as in Dakar and Abidjan) in Brazzaville, Lomé, Cotonou, Douala,

Conakry, and the other major towns of *Afrique noire*, but these Frenchmen were mainly *petit-colons* and colonial bureaucrats; in no French sub-Saharan territory did their numbers exceed 1 percent of the local population.

The difference had its impact on the intensity with which the Maghrebian *évolué* expressed his political schizophrenia. The most assimilated tended to become revolutionary; one has only to trace the careers of Habib Bourguiba and Ferhat Abbas to confirm the point. As Isaac Yetiv has put it, "Both Bourguiba and Ferhat embraced French culture at the expense of their own culture; both began their political struggle 'with' [on the side of] France, [both] pursued it 'despite' France, and [both] ended by being 'against' France."[19]

Yetiv characterizes not only Bourguiba and Ferhat, but the Maghrebian *évolués* as a group:

The Maghrebian intellectual tasted the forbidden fruit of knowledge and, like Adam and Eve, was ashamed of his nudity. He [the intellectual] has become a cultural hybrid. . . . He is at the same time one of the rare beneficiaries of France's "civilizing mission," but also—and the one does not go without the other—one of the victims of [France's] cultural oppression.[20]

The Maghrebian revolutionary experience could not alter the Moroccan, Tunisian, and Algerian francophone elites' "hybrid" character, but it did allow them a measure of emotional distance from France and, perhaps more important, gave considerable opening to the cultural and political influences of the Arab world. Many *Maghrébin* leaders remain (to use the evocative French term) *complexé*, but at least by now they have been able to cast off their "shame" by also becoming part of an older and more familiar— though not necessarily more comfortable—Arab social and political tradition. The strong post-independence assertion of Arab identity has created its own set of psychological problems, but these do not concern us here.

On the other hand, the political-cultural schizophrenia of the francophone black African elite remains acute. This is so in part because no satisfactory alternative African cultural-political identity has yet presented itself[21] and partly because, given the amicable separation from France, the French cultural link paradoxically could be strengthened rather than weakened.

Perhaps the real French victory in Africa was that it created a self-regenerating, self-perpetuating cultural myth able to bind the elites of its former colonies with an invisible thread where it could no longer hold them on a colonial leash. Such an African elite did not grieve when the French gave up imperial power in 1960. But that members of this same black elite could weep openly at de Gaulle's funeral and later flock to Paris to be the honored guests of his successors is evidence enough that their cultural-political ambivalence—their schizophrenia—remains strong enough to be a factor in contemporary Franco-African relations.

NOTES

1. See for example, the Marxist formulation of this thesis in Majhemout Diop, *Contribution à l'étude des problèmes politiques en Afrique noire* (Paris: Présence Africaine, 1958). A nondoctrinaire socialist view is expressed by Mamadou Dia, *Nations africaines et solidarité mondiale* (Paris: Presses Universitaires de France, 1960). The theme of nationalism as an ideology of rejection is also developed in P. F. Gonidec, *Les systèmes politiques africains* (Paris: Librairie Générale de Droit et de Jurisprudence, 1971), pp. 91-96.

2. On this point, see Gerald Moore, "Literary Protest in French-Speaking Africa," in Robert I. Rotberg and Ali A. Mazrui, eds., *Protest and Power in Black Africa* (New York: Oxford University Press, 1970), pp. 807-22.

3. Albert Memmi, *Portrait du colonisé précedé du portrait du colonisateur* (Chastel/Correa: Editions Buchet, 1957), pp. 161-62.

4. Galandou Diouf, signed article in *La Démocratie*, July 18, 1915; cited in G. Wesley Johnson, *The Emergence of Black Politics in Senegal* (Stanford: Stanford University Press, 1971), p. 148.

5. Léopold Sédar Senghor, *Hosties Noires* (Paris: Editions du Seuil, 1948).

6. Paul Hazoumé, *Doguicimi* (Paris: Larose, 1938), pp. 508-9. (The translation is mine.)

7. The incident is discussed in John A. Ballard, "The Porto Novo Incidents of 1923. Politics in the Colonial Era," *ODU* (U. of Ibadan), 2, 1 (July, 1965):63-64. For further details on Hazoumé's role in Dahomey's political history, see Maurice Glélé, *Dahomey—naissance d'un état noir*

(Paris: Librairie Générale de Droit et de Jurisprudence, 1969). The name of the Hazoumé-Zinsou journal refers to the official messenger of the last, exiled king of Abomey, (G) Benhanzin. The *récade* was a short, decorated, curved staff carried only by royal messengers called *récadaires*.

8. Doudou Thiam, *La Politique étrangère des états africains* (Paris: Presses Universitaires de France, 1963), pp. 12-13. (Translation is mine.)

9. The exception in West Africa was Guinea, which opted for independence; there the French simply pulled out, lock, stock, barrels, toilets, telephones, and officials. Under the circumstances, neither side deemed negotiations necessary.

10. In sub-Saharan French Africa, only Madagascar and Cameroon experienced severe internal violence prior to independence. The Malagache revolt of 1946 was crushed by the French with massive loss of life. The *marxisant* Union des Populations du Cameroun (UPC) launched an abortive revolt in 1955; it tried to disrupt the independence celebrations in Cameroon but only succeeded in bringing in more French troops to help President Ahidjo finally crush the uprising some three years later. Prior to 1960, of all francophone African countries, only Algeria experienced a war of national liberation.

11. This thesis is commonly advanced by Marxist Africanists. See, for example, Richard A. Joseph, ed., *Gaullist Africa* (Enugu: Four Winds Press, 1980). The military power France has available for intervention overseas is not inconsiderable: see Jacques Guillemin, "L'Intervention éxterieure dans la politique militaire de la France en Afrique Noire," in *Le Mois en Afrique*, 16, 186-187 (June-July 1981):43-58.

12. *La Culture Africaine, le Symposium d'Alger* (First Pan-African Cultural Festival, Algiers: Société National d'Edition et de Diffusion, 1969).

13. *Ibid.*, pp. 83-88.

14. *Ibid.*, pp. 363-66.

15. Joseph Bipoun-Wum, "Elite et peuple dans L'Afrique d'aujourd'hui," in *Présence Africaine*, 73 (1970):54-55. The following quotation is a continuation of the same passage.

16. Victor T. LeVine, "Political Elite Recruitment and Political Structure in French-Speaking Africa," in *Cahiers d'Etudes Africaines*, 31, 3 (1968):369-89.

17. *Maghreb* is an Arab term meaning "west"; it was traditionally used to refer to the lands furthest west from the "center" (Mecca and Medina for example). It was usually understood to include what is today Morocco, Algeria, Tunisia, and Libya. However, Morocco itself is often referred to as *al-Maghrib*.

18. Again, the qualified exceptions are the revolts in Madagascar (1946) and Cameroon (1955-1963); early strikes in Senegal, Porto-Novo

(Dahomey), and the Ivory Coast; and tribal violence in the French Congo during the 1950s.

19. Isaac Yetiv, "Un sous-produit de la colonisation française en Afrique du Nord: Les 'Evolués' (le 'politique' et le 'littéraire')," in *L'Esprit Créateur*, 12, 4 (Winter, 1972):264-65.

20. *Loc. cit.*

21. I do not mean that an African identity does not exist; the point is that there is as yet no agreement on exactly what it is, what it contains, and how it should be described. One of the latest contributions to the discussion is a United Nations University paper, "The African Personality" (United Nations University, New York: Project on Goals, Processes, and Indicators of Development, 1980), p. 29.

10
NJOKU E. AWA

Colonialism, Media Imperialism, and the Survival of African Culture

Media imperialism is defined by O. Boyd-Barrett as "the process whereby the ownership, structure, distribution and content of the media in any one country are singly or together subject to substantial pressure from the media interests of any other country or countries without proportionate reciprocation of influence by the country so affected."[1] Boyd-Barrett views media imperialism as a dominant component, outside formal education, of cultural imperialism. Herbert Schiller, one of the central characters in the media/cultural imperialism debate, writes poignantly about the hegemony of a handful of transnational media conglomerates that manufacture "culture" for worldwide consumption.

The production of movies, television programs, games, records, magazines, and books is consolidated in a few corporate superstructures and made part of multiproduct lines of profit-maximizing combines. These culture-producing business aggregations, with the acquiescence of the judiciary, confer on themselves the legal status of individuals and take for granted their protection under the U.S. Constitution's Bill of Rights. They cover their expansionist drives for markets under the principle of the free flow of information.[2]

These quotations are presented to give the reader a flavor of the technical meaning and the dimensions of the term "media imperialism." "Free flow," the pivot on which the current debate on the "New World Information and Communication Order" revolves, is a nebulous concept indeed. Originally introduced in Article 1 of the UNESCO Constitution[3] and hailed by the West as the triumph of its (Western) concept of freedom of the press, free flow came under attack by Third World countries, ironically with UNESCO's backing. I say ironically because UNESCO was until 1969 the champion of the free-flow doctrine. In that year, UNESCO convened a meeting of experts in Montreal to discuss international communication flow. During the course of that meeting, reference was made to two related concepts—"two-way circulation of news" and "balanced circulation of news." Since then, several meetings have been convened to debate the issue. One of these, held in Nairobi in 1976, culminated in the appointment of a sixteen-person International Commission for the Study of Communication Problems under the distinguished chairmanship of Sean MacBride, a Nobel laureate.

The commission's unenviable tasks included determining an ideologically unbiased definition of "free and balanced flow of information"—the central issue in the debate—and identifying strategies by means of which objectivity and independence of the media can be assured.

As in most debates, there are two parties to the present dispute, the West and the Third World. And as in other debates, each party appears convinced of the rightness of its position. Briefly stated, the West, especially the United States, claims it has a strong commitment to the freedoms enshrined in its Constitution, one of which is "freedom of speech and expression." From the perspective of the United States, especially its media conglomerates, this freedom includes the right to disseminate and receive information, the public's right to learn of events happening within and beyond its immediate environment, and the right of journalists to gain access to information in the marketplace of ideas. To the West, these are inviolable rights, the endangerment of which would constitute a serious threat to its media ideology.

But Third World countries see the marketplace concept as nothing but a cover for Western expansionism. They are concerned about the dominance of the international communication system by the

West and their own inevitable dependence on Western news media and about the distortion by Western journalists of events occurring in non-Western countries and the irrelevance of much of what is reported about the Third World. At a meeting of the Nonaligned Press Agencies Pool (NAPAP) in New Delhi, India, Vidya Charan Shukla, India's minister of information, declared:

The "free" flow of information, which was chanted in a chorus, was aimed to enable all countries in name, but only the powerful countries in reality, to pump their information into all regions of the world without let or hindrance. Nonaligned countries till today have been able to do almost nothing to protect their national interests against such onslaughts, since no safeguards are possible without (a) some degree of development of their own national media and (b) a state of cooperation among themselves. In fact, the idea of "free" flow of information fits insidiously into the package of other kinds of "freedom" still championed by the adherents of 19th century liberalism.[4]

Shukla accused Western news agencies of cultural invasion and multinational corporations of economic exploitation of Third World countries. He seemed to have reflected the general sentiment of Third World media critics, most of whom where of the opinion that "free flow" (as interpreted and implemented by the West) is inherently pernicious to the welfare of non-Western, media-poor countries of the Third World. This view is repugnant to the feelings of the West. In 1979 the U.S. National Commission for UNESCO organized a conference around the theme "Toward an American Agenda for a New World Order of Communications." At the end of the conference, the participants, while acknowledging the need to modify the doctrine of free flow to reflect "the integrity of the cultural patterns of other societies," reaffirmed America's historic interpretation of free flow. The conference stressed, for example, its "aversion to centralized control [of the media] whether by government or private sector" and its belief in the "free flow concept."[5] In fact, one of the conferees said, "It is unlikely that any regulation can stem the tide toward global free flow of information."[6]

Judging from their tones, the debaters appeared to be talking at crosspurposes, with each party seeing only the beams in the other's eyes. In other words, each party sees reality only in its own definition of what is right or wrong, free or unfree, and reacts semantically to the other's definitions and interpretations—a classic example of "rights in collision."

With a few exceptions, Western academics who have contributed to the debate have generally been dogmatic; their contributions seem to have added insult to injury, thereby rendering the doctrine unpalatable to Third World authorities.[7] Consider, for example, Ithiel de Sola Pool's view on the debate:

> Another set of obscuring cliches are used by authorities who fear the free flow of information to their population. They justify restrictions as necessary to the preservation of their culture, or as preventing dependency, or as protecting their own production from cultural imperialism. For social scientists there are important and difficult issues here that have been studied for centuries. . . . Politicians, however, often make simple minded incomplete arguments that appear to the prejudice that if something is of foreign origin the receivers are hurt and the source benefits. At that unsophisticated level . . . an American politician takes it as proof enough that Americans are hurt if he can show that Italian shoes are gaining a growing portion of the market.[8]

Pool's argument may be summarized as follows: opponents of the free-flow doctrine are myopic, shallow, and unsophisticated; they are unable to see the advantages that can accrue to A and B as they (A and B) share A's values, legacies, and prejudices to the exclusion of B's.

Pool's argument overlooks the fact that like "free trade," free flow assumes competition in the marketplace. The West—through its media conglomerates, especially its four wire services, Reuters, AFP, AP, and UPI—can afford such competition. Poor and low-technology nations have little ability to establish and operate expensive and technologically sophisticated information systems to match the giant information systems of the West.[9] So what we have is a one-way flow of information, from technologically advanced countries (including the USSR, which operates TASS) to Third World countries. The global information and communication system is thus sealed: Third World countries, neither owning nor directly participating in the technology, remain at best avid consumers of "Westernized" and "Sovietized" information.

One other aspect of Pool's argument that bears examination is his metaphor of Italian shoes in the American market. This is just the type of illustration needed to buttress belief in the claim that country A will gain at the expense of country B, if the latter is made the dumping ground for the former's products—information, shoes, or other manufactured commodities. The effect of Japanese imports, especially automobiles, on the American economy is a case in point. In Detroit thousands of workers have been laid off or dismissed by the major automobile companies—General Motors, Ford, and Chrysler—as a result of the trade imbalance between Japan and the United States. Also, in Cortland, New York, Smith Corona has reduced its staff by about one-third because the typewriter market is saturated with Japanese-made, relatively inexpensive machines. To redress the imbalance, the United States has made representations to the Japanese government and its auto makers. The goal of these representations is to stem the tide of the unilateral advantage accruing to Japan under the free trade ideology.

One of the reasons why Third World nations have refused to countenance the old tag of free flow of information is that under the doctrine the West exports a wide range of entertainment material to the so-called free world. With respect to movies, Thomas Guback observes, "In the early 1970s the nations of the world were annually producing about 3,500 feature motion pictures. Although only about 5 percent were of American origin, American films occupied about 50 percent of theatrical screen time in what is called the Free World."[10]

Filmmaking is an area in which Africa has failed to develop a realistic policy at both the national and continental levels; indeed, Africa lags behind Asia and Latin America in the domestic production of films. In fact, Guback laments that

After . . . two decades of independence, few African states have been able to develop a national policy for cinemas. Consequently . . . a *de facto* policy has been imposed by American and European interests, and its essence is decidedly commercial, with little concern for cultural identity. Unless drastic changes occur, African states will be cinematically isolated from one another.[11]

Guback's statement about "cultural identity" is reminiscent of UNESCO's concern that Africa should develop film production and distribution capabilities that would allow it to create pictorial dramas that are "truly African in style and content," especially films that "reflect African realities as exactly as possible."[12] Obviously, UNESCO's concern failed to elicit the response it was supposed to, but Africa's inaction in this matter stimulated interested media conglomerates to plan what they described as "a united invasion of the Dark Continent."[13] That goal (the invasion of Africa) has been accomplished along with its concomitant social and economic effects demonstrated by Africa's increasing dependence on Western technology and the erosion of its own culture.

DISTORTION IN THE MIRROR

The claim has frequently been made that mass communication systems are reflective and supportive, rather than directive, in their presentation of cultural values.[14] But it is evident that when the cultural values subsumed in the message are not those of the recipients, an apparently neutral and innocuous message may have important political and social effects. Programming thus becomes of crucial importance. George Gerbner, for example, calls programming "a synthetic representation of the dominant values and power structure of . . . society."[15] Television entertainments do not simply entertain; they teach assumed cultural and material values that may well be contrary to the social or the political aims of the government of the importing country. Viewed in this light, the significance of the wire services becomes more readily apparent: they provide a good example of the imperialistic effects of dominant values when applied to and forced on other, technologically weaker nations.

Tapio Varis in his study of program imports throughout the world, examines the cultural content of programming in television. He notes that exporting companies "often aim at enhancing the national image of the producing country: that program exchange is commercially based rather than in any real sense 'international,' that Third World nations import a disproportionate amount of programming, and that foreign material dominates prime-time viewing in weaker nations."[16] He also notes that viewing is frequently limited to the rich and elite of the Third World—precisely the people whose assumed responsibility is to counteract the cultural effects of the industrialized world's dominance of the international media.[17] These conclusions can be applied *mutatis mutandis* to the relationship in the print media between the West and Africa.

The wire services gather, process, and disseminate information. Each of these functions implies an editorial choice, determining and selecting what appears to be "newsworthy" or "what will sell." These processes are intimately affected by the stereotypes held by reporters and editors—the "gatekeepers" of information flow, both in Africa and in the West. Stereotyping in its widest sense indicates a simplification or oversimplification in our perception of the world and, as Andrea Rich has shown, "we learn to stereotype through the mass media."[18] One of the results of the self-perpetuating stereotypes of Africa is the inadequacy of information on the continent and an overemphasis on the few available stories about African countries and people. We are conditioned to expect, for example, mass violence as a necessary part of the political process in Africa. Orderly change in African politics, for example, the peaceful transition of power after the deaths in 1978 of presidents Houari Boumedienne of Algeria and Jomo Kenyatta of Kenya, and the retirement in 1981 of President Léopold Sédar Senghor of Senegal, go largely unreported. By failing to report such positive events as the orderly transfer of power, the wire services act to reinforce existing stereotypes.

President Julius Nyerere's experiments in social justice in Tanzania have provoked many academic investigations, but the 1979 conflict between Tanzania and Uganda resulted in far more "news coverage" of Tanzania than any of its longer-term achievements. The establishment of President Agostinho Neto's government in Angola was widely covered in the West only because of Cuban military involvement in the final phases of his success. That Cuban involvement, however, was alone worth more newsprint than the fifteen years of struggle against Portuguese colonialism.

The distortions and misunderstandings that grow from the near monopoly of coverage which the wire services possess over events in the Third World, especially Africa, and the interpretations of those events may be summarized under three main headings:

1. Africa and the rest of the Third World provide disaster stories: earthquakes, palace revolutions, war, famine, large train crashes, and massacres. An example of the last named was the massacre of six hundred Moslems in a provincial town south of N'Djamena in February 1979. This story was widely reported in the Western press and television, although Chad does not usually appear among the headlines of the world media.
2. When political events are reported, the concentration is almost entirely on the leaders of the country concerned. Such "personality cults" (for they are no less than this) tend to present both dictators and democratically elected leaders in precisely the same terms. Further, it is probably worth noting that a higher standard of probity is demanded of such leaders than is expected of Western politicians and officials.
3. The coverage of the personality of a leader will tend to mask the events in his or her country, so events, even when reported directly, tend to be masked by convenient tag explanations. How many African events have been explained to the West as outbreaks of "tribalism?" This term alone has explained so many disparate events that it could by now be applied to any event in any part of the world with as much meaning as it now possesses in the African context, yet it is still generally reserved as a typifying modifier of African events.

But the expectations of disaster, instability, and personality cults are significant not simply because of the negative impression they create in the Western world about events in the Third World. Because Third World countries are dependent on occidental sources of information, this negativism is fed back precisely to those countries it denigrates and misrepresents. This fact introduces us to a wider consideration.

POLICY AND INFORMATION

Although the United States government has long supported the doctrine of the free flow of information, it has always recognized in its budgets that information is anything but free. From a nameless organization in Langley, Virginia, to the various economic and political intelligence officers attached to embassies and consulates throughout the world, the costs of information are recognized as vast. John Merrill and Ralph Lowenstein provide a partial, albeit adequate, inventory of the media owned and operated by the United States government:

Through the Government Printing Office, the U.S. is one of the major book publishers in the country. It owns two wire services . . . , produces hundreds of magazines through its federal agencies, publishes numerous military camp and service-wide newspapers, produces motion pictures for the United States Information Agency, and broadcasts throughout the world over armed forces radio and television networks and the Voice of America. Quite obviously, the government is a gatekeeper in each one of these wholly owned enterprises.[19]

The information gathered and processed by these United States government agencies is, of course, private and expensive rather than public and free. Further, the information gathered is gathered for a purpose. That purpose is the formulation of policy.

It is axiomatic that policy is based on the available information. The less the information, the less likely it is that policy will comport with reality. So policy formulated without adequate data will, at best, have a coincidental relationship to reality.

We have already noted the cost of information. The national budget of a Tanzania or a Mali is unable to buy as much private information as that of the United States or Great Britain. To the extent that private information is unavailable or too expensive, smaller countries are likely to base policy decisions on a mixture of private and public information. But we have already noted how much of that public information favors the industrialized countries of the world through, for instance, "wire service nationalism," and, further, much of the information involved is decidedly negative toward African and other Third World countries.

It follows that Third World policy making is doubly disadvantaged, because it works on less private information and it relies more heavily on public information tailored to favor the industrialized world. These disadvantages force Third World nations to build their policy on the basis of distortions of reality. As a basis for action and development, such information is grotesquely inadequate and is likely to result in disaster. (This is, incidentally, one of the ways in which the predilections of wire-service stereotypes tend to be self-fulfilling.) And such a situation is perpetuating itself. There is no obvious or immediate way to correct the radical imbalance between the information-rich and the information-poor countries of the world.

But the effects of this relationship on African and other Third

World countries are ominous indeed. John Lent has noted that in the Caribbean, rock and soul music have replaced calypso and steel bands and that "Hollywood movies fill radio and television logs and movie marquees."[20] In many parts of Africa, magazines with prurient content are now sold openly; creativity in music, especially "highlife" and "rhumba," has declined as the disco fever has assumed an epidemic proportion.

Communication among nations is presently, as I have indicated, unidirectional. The imbalances in flow tend very largely to favor the countries of the industrialized West. And the information received in the countries of the Third World is largely treated to aid the goals of the sender. The Third World's hard won independence from political dominion is thus immediately challenged in the crucial area of the formulation of national policy by a colonialism of information and an apparently inescapable circle of misapprehension and partiality.

No country is an island: no country or culture can survive without maintaining some ties with other countries and cultures. On the verge of the twenty-first century, the countries of the world are becoming more interdependent. No part of the world, including the most technologically advanced, can claim to be self-sufficient. We know this to be true from the standpoint of natural resources because of the crises created in the industrialized nations by the oil policies of OPEC. Many of the low-technology nations of the Third World have vast natural and mineral resources. The industrialized nations possess the technology to exploit these resources. The development of mutual technological cooperation is essential to the survival of high- and low-technology nations. The West can train African and other Third World nations in the application of technology to production.

The same is true of communications. Colonialism halted the growth of indigenous culture, especially in Africa. Media imperialism effectively extends and reinforces the suppression of indigenous culture. Yet, one's understanding of one's own condition and one's view of world affairs are both largely determined by culture. All events take place within some cultural setting and indeed derive their significance from the culture in which they occur. The same event could be and indeed is interpreted in entirely different ways, depending on the viewpoint of the reporter. The writing of the history of one culture from the milieu of another raises serious questions of cultural bias and distortion.

Deeper than the manifestations of cultural bias and distortion that the West has so often displayed toward Africa and other Third World regions are the actual effects of one culture imposing itself upon another in a superordinate/subordinate relationship. Such effects have shaped the Africa that emerges today. Cultural bias, distortion, and racism, largely a result of colonialism, dimmed the light on Africa's history, culture, and civilization. Africa's culture and mores, spiritual and temporal concepts, and ideals were dismissed as paganistic irrelevancies that blocked the path of Christian progress and European enlightenment. The scramble for Africa occurred in the name of these Western ideals.

Since the colonial period Africa has struggled to survive under a new order imposed upon her by Europeans. Before the European presence, new ideas or religions were not unfamiliar in Africa. In the seventh century A.D. Islam swept through Africa. But there is a profound difference between the ways Islam and Christianity established themselves there. African religion and culture formed the primary base of society; and, therefore, to survive, Islam underwent a series of changes and accommodations. Thus, in a sense, Islam became Africanized.

The erosion of African culture began when the essence and structure of traditional society gave way, adapting and reemerging, reshaped and reformed, ready to move Africa another step forward in history. Nevertheless, Africa still retains much of the traditional culture, and the strength of this culture continues to provide the framework in which Africa's evolution takes place.

Africa has a rich and vibrant culture; so does the West. The prospects for cooperation exist. Yet communication has remained unidirectional. Although in large part the result of the patterns established since the precolonial period of the imposition of Western values on Africa, this unidirectionality is also the result of the failure of African and other Third World countries to develop and assert their own communications technology or, at least, to achieve a measure of media independence. Just as technology can be transferred to effect the exploitation of natural resources, so it can be transferred to assert, to disseminate, and to share cultural resources.

NOTES

1. O. Boyd-Barrett, "Media Imperialism: Towards an International Framework for the Analysis of Media Systems," in *Mass Communication and Society*, ed. J. Curran, M. Curevitch, and J. Wollacott (London: Arnold Publishers, 1977), p. 16.

2. Herbert I. Schiller, "Transnational Media and National Development," in *National Sovereignty and International Communication: A Reader*, ed. Kaarle Nordenstreng and Herbert I. Schiller (New Jersey: Ablex Publishing Corporation, 1979), p. 25.

3. United Nations Educational, Scientific and Cultural Organization, *Constitution of the United Nations* (New York: United Nations, 1945).

4. Dante B. Fascell, ed., *International News: Freedom Under Attack* (Beverly Hills, Calif.: Sage Publications, 1979), p. 130.

5. Roger Tatarian, ed., *Toward an American Agenda for a New World Order of Communication*, The U.S. National Commission for UNESCO, January 1980 (Washington, D. C.: Department of State, 1980), pp. 13-14.

6. Tatarian, *op. cit.*, p. 13.

7. One exception to this general rule is Erwin Atwood and Sharon M. Murphy, "The 'New World Information Order' Debate: Assessments and Recommendations" (32nd Annual Conference of the International Communication Association, Boston, Mass., 1-5 May 1982).

8. Ithiel de Sola Pool, "Implications of Communication Technology For National and International Development" (27th Annual Conference of the International Communication Association, Kongresshalle, Berlin, Germany, 29 May-4 June 1972), p. 3.

9. Njoku E. Awa, "The Cultural Dimensions of the Right to Communicate," in *Contemporary Black Thought: Alternative Analyses in Social and Behavioral Sciences*, ed. Molefi Kete Asante and Abdulai S. Vandi (Beverly Hills, Calif.: Sage Publications, 1980).

10. Thomas H. Guback, "The International Film Industry," in *Mass Media Policies in Changing Cultures*, ed. George Gerbner (New York: John Wiley, 1977), p. 21.

11. *Ibid.*, p. 36.

12. United Nations, Reports and Papers on Mass Communication, *Developing Information Media in Africa* (Paris: United Nations, 1962), p. 31.

13. Guback, *op. cit.*, p. 36-37.

14. See, for example, Mary B. Cassata and Molefi K. Asante, *The Social Uses of Mass Communication* (Buffalo, N. Y.: Communication Research Center, SUNY at Buffalo, Dept. of Communication, 1977).

15. George Gerbner, ed., *Mass Media Policies* (New York: Wiley Interscience Publishers, 1977), p. 2.

16. Tapio Varis, "Global Traffic in Television," in *Journal of Communication*, 24, 1 (Winter 1974): 102-09.

17. Kaarle Nordenstreng and Tapio Varis, "Television Traffic—A One-Way Street?" United Nations, Reports and Papers on Mass Communication, 70 (Paris: UNESCO Press, 1974).

18. Andrea L. Rich, *Interracial Communication* (New York: Harper & Row, 1974), p. 47.

19. John C. Merrill and Ralph L. Lowenstein, *Media, Messages and Men: New Perspectives in Communication* (New York: David McKay Company, Inc., 1971), p. 207.

20. John A. Lent, *Third World Mass Media and Their Search for Modernity: The Case of Commonwealth Caribbean 1717-1976* (Lewisburg, Pa.: Bucknell University Press, 1977), p. 314.

11

TASLIM O. ELIAS

Judicial Process and Legal Development in Africa

It has with a good deal of truth been claimed by many that the jury system and the habeas corpus procedure are the pillars of the English common law. Even more than either of these, however, is the doctrine of judicial precedent as the main characteristic of the common law as it operates in the Commonwealth, in the United States of America, and in certain marginal areas that have been influenced by the common law, such as the Sudan, Ethiopia, and Liberia. The importance of the doctrine lies in the fact that, in contrast with the civil law systems of continental Europe and Latin America, it envisages a legal system that derives its source from a developing legal order based upon a series of judicial decisions embodying the common customs of the realm. This is in contradistinction to the civil law which derives its source from codes. In simple terms, the distinction is between case-law and codification as the underlying basis of the legal system.

The doctrine of judicial precedent is the concept and practice whereby decisions of the highest court in the land are binding upon all courts subordinate to it, those of the court or courts immediately below the highest courts bind all courts subordinate to them and so on until the lowest courts are reached at the base of the pyramid. Thus, in the United Kingdom, the highest appeal court for British Courts is the House of Lords, the decisions of which bind the English Court of Appeal, the High Court, the Crown Courts, and the Magistrate's Courts in the same way as they bind the Scottish Court of Sessions and subordinate courts in Scotland. While decisions of each of the other courts just mentioned bind the courts respectively subordinate to it, the decisions of the Court of Sessions in Scotland bind only Scottish Courts subordinate to it, but English and Scottish decisions are mutually exclusive as regards their binding character below the House of Lords. Her Majesty's Judicial Committee of the Privy Council was, and in a number of cases still is, the highest court of appeal for the British colonies (and for a few English tribunals like those of the legal or medical professions in matters of discipline) and its decisions, commonly referred to as opinions, are binding on such courts and not on English courts as such.

In its operation in Africa, the doctrine implies that, for instance in Nigeria and Ghana, the decisions of the Supreme Court as the highest court bind the High Court, those of the High Court bind the District or Magistrate's Courts, while those of the latter bind, at least in theory, the customary or local courts. We need not stop to consider how far customary or local courts do, in practice, observe the doctrine of judicial precedent, particularly having regard to decisions of superior courts on issues within their jurisdiction. But we must mention in passing that in a federation like Nigeria, while the decisions of the Supreme Court bind all the State High Courts, no decision of one High Court such as the Bendel State Court of Appeal binds another State High Court. This is because all the State High Courts are of coordinate jurisdiction. When there was the West African Court of Appeal, its decisions bound the courts of each of the four countries subject to its sway. Since independence, however, the old West African Court of Appeal decisions have only a persuasive authority in each West African State. If we may explain this a little, we should say that there is well-established principle to the effect that precedents are classifiable into the two categories of authoritative and persuasive: that is to say, that precedents are authoritative within a particular hierarchy of courts under one territorial jurisdiction, as is the case with the Supreme Court decisions of each state vis-a-vis courts subordinate to it, while with respect to the Supreme Court of one territory, its decisions have only a persuasive authority in any other territory and may be followed or not at the will of the courts of the latter. In other words, such persuasive precedents are not binding. These considerations apply with equal force to the Court of Appeal for Eastern Africa, which was the final court of appeal for Kenya, Uganda, and Tanzania. Although the decisions of the East African Court of Appeal were binding on all the Supreme Courts of the constituent states, no decision of the Supreme Court of one state constituted an authoritative precedent for the courts of another state.

In the distinction between authoritative and persuasive precedents, we may note briefly that, for much the same reason as we have just given, the decisions of the former West African Court of Appeal were never binding upon the Court of Appeal for Eastern Africa or, indeed, upon the defunct Central African Federation Court of Appeal. While each was free to consult the decisions of the other for parallels or analogies, it was not bound to follow such decisions. We shall return to this subject later when we come to consider the problems likely to arise where there was a decision of the Privy Council upon identical issues of law previously applied in cases before the courts of one or more of these territorial courts of appeal in Commonwealth Africa. For the present, we need say no more than this: when the Privy Council was the court of last resort for both the West and the East African groups of territories, its decisions were binding upon both appeal courts equally. Today the Privy Council is no longer a court of appeal for both groups of states, although the problems of its erstwhile hegemony still remain with us and will be considered anon.

ATTITUDE OF AFRICAN STATES TOWARD ENGLISH DECISIONS

Because of the reception of English law, including in particular the use of the so-called residual clause providing for the application of English law wherever a particular dispute before the court is not covered by customary law or a local enactment, judges—African and non-African—tended all too readily during the colonial era to resort to English law to fill the gaps. This was often the case when dealing with such sensitive areas as the application of the doctrine of repugnancy or issues relating to public policy or morality; English notions of these concepts were freely imported by the judges to deal with the situation. There was not sufficient knowledge of the sociology of our peoples or of the ethos underlying our policy; so the early judges fell back on the "unruly horse" of English public policy with which they had probably a nodding acquaintance in their study of English law and political thought.

We must hasten, however, to add that there were exceptions to this general tendency for instance, when, even an English judge during the colonial period showed true judicial technique in refusing to apply English decisions to a local case before him involving the determination of trade marks. Thus, in *MacIver & Co., Ltd. v. CFAO*,[1] J. Weber observed: "To the trained eye of a civilized community, there is undoubtedly a considerable difference in the two designs set side by side and the one would hardly be likely to be mistaken for the other, but while the broad principles laid down in English cases should be applied, the Trade Mark laws of this country should be administered with due regard to local conditions."[2] A little further on, the same opinion is expressed by C. J. Speed in these words: "It seems clear that the learned judge in the court below was inclined to refuse registration of this mark and would have done so had he not felt constrained to a contrary conclusion by the decisions of the English courts. These decisions are of course binding on us, but they must be construed having regard to the local conditions which are widely different from those that obtain in England."[3] These various observations clearly show that even English judges have sometimes decided to depart from English precedents when they felt that local circumstances precluded the application of English authorities to local conditions that were widely different from those in England.

Since political independence, however, a more strident note for judicial independence from English decisions has been struck in various parts of Africa. This proclamation of the new freedom is typified by an observation by Mr. Justice Ollenu: "Again as to the common law, from its English source, the courts of Ghana have hitherto paid regard to decisions of the courts in England; now they may pay regard to expositions of the common law by the courts of any country which exercises jurisdiction in the common law, namely, the English common law." What has in fact happened after political independence has been that English decisions, whether of the House of Lords or of the Privy Council, now have only a persuasive authority in Commonwealth Africa. It follows that the decisions of other common law countries like the United States of America, Canada, Australia, and India have at best only a persuasive authority in African courts.

This raises the general question as to how far Commonwealth countries follow English decisions. In *Parker v. R*,[4] Discon, L. C. J., of Australia in a very illuminating judgment held that the controversial English decision of *D.P.P. v. Smith*[5] had been wrongly decided and was, therefore, not to be followed in Australia. This same English decision fell to be considered in the East African case of *The Queen v. Sharmpal Singh*,[6] where the accused had been convicted of the murder of his wife by the Kenya High Court sitting with three assessors who said that the accused was not guilty since the wife's death occurred in the process of the husband having intercourse with her. The Court of Appeal for Eastern Africa substituted a verdict of manslaughter, and the state appealed against this judgment to the Privy Council for the restoration of the verdict of murder. The Kenya Government counsel cited *D.P.P. v. Smith* as authority for the proposition that "knowledge" within the meaning of "malice aforethought" under the Kenya Penal Code does not mean actual knowledge but only such knowledge as a reasonable man would have that death might be the probable consequence of his acts or omissions. It was further argued that the Court of Appeal for Eastern Africa had wrongly ignored the English decision in *D.P.P. v. Smith* in substituting its verdict of manslaughter only. The Privy Council refused to follow *D.P.P. v. Smith* because, in its view, the Penal Code provision of what constituted grievous harm was not affected by the English decision. Their Lordships accordingly affirmed the decision of the court of Appeal for Eastern Africa.

Another decision showing that judges—African and non-African—are increasingly conscious of the need to safeguard local judicial precedents against English decisions in certain situations is *Ezeani & ors v. Njidike*.[7] This was a case involving, inter alia, the tort of conversion and the measure of damages therefore. Brett, J.S.C., in delivering the judgment of the Supreme Court of Nigeria, observed in reference to the House of Lords decision in *Rookes v. Barnard*[8] regarding the award of exemplary damages: "It is not necessary in the present case to decide whether the Courts in

Nigeria should adopt this decision in toto, but as a warning against the over-free award of exemplary damages it is of strong persuasive authority." Incidentally, the question whether or not *Rookes v. Barnard* was applicable in Kenya was considered in *Orude and Nwangi v. The Municipal Council of Kisumu*.[9] The Court of Appeal for Eastern Africa, relying on the Privy Council test in *Australian Consolidated Press, Ltd. v. Uren*, held that there was no local body of law inconsistent with *Rookes v. Barnard* which must be treated "as authoritatively setting out the law of England as to exemplary damages in tort, which was applied in Kenya by the Judicature Act, 1967." This decision was soon to be upset by *Broome v. Cassell & Co., Ltd. & anor*,[10] in which the English Court of Appeal cast serious doubts on its validity, but the House of Lords has since restored *Rookes v. Barnard*. But for this restoration by the House of Lords in England, the law as to exemplary damages in East Africa would have remained chaotic as a result of the slavish application there of this English decision. It would have been wiser for the Court of Appeal for Eastern Africa to have followed the example of the Supreme Court of Nigeria by regarding the English decision as having only a persuasive authority.

In *Rashid Muledina & Co., (Mombasa) Ltd. & ors v. Hoima Ginners Ltd.*,[11] one of the arguments of counsel for the respondent was that, in interpreting the Arbitration Act of Kenya (Cap 49), the Court of Appeal for Eastern Africa should not consider English decisions nor even the decisions of the Court itself, since they were subject to appeal to the Privy Council. Sir Charles Newbold, C.J., observed:

It has been urged on behalf of the respondent that this court is not bound to English decisions and that it should overrule the decision in the Sohan Lal Case[12] as that decision was given at a time when this court was subordinate to the Privy Council. It is clear that this court is not bound by any English decision, whether given before or after independence. Nevertheless, this court will pay due regard to the decision of any Commonwealth Court where a similar system of law to that apertaining in East Africa exists, and will, of course, pay especial regard to the decision of the English courts, especially where those decisions enunciate the common law or equity or interpret statutes of general application or statutes which have been substantially copied in East Africa. As regards previous decisions of this court, whether before or after Independence, I would not wish to express an opinion as to the precise application of the doctrine of stare decisis as the matter was not fully argued before us and in any event I am quite convinced that the decision in the Sohan Lal Case was correct and should be followed.

As regards the reservation of the learned chief justice in his last sentence, J.A. Spry, explained the position further in these words:

I would, of course, agree that this court is bound by English decisions but in the interpretation of the Arbitration Act, much of which (including sections 11 and 12) is clearly derived from the English Arbitration Act, 1889, respect should be shown to English decisions on that Act, particularly those given prior to the enactment of the Kenya statute because, in the absence of any indication to the contrary, it is reasonable to suppose that the legislature enacted the Kenya statute with knowledge of those decisions. As regards the pre-Independence decisions of this court, the legislature has on each of the constitutional changes, expressly maintained the existing law and therefore those decisions should carry just as much weight as if there had been no constitutional changes.

In *Ahmed & anor v. R*,[13] the question was whether the joinder of two accused persons which constituted a procedural defect under the Kenya Criminal Procedure Code was a mere irregularity or whether it was a fundamental illegality which vitiated the whole trial. On an appeal from the Kenyan Supreme Court, the Court of Appeal for Eastern Africa first considered *Mubarak v. R*,[14] one of its own earlier decisions on appeal from the High Court of the Somaliland Protectorate, which, while involving a similar problem, really turned on the application of a Criminal Procedure Code based on that of India. The Court of Appeal pointed out, however, that one of the differences between the Indian (and Somaliland) Code and the Kenya Code, was the omission in the Kenya Code of any provision for separate trial of every charge; and the court was of the opinion that, as the Kenya Code had been based on the English Indictment Act, 1915, and not on the Indian Code, the English decisions must be followed.[15] The Court of Appeal took the view that "it is the English law and practice to which it is right to turn to ascertain the effect of an irregular charge or information and that the Indian law and the decision made thereunder are not impugned."

When a Privy Council decision was based on an Indian Act which applies in East Africa, the Court of Appeal for Eastern Africa might very well decide not to follow it. Thus, in *Zamburakis & anor v. Rodussakis*,[16] the appellants had argued at the trial that the claim against them was barred by the Indian Limitation Act, 1908, which, with the Indian Code of Civil Procedure, was applied in Tanganyika in 1920 by Order-in-Council. J. Mahan, who tried it as a preliminary issue in the pleadings, rejected the plea. When the matter was taken to the High Court, C. J. Cox upheld this ruling and ordered that the account should be taken. On appeal, the Court of Appeal for Eastern Africa affirmed Mahan's ruling for the reason that section 97 of the Code of Civil Procedure forbids appeal from a preliminary ruling on any appeal from the final decree. On a final appeal to the Judicial Committee, Their Lordships followed an earlier decision of their own on the interpretation of the same act on appeal from India in 1917 in Fricomdas Cooverji Bhojav Gopinath Fiu Thakur.[17] The question now is: Would such a decision of the Privy Council be followed in any East African court today? The issue is important in view of the sizable number of Indian Acts which apply there as part of the received law.

There may occasionally arise a case before an African court in respect of which there are two inconsistent decisions, one of the English House of Lords and the other of the Privy Council. As the doctrine of judicial precedent operates in Africa, the better opinion is that Privy Council decisions prevail. Thus, in *Clyde-Wiggins v. Maba Estates Ltd.*,[18] J. Goldin preferred to follow *Baines v. Pick*[19] rather than *Scharfeneker v. Duley & Co., Ltd.*,[20] thereby affirming the principle that decisions of the South African Appellate Division, given before the abolition of its appellate jurisdiction over the High Court of Southern Rhodesia, are binding on a single judge of the High Court of Southern Rhodesia. The South African chief justice had in the course of his judgment in *Van der Linde v. Calitz*[21] discussed *R v. L*[22] on appeal from Rhodesia, wherein the view was expressed that, despite statutory wording that evidence was to be admitted "as if the matter were depending in the High Court of Judicature," regard must be had to the fact that the Privy Council was the Court of Appeal and not the House of Lords. Accordingly, in the event of a conflict between the two, Privy Council decisions will prevail. J.L. Davies in *ex parte Boland* gave a salutary reminder that, where courts are given a judicial discretion, reported cases are only examples of how past judges have thought fit to exercise that discretion and cannot either fetter or limit the discretion conferred by statute or create a binding rule of practice.

POST-RECEPTION DATE ENGLISH DECISIONS IN AFRICA

The treatment in Orude and Nwangi Case and the authority of *Rookes v. Barnard* by the Court of Appeal for Eastern Africa has once again focussed attention upon the binding character in an African State of English decisions given after the reception date. Let us illustrate with an example where the reception date is January 1, 1920. Should an English decision given in 1930 on a rule of common law which extends its scope by creating new law be binding upon that particular state? There have been two views on this matter. The first view is that such a post-reception date English decision, insofar as it is a legitimate extension of existing common law rule, should be regarded as binding on the courts of that state provided that it is a decision of the appropriate English court.[23] The other view is that only those English decisions at the cut-off date will be binding.[24] The problem will be thrown into bold relief if we take one or two concrete cases, one from the law of contract and the other from the law of tort. Consider what is known as the rule in *Chandler v. Webster*,[25] which is to the effect that if I hire a room in your house along the main road in town in order to view a procession, and that procession is subsequently cancelled, I cannot recover any money paid in advance; the contract is frustrated, and the loss "lies where it falls." This was the English common law up to *Fibrosa v. Fairbarn, etc., Ltd.*,[26] in which the House of Lords overruled *Chandler v. Webster* and held that the payer of money for a consideration that was wholly failed should be able to recover it. On the second view, a Commonwealth African country would not be able to claim this logical extension of the English common law rule except by means of fresh legislation. Again, let us take in the law of tort the development of the tort of negligence. According to the decision in *Winterbottom v. Wright*,[27] if A sold a defective chattel to B and if C was injured by using it, C could not sue A because C was not a party to the contract between A and B. Then, after a series of decisions, *Donoghue v. Stevenson*[28] was decided by the House of Lords on a Scottish appeal to the effect that if A puts a deleterious manufactured substance into circulation by means of a sale to B and if C is injured, C can sue A for negligence independently of the fact that C is not a party to the contract. On the second view, this worthwhile extension of the principle of tortious liability for negligence would not be available to the state concerned.

An interesting example of the interstate use of judicial precedents is afforded by the Ghanaian case of *Wallace Johnson v. R*[29] which, it will be recalled, was to the effect that, where a provision in a code was intended to be exhaustive of the applicable law, it should be considered free from any glosses or interpretations based upon English or Scottish law. In *Ogbuagwu v. Police*,[30] in which there was a charge of seditious libel under section 51 of the Nigerian Criminal Code, J. Bairamian approved and applied Wallace Johnson's case in holding that a defence which was available under English law but which had not been expressly incorporated into the Nigerian Code was not available in Nigeria, since the Nigerian Criminal Code was "meant to be complete and exhaustive." Similarly, in the Ugandan appeal of *Yonasani & ors v. R*,[31] the Court of Appeal for Eastern Africa applied the dictum of the Privy Council in the Wallace Johnson's case where the question was whether, in a trial of accessories after the fact, the English rule that the principal offender must first have been prosecuted to conviction before the accessories after the fact could be charged was held applicable in Uganda. The Court of Appeal for Eastern Africa made the following pertinent observation: "What is true of the Gold Coast Law of sedition is true also of the Uganda Law of accessories after the fact, and it is unnecessary in our opinion to engraft anything onto it from English Law."

In the Zambian case of *John Chitenge v. The People*,[32] the trial judge held that, if the intent to commit a felony was proved, malice aforethought was conclusively established, and the Zambian Court of Appeal accepted this view. What had happened in the case itself was that A, after a quarrel with B at a beer party, later went at night to set fire to B's house, in which C, a visitor staying with B, was asleep at the material time. A honestly thought that the house was empty at that time, but C suffered injuries from which he later died. A was convicted of the murder of C and then appealed. But the Court of Appeal pointed out that the law of Zambia differed from the English law prior to the enactment of the Homicide Act of 1957. The learned trial judge had, in reaching his conclusion, applied Wallace Johnson's case and some other decisions of the Court of Appeal for Eastern Africa.[33] The Zambian Court of Appeal held, however, that the law of Zambia was in fact the same as that of England before the Homicide Act of 1957 and said that the Zambian Penal Code contained a provision in section 4 which was different from the provision of the Gold Coast Code. It accordingly held that Wallace Johnson's case was not applicable to Zambia.

We may cite one more illustration from Australia. In *Hungier v. Grace & anor*,[34] C.J. Barwick of Australia cited with approval the Privy Council judgment in the Nigerian case of *Kasumu v. Baba-Egbe*[35] in support of his conclusion to the effect that advances made by a person which were not in the course of carrying on a business of money lending could not be regarded as a loan within the meaning of section 22(1) of the Money Lenders Act 1958 of Victoria, which is the same as part of section 19 of the Money Lenders Ordinance of Nigeria.[36]

It is possible to take the view that this example of intra-Commonwealth borrowings of relevant decisions has no doubt been induced by the fact that, in applying the Nigerian case, the Australian High Court was merely applying the persuasive authority of a decision of the Privy Council. Thus, examples of direct citation of a Supreme Court judgment of Nigeria or of any other African Commonwealth country by one of the older members of the Commonwealth are rare indeed.

The attitude of Ghana courts[37] has, in recent years, been largely influenced by the provision of section 42(2) of the Constitution of 1960, which says that "the Supreme Court shall in principle be bound to follow its own previous decisions on questions of law." Commenting on this expression, Mr. Justice Ollenu said:

Now, what is the proper interpretation to be given to the words "shall in principle be bound to follow its own previous decisions on questions of law"? Are they to be interpreted in the same way as the principle of stare decisis as operates in England in the House of Lords or the Court of Appeal, namely, that the Supreme Court has no option but to follow its previous decision even though it is manifestly wrong unless it can show that that previous decision was given per incuriam? Our view is that the words "in principle" are intended to create an elastic rule, to save the Supreme Court in embarrassing situations and to enable it to re-examine its own previous decision, to correct or differ from it when it finds such decision to be either manifestly wrong, not only because it was given per incuriam, but because of inconsistency with some principle of law or custom and is therefore a decision which for some good reason or the other should not be followed. In our view the Article lays down a flexible rule intended to enable the court to mould and develop the law, the common law no less than the customary law, to meet the needs of economic and social changes which are taking place in our new and developed nation without the necessity to resort to Parliament each time to rectify an error in the law brought about by a wrong decision.[38]

The same line of reasoning may be observed in *Loga v. Davordzi*,[39] where J.S.C. (as he then was) Azu Crabbe observed as follows:

Article 42(4) of the Constitution of Ghana declares that the Supreme Court "shall in principle be bound to follow its own decisions on questions of law." To my mind, the words "in principle" connote some flexibility in the application of the doctrine of stare decisis by this Court, which cannot regard itself as absolutely bound by its own previous decisions. . . . The merit of this less strict rule of precedent is that it enables the court to mould the law and to adapt it to the changing conditions of society. . . . It follows, therefore, that this Court, like the Privy Council, must feel strongly disposed to adhere to its previous decision (see *Fatuma Binti Mohamed Bin Salam v. Mohamed Bin Salam* (1952) A.C. 1). It must only deviate from its previous decision when the previous decision is manifestly wrong, or in exceptional circumstances.

AFRICAN INTERSTATE USE OF PRECEDENTS

The extent to which the various Commonwealth African states make use of precedents from one another depends upon a number of factors. Among the factors that should encourage such use may be mentioned the common heritage of English law, the once all-pervading judicial opinions of the Privy Council, geographical contiguity, and similarity of reactions of the several customary laws to the current social and economic stimuli. Of the various

Judicial Process and Legal Development

countries in Commonwealth Africa, Nigeria and Ghana have probably the closest relationship in legal and judicial matters. This is because the old Lagos Settlement was administered as the Eastern Province of the old Gold Coast Colony between 1866 and 1874; the two legal systems derive their common source from the Supreme Court Ordinance No. 4 of 1876; there has also been an intermingling of lawyers and of political leaders on such issues as the West African land question and the National Congress of British West Africa.

In practical judicial terms, this rapprochement in legal and allied matters has been reflected in the judicial sphere. Thus, in *Ekpendu v. Erika*,[40] the Supreme Court of Nigeria decided that the purported lease of a portion of family land without the consent of the family head was void ab initio. The court further laid down the following propositions of customary land tenure: (a) that a sale or lease of family land carried out by the family head, without the concurrence of the principal members of the family, is voidable, and that this had been so decided by the West African Court of Appeal in *Esan v. Faro*,[41] and (b) that a sale or lease of such land by the principal members of the family without the concurrence of the family head is void ab initio, and that this had been so decided by the West African Court of Appeal in *Agbloe v. Sappor*.[42] The Supreme Court pointed out that it was immaterial that *Esan v. Faro* relates to Lagos land while *Agbloe v. Sappor* relates to Accra land, since both cases were decided by the same three judges of the West African Court of Appeal within two months of each other.[43] In *Shang v. Coleman*,[44] a strong Court of Appeal of Ghana consisting of Ag. C.J. (as he then was) Van Lare, Granville Shapr, and Ollenu quoted with approval the Privy Council decision in *Bamgbose v. Daniel*[45] to be governed by the lex domicili, that is, the customary law of succession in that case. The court observed, inter alia, that African interpretations should, wherever possible, be given to English statutes which apply in Africa. Sometimes, however, the courts of Nigeria may not follow a Ghanaian precedent and vice versa. Thus, in *Taiwo v. Dosunma*,[46] where the issue was as to the accountability of the family head to members of the family, the Supreme Court of Nigeria, to which a number of Ghanaian cases[47] had been cited by counsel, pointed out that "although we are content to assume that it might be judicially noticed in Ghana that in certain areas, at least of the country, the junior members of the family cannot call on the head of the family for an account, we do not consider that that in itself means the existence of such a custom in Ghana can be judicially noticed by the High Court of Lagos." The court would seem to be saying no more than that since under Nigerian law an alleged rule of customary law has still to be established as a matter of evidence, this particular Ghanaian custom which obtains only at certain places in Ghana must be proved to be the custom of Lagos. Quaere whether, if the alleged custom had been held in Ghana to be a general custom, it would have been accepted by the Supreme Court of Nigeria. It would not have been, for the reason that it could not be taken judicial notice of, since as foreign law, it still has to be proved by evidence. Finally, it will be sufficient to refer to *Awonor-Williams v. Gbedeman*,[48] in which, as we may recall, the Ghana Supreme Court referred to its Nigerian counterpart's decision in *Lakanmi & anor v. The Attorney-General (Western State) & ors*[49] in dealing with the question of the validity of the decrees issued by the military governments of the National Liberation Council.

We may now turn to other instances of interstate uses of precedents in Africa. An epoch-making judgment of the Court of Appeal for Eastern Africa in which the fundamentals of the applicability of judicial precedents were examined and restated for that part of the continent is *Dodhia v. National and Grindlays Bank, Ltd. & anor.*[50] The immediate questions for determination were: (a) whether the Court of Appeal for Eastern Africa was bound by decisions of the Privy Council given in appeals from East Africa, and (b) whether the Court of Appeal for Eastern Africa was bound by its own previous decision. Alongside these points was also the question of the application of the doctrine of stare decisis by the High Court and subordinate courts in Kenya. But before we deal with this particular case, let us look at the state of the law as declared by the Court of Appeal for Eastern Africa in *Vallabjhi v. National and Grindlays Bank, Ltd., & anor.*[51] There, it was held that unattested letters of hypothecation were wholly void. When the matter was taken on appeal to the Privy Council, it was held that such letters were valid inter partes.[52] The Vallabhji case, which was the last decision delivered by the Privy Council in an East African appeal before the abolition of appeals to the Judicial

Committee, raised a point of law identical with that involved in the instant Dodhia case.

The Vallabhji case raised the question of the applicability and authority in Kenya and New Zealand decisions on New Zealand Acts which formed the basis of the Kenya Chattels Transfer Act. P. Newbold, after scrutinizing the terms of the applicable statute law against the background of the received English Common Law and Equity in order to discover whether there was anything in the local circumstances of Kenya which made these inapplicable there, held that the Court of Appeal for Eastern Africa was bound by the decisions of the Privy Council when the latter court was the final court of appeal; that the Privy Council had the necessary flexibility in following its own previous decisions; and that the court of appeal is not bound by any prior decision of the Privy Council, including that in the Vallabhji case. The other two justices of appeal agreed with him. The court was also unanimous in the view that "while it would normally regard a previous decision of its own as binding," it "should be free in both civil and criminal cases to depart from such a previous decision when it appears right to do so." The court also "accepts that subordinate courts are bound by the decisions of superior courts and that a subordinate court of appeal should normally be bound by a previous decision of its own." Newbold, while adhering to the position he had taken in the Vallabhji case, thought the majority of the judges of the Privy Council in that case were "unaware of the conditions and needs of the people of Kenya"; that the Vallabhji case was wrongly decided, but that this was a comparatively minor matter of the construction of a section, and to change the construction of it three times in as many years would cause uncertainty in law for the business community; hence the court of appeal would not depart from the Privy Council view in Vallabhji. Duffus, V-P, thought that to reverse the Privy Council now would lead to complete uncertainty, while Spry considered that "the majority judgment . . . represents a logical and reasonable view which has formed part of the law of Kenya for the past three years," and that "there was no compelling reason for departing from that decision." Thus, by a self-denying ordinance, the Court of Appeal for Eastern Africa refrained from upsetting an inconvenient decision of the Privy Council and chose to allow it to remain on the ground of convenience.

PRECEDENTS IN THE SERVICE OF LEGAL DEVELOPMENT

We may now take a look in the round at the operation of stare decisis as inherited by Commonwealth African states as part of the received English common law. There can be little doubt that, despite the disadvantages that inevitably attend upon the strict application of the doctrine of judicial precedent, it has been an agent of evolutionary legal development. Among its notable disadvantages are, to be sure, its tendency towards bulk and complexity in the growth of the common law; the possibility of having to make sometimes illogical distinctions between cases that are apparently similar in order to avoid having to follow inconvenient precedents,[53] the sometimes continued application of old and outmoded decisions to current social and economic problems; and the difficulty of determining the ratio decidendi of a case where different reasons were given for reaching the same conclusion.[54] On the other hand, the advantages of the case-law system are reasonable certainty of the law at any particular stage and also flexibility of growth of the law according to changing notions of legal development dictated from time to time by changing social and economic conditions. Such changes in the law as are considered to be necessary are made after the fullest possible arguments in open court by counsel for both sides followed by careful scrutiny and consideration by the bench of all the relevant factors urged in favor of or against change. Where a change is more than the normal modification or extension of existing legal principle so that it amounts to a radical departure from established notions of justice according to law, the judicial function is at an end and the legislative initiative comes into play to effect the needed change. We noticed this phenomenon when we considered earlier the judicial modification of the rule in *Chandler v. Webster*, which held that where there was a frustration of the adventure of a contract, the loss lay where it fell and the payer of money or the renderer of services could not recover anything under the contract, into a new rule in the Fibrosa case, whereby if, under the frustrated contract, there was total failure of consideration, money paid or services rendered could be recovered or compensated for respectively. But where the failure of consideration is only partial, so that only a part of the payment had been made in advance but the payee has been put to reasonable expense in executing the contract, there is need for apportionment of the rights and obligations of the parties to the contract. The House of Lords could not, however, do this; what it did, and what all courts faced with a similar situation should do, was to draw the attention of Parliament to the desired change. In the particular instance under consideration, we may note that the fundamental change required in the law was effected by the Law Reform (Frustrated Contracts) Act, 1945. The common law system thus recognizes the respective spheres of the judicial and the legislative processes in the development of the law.

If we seem to favor the case-law approach to the problems of legal development, it is mainly because it is the rational and dynamic interpretation of a situation in each African territory in which polyethnic communities abound. The advocates of codification would be up against great difficulties in any attempt to codify the customary laws of the respective communities that make up the state. How are we to organize the compilation of such codes? What types of personnel should be engaged in the task—lawyers, sociologists, historians, and other research workers? Should these work singly or as a team? Then, we may also ask whether they should employ questionnaires or combined questionnaires with visits to the towns and villages. Whom should they consult—the old or the young or both? How should they reconcile the data thus obtained from both? These and similar problems have been agitated at considerable length elsewhere, and it would deflect us from our present course to repeat all the relevant arguments here. Suffice it to say that case-law is clearly preferable to codification as a means of legal development in Commonwealth Africa today. The recent efforts in the form of restatements of African law in parts of East Africa are useful as stop-gap measures, but they are hardly a substitute for case-law as a dynamic of social change in African legal development.

It may be pointed out that the mere proliferation of codes within a state is not conducive to the early emergence of a body of common law toward which each territory is or should be striving as a worthwhile goal of its legal development.[55] The coexistence of a multiplicity of codes within the same territorial entity might encourage tribal particularisms if it did not also breed ethnocentric prejudices. In this connection, it should be mentioned that Ghana has given the first and most explicit statutory expression to the concept of a common law as the aim of its legal system. Here is Ollenu's summary of the Ghanaian situation:

But what is the "common law," and what is the "customary law," which together with the principles of equity and the statutes of Ghana constitute the law of Ghana today? They are the English common law as assimilated to the circumstances of Ghana through the years that justice has been administered according to the English law, and the customs that have passed the tests I have already described and are thus contained in the body of case-law on the subject. These two laws are defined in the Interpretation Act, 1960, sections 17 and 18. Without wearying you with a recital of these sections, their effect as I understand it means "the common law of Ghana," the two different sources of which I have already described. All persons are subject to this common law; but over and above this, when a person shows that he, as a member of a particular locality or community, is entitled to the benefit of a local custom, then he will be given the benefit of that custom. Thus in Ghana today, a Local Court is by statute vested with full jurisdiction to administer, as part of the law of the land, principles of English law and the principles of equity which, before, were foreign to it. Again the customary law is no longer a fact to be proved in a Supreme Court; consequently the provisions in the High Court (Civil Procedure) Rules requiring customary law to be pleaded must disappear. Henceforth any mist which has surrounded the customary law is guided by the principle of repugnancy, and by precedents, the judges will be able to set out authoritatively the law of Ghana, and thus make possible the compilation of books on the common law of Ghana.[56]

It is thus clear that the common law of Ghana, as indeed of any Commonwealth African country, is made up of the English common law, the principles of equity, applicable English statutes, local statutes, and those rules of customary law which form part of the country's case-law and which apply to the relevant local communities. All the other elements of this common law apply to all persons within the state generally, while the customary law elements apply to particular groups. There is also the desired mechanism of legal development—the production of legal textbooks from time to time out of the whole judicial process. The method of case-law permits the possibility of similar, if not uniform, development of bodies of customary law by the application of juridical technique to the moulding of the raw materials along scientific lines. "The English common law," as Oliver Wendell Homes observed, "has not been logic; it has been experience."[57] It is the result of a slow but steady evolution, through generations, of the once disparate Anglo-Saxon customs fashioned from the time of Henry II onward by itinerant justices (often referred to as justices in eyre) and later by the royal courts until these customs gradually became for the most part the common law, that is, "the common custom of the realm." It seems reasonable to assume that, as inheritors of the English common law, especially of its spirit and practice, the various Commonwealth African states, given the polyglot nature of their communities and the interplay of the ever-changing economic and social forces, would do well to maintain the method of case-law as the means of developing a common law within their respective borders.

In each state, the judicial process will inevitably produce not only similarities of development, as between the main bodies of customary law, but also a measure of mutual borrowings often resulting in a uniformity of rules. One would make bold to say that if the operation of the case-law system should lead to the adoption of a rule of one of the dominant bodies of customary law as the new law, that would not necessarily be a bad thing. For instance, one would not be surprised if a matrilineal system of succession becomes under the stress of prevailing economic and social circumstances gradually patrilineal, patrilocal, and even patripotestal.[58] After all, fathers are now more often than not expected to pay their children's school fees; the children themselves are expected to bear their father's name and to inherit his estate upon his death. The increasing individualization of holdings and possessions encourages the tendency towards placing greater reliance on the nuclear family, with the father as the head. On reflection, it seems better that one body of customary law should, where necessary, adopt a rule from another body of customary law and make it the universal rule within the state, than that, under the rule in *Cole v. Cole* or *Coleman v. Shang*, the court should continue to apply the ancient and discarded Anglo-Saxon rules of succession prescribed under the Statute of Distributions, 1670 and 1685, which, by the way, was done away with in England itself well over fifty years ago.

By the use of judicial precedent in our system of case-law, there has been a significant development of our customary laws. A number of customary rules and traditional practices have been evolving since the advent of English law: it has been due to the courts that the concept of family land has been gradually analyzed and clarified in such a way that the rights of the individual family members therein have been defined from case to case, that the chief or the family head has been shown to be a kind of trustee or caretaker in relation to the family land, that the characteristics of the customary tenancies have been defined in precise legal terms, and that the customary pledge of land as a perpetually redeemable interest has been compared and distinguished from the English mortgage. Nor has the judicial process neglected the problems associated with the customary marriage and divorce, especially in relation to marriage under statute or what is sometimes erroneously called English or Christian marriage, although some crucial aspects of this relationship have yet to be resolved by legislation in order to produce a rational and coherent body of law in many Commonwealth countries. The customary laws of succession and inheritance have been elaborated by judges in a number of leading cases by the well-known methods of case-law. On the whole, it can be said that the application of the judicial techniques of the English common law to our customary laws has often resulted in the remoulding of the traditional rules and concepts along lines of rational development to suit our evolving economic and social characteristics. Through the use of the doctrine of repugnancy, customary law has been largely shorn of its obnoxious aspects, while at the same time the judicious use of precedents in our superior courts has helped in the gradual buildup of bodies of legal principles and practices which have enriched our various bodies of customary law. Some mistakes have, no doubt, been made in the process, resulting sometimes in misapplication of one type of customary rule or observance to the wrong groups and sometimes in overeasy generalizations which might obscure real differences. But such errors, where they have in fact occurred, can be and in fact have often been corrected by legislation or through the normal operation of the judicial process; they do not detract from the overall benefit to the development of customary laws that accrues from the judicious use of judicial precedents.

If we turn to the other areas of our laws, we shall find that our judges have tried within the limits of their vision and resources to introduce order into chaos by the rational application of the judicial process. Let us take, for instance, cases of the conflict of laws. The principles enunciated in a series of cases in which English law has come into conflict with customary law, or in which customary law has been at variance with statute law (whether English or local) or in which one body of customary law is opposable to another body of customary law, have over the years been evolved by the courts to meet the peculiar needs and circumstances of our pluralistic societies and the resultant profusion of laws. For one of the factors that make the laws of each of the Commonwealth African states so complex is the simultaneous application of at least three streams of laws, often to the same set of people. The sometimes bewildering variety of the interactions between these bodies of laws reinforces the growing need and even desirability of fashioning a body of common law for each state as the prime goal of the legislative policy and the judicial process.

What we have said earlier concerning the attitude of our courts towards English judicial precedents applies with equal force to the judicial interpretation of the various constitutions, in peacetime as in times of national emergency or war. We saw how ready the courts were to follow English precedents that afforded clear and pertinent guides; yet we also saw how the courts did not hesitate, on occasions, to depart from inconvenient precedents and how, if need be, the local legislature stepped in to nullify a Privy Council decision considered to be inappropriate to local circumstances. But perhaps it is in dealing with the constitutional problems arising out of *coups d'état* that the judges have shown their most notable resilience and independence of approach to unorthodox legal situations. What is worthy of note, however, is the steady fidelity of the judges to legal techniques no less than to the basic requirements of the rule of law.

CONCLUSION

The role of the judge in a Commonwealth African court is ex hypothesi a truly dynamic one. Unlike his counterpart in other common law jurisdictions in the older Commonwealth, the African judge is faced with tasks or a series of tasks that require a good deal of judgment and stamina. In the first place the law he has to apply is almost everywhere complex and often unsettled in that he must make a choice of alternatives among the competing claims of English common law, equity and statutes of general application, various bodies of customary law, and local statutes—all of which may apply to the subject matter of the dispute before the courts. In the second place, the judge has to consider his task in applying this complex law not only ratione personnae but also ratione materiae; this is because he is very often required to ascertain which law to apply to which parties where at least one of these is a non-African and also to have regard to the subject matter of the dispute as well as to take into account whether one or more of the parties have made a choice of law and whether such a choice should be permitted. In the third place, the judge must have an underlying philosophy that should guide his action from case to case, because it is this "inarticulate major premise," to use Oliver Wendell Holmes' expressive phrase, which supplies the rationale of his conclusions. Without such an underlying assumption the judge's task in the judicial process becomes unconvincing because it loses a proper sense of direction. Although trial judges are very much in need of such a philosophy, it is judges of appeal that cannot truly discharge their functions fully without it.

Yet, the nature of the judicial process in a Commonwealth African court is such as to induce in the judge a disposition towards judicial law making in certain areas of the law where there is either some uncertainty or no precedent at all. This is most noticeable in the sphere of the judicial treatment of certain aspects of customary law. African judges of today sometimes find the evolving customary law as malleable as Chief Justice Holt and Lord Mansfield found the English common law in the seventeenth and the eighteenth centuries.[59] Whether as trial judges or as justices of appeal, they need courage and a sense of conscious purpose in moulding the evolving law, but above all they need also the resources of intellect and character without which the law they attempt to nurture and tend would be but a poor and sterile thing. Since judges in each Commonwealth African country have the additional responsibility to administer the received English law as well as the locally enacted law in commerce and industry, the task of achieving an amalgam capable of meeting the needs of a developing society becomes all the greater.

Judicial Process and Legal Development

The ultimate aim of the judicial process is to effect a dynamic compromise between law and society, between the technicalities of legal science and the requirements of social justice. As the law develops on the basis of a flexible application of the doctrines of repugnancy and of judicial precedents, there will emerge in due course a common law in each Commonwealth African country as the goal of its judicial process.

NOTES

In much of the world, judicial decisions are published either officially or unofficially in what are generally called "Reports." Typically, a complete case citation includes the number of the volume in which the decision appears, the page on which it begins, and, in parentheses, the year in which the case was decided. Accordingly, note 10 means that the decision in the case of *Broome v. Casseu & Co. Ltd. and Anor* can be found in volume 2 of the *All England Reports* beginning on page 187, and the decision was rendered in 1971. [Eds.]

1. (1917) 3 NLR 181.
2. *Ibid.*, p. 19.
3. *Ibid.*, p. 22.
4. (1963) CLR 569.
5. (1960) CLY 739, (1961) AC 290.
6. (1962) EA 13 (PC).
7. (1965) NMLR 95.
8. (1964) 2 WLR 269.
9. Civil Appeal No. 37 of 1970. Judgment delivered on 27 November 1970.
10. (1971) 2 All ER 187.
11. (1967) EA 645.
12. Sohan Lal v. East African Builders' Merchants (1951) 18 EACA 50.
13. 1 Criminal Appeal No. 31 of 1962. Judgment delivered on 2 May 1962.
14. (1959) EACA G. App. No. 172 of 1969, unreported.
15. This decision was in accordance with the rule in Trimble v. Hill (1879) 5 AC 342 to the effect that where the local legislation was substantially the same as the English legislation, the English decision on such legislation should be followed. Indeed, this was done in Jeremiah v. R (1951) 18 EACA 218.
16. PC Appeal No. 5 of 1957. Judgment delivered on 16 July 1968.
17. ILR 44, Cal 759.

18. (1967) (1) SA 240 (R).

19. (1955) (1) SA 534 (AD).

20. (1940) SR 223.

21. (1967) (2) SA 239 (AD) pp. 250-51, per C. J. Steyn.

22. (1951) (4) SA 614 (AD). (1967) (3) SA 655 (R).

23. See Taslim O. Elias, "Judicial Precedents in Colonial Courts," *Modern Law Review*, 18 (1955):361-70; A. W. E. Park, *The Sources of Nigerian Law* (Lagos: African Universities Press, 1963).

24. See A. N. Allot, *Essays in African Law, with Special Reference to the Law of Ghana* (London: Butterworth, 1960), pp. 31ff; and "Judicial Precedent in Africa Revisited" (1968), *Journal of African Law* (1968):3-31.

25. (1904) 1 KB 493.

26. (1943) AC 32.

27. (1842) 2 M and W 519.

28. (1932) AC 562.

29. (1940) 1 All ER 241.

30. (1953) 20 NLR 139.

31. (1942) 9 EACA 65.

32. Judgment No. 15 of 1966. Ciminal Appeal 14/66, unreported.

33. Eg Petero Sentali v. R (1953) 20 EACA 230; Seronga Ole Gidi & ors v. R (1953) 20 EACA 241; and Abdu Rabi v. R (1956) 20 EACA 555; and Handulwe v. R (1962) R & N 47 (a decision of the Federal Supreme Court of the defunct Federation of Rhodesia and Nyasaland).

34. (1972) 127 CLR 210.

35. (1956) AC 539, pp. 546-47, 551.

36. *Ibid.*, p. 215.

37. For example, in West African Bakery v. Miezah (1972) 1 GLR 78, pp. 86-88.

38. "Judicial Precedent in Ghana" (1966), 3 UGLJ, pp. 160-61.

39. Court of Appeal Judgment delivered on 13 June 1966, unreported. See also CFAO v. Zacca (1972) 1 GLR 366. The flexibility referred to in the text as essential to a developing society would seem to be reflected in the holding that the High Court of Ghana is not bound by its own decisions: Saarah v. Asuah (1962) 1 GLR 536, p. 538 (bottom).

40. (1959) 4 FSC 79.

41. (1947) 12 WACA 135.

42. (1947) 12 WACA 187.

43. See also N. A. Ollenu, "The Changing Law and Law Reform in Ghana," *Journal of African Law*, 15, 2 (1971): 52-53 on the accountability of the family head in Ghana.

44. Civil Appeal No. 41/59 delivered on 23 November 1959; see also Coleman v. Shang (1961) AC 481, where the Privy Council affirmed the Court of Appeal of Ghana.

45. (1955) AC 107 (PC).

46. (1966) NMLR 94.

47. For example, Nelson v. Nelson (1932) 1 WACA 215.

48. (1969) Court of Appeal sitting as the Supreme Court, Const SC 1/69 dated 8 December 1969.

49. (1970) SC 58/69.

50. Kenya Civil Appeal No. 53 of 1968. Judgment delivered on 21 November 1969.

51. (1964) EA 442.

52. See (1966) EA 186.

53. For a perceptive study of these problems, see W. E. Geldart, *Elements of English Law* (London: Macmillan & Co., 1966).

54. See the famous essay by A. L. Goodhart, "Determining the Ratio Decidendi of a Case," in *Jurisprudence and the Common Law* (London: Cambridge University Press, 1931), pp. 1-32; A. W. B. Simpson, *Oxford Essays in Jurisprudence* (Oxford: Clarendon Press, 1961), p. 148.

55. See T. O. Elias, ed., *Law and Social Change in Nigeria* (London: Evans Bros., 1972), ch. 12.

56. T. O. Elias, "The Influence of English Law on W. Africa", *Journal of African Law*, 5 (1961):34.

57. Oliver Wendell Holmes, *The Common Law*, p. 1.

58. One example in which the Fante rule of matrilineal succession has sometimes been confused with the Ga custom of patrilineal inheritance occurs in Solomon v. Botchway (1943) 9 WACA 127.

59. Bora Laskin, a judge of the Supreme Court of Canada in his lecture entitled "The Institutional Character of the Judge," observed as follows:

A final court which is prepared to overrule its own precedents puts itself, institutionally, into a partnership, albeit a junior one, with the legislature. Especially in the field of private law, such as contract, tort and property, where the courts themselves have fashioned many of the rules, they have some responsibility for keeping the rules under surveillance with a view to modifying or changing them as changing conditions may at a particular time warrant. . . . They may, hence, properly rely on the courts to share in the burden of law-making in those areas congenial to judicial legislation, as, for example, in the private law fields that I have already mentioned.

See also the *Lionel Cohen Lectures* (Jerusalem: Hebrew University of Jerusalem, 1972).

12   J. H. KWABENA NKETIA

Perspectives on African Musicology

A few years ago a group of African scholars at the University of Nairobi decided to found a journal which would be devoted to the scholarly study of African music as well as reports on creative work and related matters. They decided to call the journal *African Musicology* rather than a *Journal of African Music*, presumably because a journal of that name already existed. Although the proposed title seemed attractive because of its apparent novelty, the reaction to it was mixed, for it seemed to suggest the existence of an African tradition of musicology which is distinctive and separate from musicology in the Western tradition. There was no doubt, however, about the intention of the founders: they wanted to create a journal that would specialize in African materials and which would encourage an Africa-centered approach to the presentation and interpretation of data.

The term "African musicology" is of course not new, even though it has hardly gained the currency it deserves. It was used by Klaus Wachsmann, an eminent musicologist who worked in Uganda for twenty years (1937-1957), in a number of articles he wrote between 1966 and 1971 when his awareness of the institutional changes that had taken place in Africa led him to take stock of the changing musical scene and the new status and role musicology had assumed. Not only had a number of African scholars and composers emerged, but also ministries and departments of culture were giving support to music and music research in a manner that could not have been envisaged in the period before political independence. Since research in African studies and, in particular, African music had been done in colonial Africa by Western scholars who had sustained their interest in the post independence period, it seemed that a new era had dawned and that it called for partnership in research and the cross-fertilization of ideas through dialogue. As there was much to be gained from the collaboration of African scholars and their Western colleagues, the possibility of bringing them together, at least conceptually, needed to be explored.

African musicology provided the desired conceptual focus. It would be an area of scholarly activity in which Africans and non-Africans who shared a common concern for knowledge about the music of Africa could participate, each from his own perspective, background, and interest but linked by common field interests and a common concern for the collection, analysis, and systematization of data. Specifically, African musicology would encourage:

1. critical and analytical studies that examine or exemplify musicological issues in the light of field data;
2. studies that take into account the history, archaeology, and ethnology of the geocultural region of Africa or specific areas in which field work is undertaken;
3. development studies that respond to the intellectual, sociocultural, or political environment in which music is cultivated and practiced; and
4. the dissemination of information and materials on African music both within and outside Africa—that is, wherever there is a readership and a public for live performances or recorded African music.

The goals of African musicology would thus be scholarly and humanistic not only in terms of its quest for a knowledge and understanding of African man as music maker and music user but also in regard to practical issues related to music as language or a mode of communication, to music as an object of aesthetic interest, and to music as culture.

For African scholars involved in the development of their contemporary culture, humanistic goals extend beyond these to pragmatic considerations which are not unlike those spelled out by Richard Schlatter for the humanist scholar. In reply to the rhetorical question: "What is the purpose of humanistic sholarship? What, in fact, does the humanist scholar do?" Schlatter observes that

> The job of the humanist scholar is to organize our huge inheritance of culture, to make the past available to the present, to make the whole of civilization available to men who necessarily live in one small corner for one little stretch of time . . . to clear away the obstacles to our understanding of the past, to make our whole cultural heritage . . . accessible to us. He must sift the whole of man's culture again and again, reassessing, reinterpreting, rediscovering, translating into modern idiom, making available the materials and the blueprints with which his contemporaries can build their own culture, bringing to the center of the stage that which a past generation has judged irrelevant but which is now again usable, sending into storage that which has become, for the moment, too familiar and too habitual to stir our imagination, preserving it for posterity to which it will once more seem fresh.[1]

Schlatter then goes on to point out that "the humanist does all this by the exercise of exact scholarship." And this is precisely what has been of interest to African scholars: the combination of scholarship with a sensitivity to its application, for music is such a practical and purposeful subject that one cannot meaningfully separate its study as an expressive system from its practice and the issues that surround it in its social and cultural contexts. What has continued to interest many scholars in Africa at this critical time in their history, therefore, are studies that enable them to reestablish or renew their connection with their own people in cultural matters so they can become active rather than passive participants or mere spectators in the contexts in which they encounter music and dance in their daily lives.

It will be evident, therefore, that the factors which have stimulated African interest in the study of African music and nurtured the growth of African scholarship are naturally different from those that brought Western scholars to Africa during the colonial period or those that continue to generate interest in the study of African music among scholars abroad. The history of Western scholarship in Africa is substantially a part of the history of comparative musicology and ethnomusicology, whereas African scholarship began in response to the challenge of colonialism and the need for developing a consciousness of identity. It then went through a period in which African writers were able to apply the positive scholarly skills acquired in the process of acculturation before it gradually integrated itself into international scholarship in music. Accordingly, African scholarship can be related to the period of colonial development (1920-1950), the period of cultural awakening and cultural revival (1950-1960), the period of great transition (1960-1970), and the period of cultural development and cultural studies (1970 to the present).

As the story of the development of African interest and scholarship in African music is not generally known, this essay will provide a brief historical review of African scholarship and conclude with a brief discussion of the orientation that current African musicology seems to require of African scholars.

THE BEGINNINGS OF AFRICAN SCHOLARSHIP, 1920-1950

Although the need for studying African cultural expressions was stressed by African nationalists in the late nineteenth and early twentieth centuries, African scholarship in music did not begin until the 1920s when the development of human and material resources in the colonies began to be emphasized by the major colonial powers. There was a need for better knowledge and understanding of colonial peoples in respect to their histories and cultures as well as their physical environment. Accordingly, journals and magazines were founded in the colonies to provide a forum for literary, scientific, and other scholarly contributions by colonial administrators, educators, and missionaries as well as by local authors. International journals devoted to African affairs, African languages, cultures, education, and development were also established at this time and provided additional outlets for African writers.

Most of the African writers who contributed articles on music to such journals and magazines or to newsletters and local papers adopted a journalistic approach, reporting what they knew or felt as carriers of African traditions,[2] while others dealt with specific topics such as drums and other musical instruments,[3] songs,[4] or observations on some aspect of music and dance.[5] There were also a few reports on the state of music in a given territory or ethnic group.⁶

The significance of these writers lies in what they symbolize, the information they provide, their speculations, and their attitudes rather than in their scholarly perspectives; for what most of them wrote was the outgrowth of their awareness of their own musical environment rather than the result of systematic enquiry. There is evidence that some of them, and others who followed, were encouraged to share what they knew or what they had collected from their community because of a positive attitude toward African music and culture. Such encouragement was given to Ugandans, for example, by the East African Music Research Scheme, which was funded by the Colonial Office Social Science Research Council of the United Kingdom and directed by Klaus Wachsmann, who, as curator of the Uganda museum in Kampala, actively involved African musicians and school teachers in his programs.

Another development which stimulated African interest in traditional music during this period was the opening up of prospects for education abroad for a small number of students. Precedent for such studies had been established in the late nineteenth and early twentieth centuries by a few enterprising individuals who enjoyed the sponsorship of secular or religious bodies. For example, A. C. Coker of Nigeria studied music in Germany in 1874, and he was followed forty years later by Ekundayo Phillips who studied at Trinity College of Music in London from 1911 to 1914; he in turn gave private tuition to other aspiring musicians such as Fela Sowande, the eminent Nigerian composer and organist.

Literate African musicians who were unable to go abroad immediately could, in addition to such private tuition, also take advantage of correspondence courses and external examinations in Western music offered by some institutions in London, such as Victoria College of Music, Trinity College of Music, and the Associated Board of the Royal Schools of Music, for the diploma-testing facilities of these bodies were made available to countries in the British Commonwealth. Local representatives were appointed to supervise the written examinations, while visiting examiners were sent around for the practical examinations. This practice encouraged not only the systematic study of Western music and music theory but also, here and there, some reflection on possible analogues of such theory in African music as well as on areas of difference between the two musical traditions and on the sociocultural importance of music in Africa.

The Contribution of George Ballanta

Of the trained African musicians who turned to the study of African music, two deserve particular mention: Nicholas George Ballanta of Sierra Leone and Ephraim Amu of Ghana. A biographical note written by the editor of *Musical America* shows that George Ballanta took correspondence courses in music. "He made such progress that he was able, prior to 1921, through submitting compositions by mail, to pass the intermediary examination of Durham University, England, for the degree of Bachelor of Music."[7]

Ballanta subsequently studied music at the Institute of Musical Art in New York and received a diploma there in 1924. Under the sponsorship of Penn Normal Industrial and Agricultural School on St. Helena Island in South Carolina, he studied black music in Alabama, Georgia, and South Carolina. We are told by the editor of *Musical America* that "while at Penn School, he recorded 103 spirituals of St. Helena which are now available in one volume."[8]

The knowledge that George Ballanta gained from his study of black music and the field experience he had in collecting and transcribing the music of black people in the United States prepared him for similar activities in Africa with the sponsorship of the Guggenheim Foundation. He claims to have spent two years in West Africa doing extensive research, travelling a total of 7,000 miles and collecting over 2,000 examples of African songs from Sierra Leone, Liberia, Senegal, Guinea, Gold Coast (Ghana), and Nigeria. It is not clear what he intended to do with this collection, for it had no programmatic consequence for music education or musicology in West Africa. It appears that he operated like an outsider coming to Africa to collect examples of music rather than as an insider collecting materials that could be used in some creative or educational program.

Ballanta, however, did not merely collect. He wrote articles on "An African Scale" (1922), "Gathering Folk Tunes in the African Country" (1926), and "Music of the African Races" (1930).[9]

Because of his training and background in composition, he took particular interest in the technical aspects of the music, the subject matter of the song texts, the relationship between intonation and melodic contour, and musical instruments. In addition he observed the effect of social change on the music of West Africa and attempted a rough classification of the region on the basis of the presence or absence of "Western or Eastern influence." As far as his own approach is concerned, he claims to have been objective in spite of his Western background, for he notes that it is "essential for an investigator to dispossess himself of his acquired conceptions if he is to appreciate African music."[10] Some of the observations he makes on aspects of form and structure (call and response, speech tone and melodic contour, and the problems these pose in hymns translated into African languages, drum language, and the nature of African musical traditions) anticipate those made subsequently by other writers. It is evident in his writings, however, that he was not able to achieve complete objectivity, for he also makes a number of inaccurate statements and assertions, such as "all African melodies are constructed upon harmonic background" and "duple time is the only time used by Africans."[11]

It is clear also that Ballanta's interest was in comparative studies—in providing an overview of African music rather than in carrying out detailed ethnographic studies of individual musical cultures. Although he took note of the use of music in customary rites such as puberty festivals and funerals, he did not investigate the correlation between "use" and "structure." His categories of investigation, however, did include social categories of music,[12] although the hierarchies he set up in this regard are open to question. His significance in the history of African musicology lies less in his conclusions, many of which were tentative, than in his emphasis on extensive field research, which was not common among African musicians during the period 1920-1950, and his regional and comparative approach to African music.

Although George Ballanta did not spearhead any movement against the institutional barriers that prevented the study and use of African music in Africa during the colonial period, his research did make him conscious of the need for change, because his own attitude toward traditional African music was essentially positive. When he was invited to a 1926 conference on "African culture and the Christian church" in Le Zoute, Belgium, he stressed the importance of using African music, at least as a tool of evangelism. He argued that, because

> the African loves music intensely . . . , one way of approaching him is to get him to sing about the love of God in his own way. The songs you hear in Africa may not be suitable for use, but substitute other words and adopt the tunes. Fit words to his tunes telling the truth of the Gospel and you will do a great deal towards getting that truth into his mind.[13]

The Contribution of Amu

A different picture emerges when one turns to Ephraim Amu of Ghana, for his encounter with the traditional music of his people completely changed his orientation and values. The challenge that issued from it created an identity crisis that turned him away from Western music and toward the serious study and creative use of the traditional music of his own people. He combined the kind of interest in field research that Ballanta developed with a strong determination to break the institutional barriers in the way of traditional African music. However, unlike Ballanta, it was not studying abroad but local circumstances that first made him conscious of his own music.

Amu acquired his basic knowledge of Western music locally when he attended elementary school in his hometown of Peki-Avetile (1902-1915) and the Basel Mission Seminary at Abetifi (1916-1920). After he left the seminary, he continued to study on his own and to take private lessons in harmony and counterpoint (1920-1924) from Allotey-Pappoe, a Ghanaian musician. After teaching for six years at an elementary school in his hometown, he was appointed to the staff of the Presbyterian Training College at Akropong in 1926. There he taught music and other subjects until 1933. His "conversion" from Western music to African music took place when he was on the faculty of the Training College. As a teacher of music and a composer, he had been going along happily with what the missionaries had bequeathed to Africans when one day a colleague—ironically a missionary—asked him about the songs he heard labourers sing as they worked on the campus of the college. As the missionary was an educator who believed in proceeding from the known to the unknown, he asked Amu why he was not writing those songs down to teach to students. Amu reacted to the suggestion with enthusiasm, for it confirmed an observation that he himself had made on the status of music in traditional society. The contrast between the enthusiasm and intensity with which Ghanaians sang their own traditional songs during ceremonial and festive occasions in the community and the way Christian hymns were sung in church had puzzled him for some time. He had also noticed differences in the extent of participation. Every member of a traditional performing group sang, while many members of the Christian congregations he observed sat quietly through the hymns. He was convinced that something needed to be done about this situation.

The problems he encountered as he attempted to write down those supposedly simple tunes were, however, considerable, but they opened up a whole new world of music to him and made him conscious of his own people's traditions, which he then set out to study seriously. He collected several traditional songs and learned to sing them. He wrote down the texts and became fascinated by their expressions and idioms as well as by the evident relationship between speech tones and rhythms. His field notebooks, which I have inspected, show that he wrote tonic solfa here and there above the texts he took down so that he could remind himself of what he learned to sing. However, he omitted the time values from the notation because they could be deduced from the speech rhythms of the texts.

After collecting songs and learning about the traditions associated with them, he turned his attention to instrumental music. His father, who was a drummer, had given up drumming when he became a Christian; thus, Amu never learned this art as a child, and he was indeed expressly forbidden to do so when he grew up. The first thing he did, therefore, was to go back to his hometown and learn from another drummer. From there he studied with a master drummer elsewhere as well as with players of bamboo and cane flutes and the *seperewa* harp lute. He learned how to make some of these instruments but later specialized in the making of bamboo flutes.

Although Amu did not write a treatise on the materials he collected or learned, there is evidence that he approached his task:

1. as a creative person interested in understanding the musical culture of his people and in using the traditional idiom in his own way;
2. as an educator who shared the knowledge he acquired with his students, including the making of bamboo flutes; and
3. as a scholar who systematized knowledge of traditional music for himself, at least to the point of being able to give systematic instruction in African rhythm (to use his own designation) to students at the Presbyterian Training College where he taught, and also in the extension or refresher courses he offered to teachers in the field. The introduction to his volume of original compositions published in 1933 by Sheldon Press contains ninety graded exercises in African rhythm, some of them based on traditional and popular tunes he had collected. The work opens with the following statement:

A full treatise on the various characteristics of African music cannot be entered into in this song book, but an attempt has been made to describe the rhythm. It consists of duple and triple time mixed, occuring either in alternate bars, or in a number of duple time bars followed by one or more triple time bars or vice versa. Once the regular alternation of those two times is understood, all other manifestations will be found easy. It must be borne in mind that in the alternation, the triple time bar is of the same length as the duple time.[14]

To help teachers in the field master African rhythm, Amu published an article on the subject in the *Gold Coast Teachers' Journal*.[15] He attached great importance to this as he was anxious that teachers should be able to read his notation of African rhythm so that they might pass the system on to their pupils.

Amu composed both sacred and secular songs for mixed voices as well as for male voices—the latter for students of the Presbyterian Training College Akropong and the former for "Singing Bands" or choral groups which he helped to establish throughout the country. These choral groups, which learned their music by rote, were intended to complement the regular church choirs, for the latter often sang Western hymns, while the former sang Amu's songs or songs written by other composers in the new African idiom Amu had established. This idiom became very popular in both literate and nonliterate communities, for Amu composed a number of patriotic songs which were widely acclaimed for what he had to say through them. One of them, entitled *Yen ara Asase Ni* and with the English sub-title *This Land is Our Own*, was so popular and so widely known that it was used as an anthem by those who spearheaded Ghana's struggle for political independence from 1948 to 1957. It can still be heard on national occasions.

Amu's interest did not stop with music making. He became so conscious of the culture in which the music was practiced that he responded to it in practical terms by changing certain aspects of his own way of life and emphasizing certain concrete symbols of culture such as African traditional costume (which was not supposed to be worn in the pulpit but which he insisted on wearing when he had to preach), traditional music and dance (which were barred from church and school but which he tried to reintroduce in some form into these institutions), and the use of indigenous languages in contexts where others would have used English. His radical approach brought him into conflict with the church, and in 1933 he was dismissed from the Presbyterian Training College where he worked. But this did not stop him. Because of his enormous reputation in Ghana as a teacher, a composer, and a "nationalist," he was immediately offered a position at Achimota School—the most prestigious institution established by the colonial government in the country. This gave him even greater scope for propagating his ideas; for as Achimota was not a church institution, it was much more receptive to cultural innovations and was able to institute "tribal drumming and dancing," as it was called in those days, as a mode of recreation and entertainment in which all students participated on Saturday nights.

Although Amu had turned from Western music to African music with great success, it was clear from his compositional techniques and later events that what he was fighting against was not Western music per se but Western "cultural imperialism" that had downgraded African music. Accordingly, after much debate with himself, he accepted the award of a scholarship in 1937 to do advanced studies in Western music at the Royal College of Music in London. He decided to study for the associate diploma of that college, with advanced harmony and counterpoint as areas of concentration. What this experience meant to Amu is summed up by a correspondent of *West Africa* as follows:

To the study of African music, Mr. Amu has brought his training in Western music, and feels that to have been able to approach it with a trained mind has been of infinite value. . . . All through his training in

London he was acquiring reasons and musical principles which finally made his interest in his national music an exercise of the mind as well as an instinctive delight.[16]

When Amu returned from London in 1942, he went back to Achimota School. However, as teacher education had been his area of interest, he joined Achimota Teacher Training College (on the same campus) in 1948. His aspirations for a new approach to music education in Ghana were fulfilled in 1949 when he succeeded in establishing a program for the training of specialist teachers of music at the Training College. This program combined instruction in both Western and African music, and it made the practical study of African drumming and the playing of bamboo flutes compulsory for all students. It was bimusical in approach, for it combined a knowledge of African music, particularly African rhythm, drumming, and the playing of flutes, with a study of Western harmony and counterpoint as well as piano. This syllabus virtually spelled out the experience from which Amu's syncretic music had grown. In 1952 Amu's School of Music was transferred to the University of Science and Technology, Kumasi, where he taught for about ten more years. Subsequently it became the basis for a National Academy of Music which was established in Winneba, a location in southern Ghana, with practically the same objective, namely that of training specialist teachers of music—teachers competent in both African and Western music—for the Ghana Educational Service.

As Amu had no time to continue the research he began in the 1920s on the scale he had envisaged, he seized the opportunity of the transfer of his school to another location to give up the leadership of that institution (his retirement was long overdue) so he could spend two more years doing field research. He was able to do this with the support of a grant from the Rockefeller Foundation and to record examples of music from selected societies in all regions of Ghana. He deposited copies of his tapes at the University of Science and Technology, Kumasi, and at the University of Ghana, Legon. When he retired from his position in Kumasi, he was reemployed by the Institute of African Studies (University of Ghana) that had by then set up a new School of Music, Dance, and Drama in Legon so that students in general music studies, as well as those in the African musicology program, could share his knowledge and experience.

Amu influenced many people in Ghana through his work as a composer, teacher, and scholar and as someone who believed in African cultural values. Although he devoted himself to the training of teachers, the research on which he based his pedogogy laid the foundation for later scholarly studies of African music in Ghana. When I was admitted to the Presbyterian Training College, Akropong, in 1937 as a student, Amu had already left, but his course on African rhythm was still an integral part of the music courses offered by that institution. It was taught by another Ghanaian, Robert Danso, who had been privately tutored by him. As my own interest and orientation at this time were towards composition, linguistics, and creative writing, Amu advised me when I met him in 1942 to collect and analyze traditional songs for my musical and textual models. Following his example and his personal encouragement, I collected over one hundred Akan songs between 1942 and 1944. (I was then a member of the faculty of the Presbyterian Training College, Akropong, in charge of music and Twi, a Ghanaian language.) The texts of this collection (with an introduction in Twi on the context of performance, aspects of performance, and various techniques of call and response) were published by Oxford University Press in 1949.

It should be noted also that nearly all other Ghanaians who have turned to musicology as a field of specialization attended Amu's School of Music before proceeding for further training at the University of Ghana and/or institutions abroad. They include Mensah, Nayo, Aning, Asiama, Fiagbedzi, and Ofei. He also influenced several of Ghana's contemporary composers including Danso, Boateng, Mensah, Nayo, and myself—to mention just a few. His influence extended from individuals to institutions.

Blessed with longevity, Amu has lived to see not only the development of the programs he initiated in music education but also the continuation of African music research in Ghana on a much greater scale. What he was able to achieve in the colonial period almost single-handedly was remarkable. Unlike other musicians and writers of the period 1920-1950, including George Ballanta, he had a tremendous impact on his country because he was highly motivated and deeply committed to education and research in African music. He was interested in tradition—in giving it recognition and some measure of continuity through the formal learning process. However, as a composer, he was also interested in change and the selective use of new musical experiences and techniques. Because his goals were humanistic, he combined three complementary approaches to African music, and they allowed him to accommodate continuity and change:

1. the analytical approach which enabled him to explore the intrinsic values of African music,
2. the pedagogical approach which enabled him to pass on what he knew or discovered in his research through formal instruction and public lectures, and
3. the creative approach which enabled him to generate interest in the African idiom in contemporary institutions and raise the level of awareness of African cultural traditions among the literate community.

Turning points in the development of scholarship or in the perspectives of a discipline nearly always hinge on individual thinkers and innovators. It is for this reason and for the progammatic consequences of Amu's research (which sets him apart as a pioneer) that I have dwelt at some length on his story, for it is a story that is hardly known in the musicological world. Although he was a great teacher during his time, he did not publish much. He worked more in oral tradition and never established formal links with the international world of scholarship; he was too preoccupied with the immense problem of cultural identity, even though it had not yet become a burning political issue at that time. Although he influenced many generations of Ghanaian students, he did not, like Ferdinand de Saussure, have devoted pupils who could put together a monumental book out of his lecture notes. Nor was he as fortunate as Samuel Johnson, who had a James Boswell to take notes on what he said.

THE SEARCH FOR BROADER PERSPECTIVES, 1950-1960

The need for studies that would go beyond the sporadic writings of the period 1920-1950 and the initial efforts of Ballanta and Amu—studies which would be more systematic and extensive in coverage but with more clearly defined objectives—was recognized soon after the University of Ghana was established in 1948 as a college in special relation with the University of London. On the initiative of Kofi Abrefa Busia, the Ghanaian professor of sociology, I was offered a faculty appointment in 1952 as research fellow in African studies to set up a program of research in "African music, language, folklore, dance and drama" in his department. Busia felt that what was needed at that time was institutional sponsorship of research in African music and related arts and that a modest beginning could be made in his department. Such an arrangement would not only ensure that research was carried out over an extended period but also that materials and theoretical perspectives would be developed, in the process, to a level that would permit the establishment of courses in African music and related arts at the degree level in the University of Ghana. He believed that the home he provided for the arts in this manner would be temporary and that the timing of their subsequent development into a separate department would depend on the progress of the research program.

The lumping together of the arts was of course deliberate, even though it seemed at first sight to ask too much of one person. It was intended to emphasis their unity in the African context while giving some flexibility to the program in terms of research topics. Since language, folklore, dance, and drama are integrated into music and musical performances, I interpreted the terms of reference as an invitation to develop an interdisciplinary approach to the study of African music, drawing not only from the materials and perspectives of these subjects but also from cognate disciplines such as linguistics, social anthropology, and history, to which I had had some exposure in addition to my training in music.

The particular school of linguistics to which I was drawn at this time was that of J. R. Firth of the University of London who emphasized analysis and synthesis, using "formal and contextual techniques." His concept of "levels of abstraction" and his principles of "contextualization" inspired by the ethnographic approach of Bronislaw Malinowski seemed pertinent to my materials. As he states in his "Techniques of Semantics" and other papers in which he elaborated on his approach:[17] when the principle of "context of situation" is applied in linguistic terms, it enables one to deal with meaning on an empirical basis, for "in that context are human participants, what they say that is going on." He describes any study which proceeds in this manner as a "situational and experiential study." Accordingly, he was critical of approaches to linguistics that "leave man out," and this is precisely what appealed to me. I found that such an approach, suitably adapted, could also be applied to the study of music as an event, enabling the musicologist to deal with formal and ethnographic materials related to music on different levels of abstraction.

Another reason why this approach appealed to me was that, unlike my colleagues in sociology, the subject of my research program was music, not society or culture. The latter was the context in which I found and studied my material and not the object of my study. Hence it was my task to search for a conceptual framework that would make music central to my thinking, rather than something on the periphery. Accordingly, while my colleagues looked at the network of social relations in individual societies considered in their totality, I looked at relationships in music making. Such relationships were not only those of kinship but also of musical representations, and they demanded observation of the distribution of musical roles and responsibilities. While my colleagues looked at different social groups or units of social organization, I looked specifically at performing groups. While they looked at cultures in their totality, I looked at musical cultures (using a musician's understanding of culture) or more specifically at musical traditions. I was aware, of course, that musical studies could contribute to some extent to the understanding of culture and society; but I regarded this as a by product of my music research, since I was also concerned with social processes related to music, for my view of music was not limited to its perception as an aural phenomenon. My African experience had taught me to view it also as a focus of interaction. My task was to harness social anthropology and linguistics to the service of studies in African musicology, just as Western musicians have harnessed history and the critical methods of literary criticism and, to some extent, philology to the service of Western musicology.

Since the music I had to study did not exist in written form and could only be reached through performances, I decided, as I planned my work, that my objectives and strategy would be as follows:

1. The focus of my field research would be on musical events, including any event that incorporated music. Accordingly, my primary data would be drawn from observation and documentation of such events in selected societies.

2. The research program would be based on the study of selected topics that allow for particular formal and contextual problems or themes to be investigated in the field and not on the detailed study of the musical cultures of individual societies in their totality.

3. The research program would document information about music and musical instruments available in oral tradition. This documentation would be related to specific topics being investigated, musical events, and interviews. A distinction would thus be maintained between "studies" and "documentation." The former would be intensive while the latter would be extensive, involving recordings of the repertoires of individual societies or events for archival purposes rather than for immediate analysis and study. The building of such an archive of sound recordings would be a major part of the program. The documentation would also include transcriptions of music, song texts, and drum language. Since such texts are created and used by musicians they must be studied by the African musicologist from the point of view of the language skills traditionally required or expected of the musician. This was part of the rationale behind my *Funeral Dirges of the Akan People*.[18]

4. The program would explore other documentary sources of data, particularly descriptive and historical studies, as well as observers' accounts—in other words, the accounts of travellers, anthropologists, and historians. As it is impossible for any single individual to undertake field work that covers the whole of a country or region, let alone the whole of Africa, one cannot but use data from such secondary sources, including unpublished materials at national radio stations, ministries, and departments of information. The latter often maintain an archive of photographs that include musical events, performing groups, and musical instruments encountered by press photographers. In areas where research has to start virtually from the beginning, every available source must be utilized.

5. The program would build up a collection of musical instruments and explore the possibility of establishing performing groups or extension courses on the university campus.

For purely practical and personal reasons, I had to begin with the study of topics in my own society. I did not see anything wrong with this, since Western musicologists study Western music, the music of their own society. I tended at this time to look at music research not only as an approach to uncharted fields of knowledge but also as a learning process which contributes to the intellectual and artistic development of the individual. There was a great deal I wanted to experience and know and share with others about music in my own society as well as in other societies of Ghana, West Africa, and the rest of Africa.

In developing an approach to the study of African music, I also fought for African orientations and reactions in the writings of previous African authors; what Western scholars and field collectors had to say about African music or how it should be approached was evident enough in the literature. One of the African writers whose remarks I found interesting was Simon Ngubane, although he did not contribute much to our knowledge of African music by way of published data. While he did not wish to minimize the importance of "scientific analysis," it was his view that "together with that intellectual attitude, one must try to get the message and the feeling behind the sometimes unusual sounds that make up African music, which thing, after all, is the most important thing in any music.' He then emphasized his point with the following anecdote:

I remember a non-African musical friend of mine who, some years ago, said to me that to him African music was interesting only in an impersonal sort of way, that is, it did not concern him and his personal feelings. He further said that African music could only arouse his curiosity and perhaps lead him to want to analyse its forms and all the scientific side of its make up; but that it could possibly be something he could love as he loved the music of Europe, was something very far from him. . . . I have since found that my friend of four years ago is not alone in this attitude towards African music. I must say that it is difficult for an African to imagine how any one can love music with only his mind.[19]

I assumed that Ngubane intended this statement to serve as a caveat for the African musicologist who may be carried away by his acquired capacity for making abstractions or seduced by the preoccupation of Western musicology with scales, measurements of pitches, tuning systems, and modes, which, along with certain types of analytical theory, constitute one particular worldview of music. It is noteworthy to find his position underscored eighteen years later by Fela Sowande, the eminent Nigerian composer and organist, when he turned his attention to systematic research into African music. He warns about the danger of establishing music education programs that might "breed a race of artistic eunuchs, through submitting to planning from the outside on African music which so far we tend to dissect as a "thing," and not as "an experienced reality."[20]

It must be noted in passing that Klaus Wachsmann also noticed similar attitudes among Africans during this period. However, he interpreted their reaction to overanalysis as a reflection of "the criterion or aesthetic principle of the music of Negritude." He continues:

Positively stated, it is a quality claimed by a Negro musician: he is a person whose body and soul respond to music as one, a man who is so sensitive to the totality of his world that he has immediate and total rapport with it. Negatively stated, it is the refusal to treat music as an object that can be analysed, dissected, and compartmentalized—a treatment that in the eyes of the philosophers of Negritude is most apprehensible in Western musical usage.[21]

These observations explain the emphasis on "the situational and experiential" approach in the period under consideration, an approach which made it possible not only to reinterpret African music to the outside world but also to communicate at the same time to the new musicological public that was emerging in Africa itself as a result of the cultural awakening ushered in by the nationalist movements of the period. This movement used traditional cultural expressions as a basis for creating consciousness of identity and as leverage for building a united front in the fight for political independence. It set in motion new trends in cultural revival by encouraging the wearing of traditional costumes by the literate community (which had been brought up to reject aspects of the traditional lifestyle), the performance of traditional rites and ceremonies hitherto branded as pagan or unworthy, and the performance of traditional music and dance at political rallies. It was felt that a new sense of history anchored in African cultural expressions needed to be generated in order to foster pride in things African. Hence what was formerly regarded only as the heritage of individual ethnic groups came to be identified as the national heritage, in other words as aspects of the achievement of the African past that might be shared in the new context.

For the same reason a national theatre movement was launched in Ghana to stimulate individual and group initiative in presenting or recreating African traditions or in developing new directions. Traditional music and dance assumed a new role in new contexts such as concert halls and theatres or improvised substitutes as a source of aesthetic enjoyment in their own right. Traditional songs were no longer to be regarded, as Ballanta and Amu had done, only as a source for developing contemporary idioms, a source of themes for composition or tunes to be set to new words for use in the Christian church. African dance was not merely something to watch in traditional settings but something to learn to perform.

The program in musicology at the University of Ghana had to take note of all these developments as well as the philosophy of African personality that later became both a political and a cultural ideology, for it was my belief that the African musicologist must be responsive to the milieu in which he works—to ideas, values, new trends, or significant cultural movements that emerge in his environment. For if he is a humanistic scholar, he has a dual commitment, to his discipline as well as to his society. The research program, therefore, had to take note of the implications of contextual changes, new habits of listening that were being formed, new communities of taste that were emerging, and new concepts of performance and modes of presentation as well as new perspectives in performer-audience relationships. It became clear as the political and cultural movements culminated in the achievement of political independence in March 1957 that our task was not just to collect, analyze, and interpret the different musical types and idioms along the lines we had mapped out. Our frame of reference had to include both traditional and contemporary forms of music as well as all aspects of music and music making in a changing society.

Another issue the program had to face was the question of the dissemination of information on music and related arts that became available through research. In the period under consideration, the new approach to African music and dance as a source of entertainment and aesthetic enjoyment in new contexts outside their traditional setting brought together audiences and spectators who did not always have a common background knowledge of everything that was presented in a multicultural or multilingual concert or festival—basic knowledge of musical instruments, traditional ensembles, categories of songs, musical types, dances, and oral traditions. It soon became clear from these encounters with different musical traditions that Ghanaians were ready to read about their own music and dance traditions as well as those of other ethnic groups in local newspapers, journals, and magazines and listen to public lectures on music.

The Ghana Broadcasting Service, which had long ago introduced traditional music in its Ghanaian language programs, now extended its offerings to include special music magazines and talks on different aspects of music in Ghana and other parts of Africa. The position of program organizer for music was established, and a former student of Amu, Attah Annan Mensah, who had just returned from further studies at Trinity College of Music in London, was appointed to fill the post. As reported in *African Music*, he was to be "responsible not only for radio programs but also for recording examples of Gold Coast indigenous music and coordinating this side of his work with the University College of the Gold Coast and Kumasi College of Technology and other interested bodies."[22] A similar position was created by the Nigerian Broadcasting Corporation at about the same time for Fela Sowande, who returned from his long sojourn in London to become actively involved in the collection, presentation, and dissemination of information on Nigerian music and musicians.

It will be evident, therefore, that in the 1950-1960 period "speech knowledge of music"—to use Charles Seeger's famous phrase—became as interesting to the literate community as "music knowledge of music." The musicology program at the University of Ghana took note of this by supporting the formation of the Ghana Music Society in 1958 as a forum for musicians and aspiring musicologists to discuss research problems as well as problems related to music and cultural development in Ghana, by contributing to radio programs on traditional and contemporary music as well as to local journals and even newspapers when invited, and by publishing the results of research in a style and form of presentation that allowed for the dual commitment to one's discipline and one's society to be fulfilled, insofar as that was possible, at the same time.

Individual Research, 1950-1960

The development of a university-based research program in Ghana did not stifle research by individuals associated with other institutions such as teacher training colleges, museums, and broadcasting organizations. Those who were working on their own writings on African music similar in perspective to those of the previous era continued to be published not only by Ghanaians but also by scholars in Benin, Nigeria, Cameroon, Zaire, Rwanda, and Uganda. Of the contributions of this period (1950-1960), four deserve particular mention because of their approach and the effort they made to provide substantial studies based on research.

The first of these consists of two essays by Seth Cudjoe, a medical doctor by profession, who set himself the task of providing a scholarly exposition of Ewe drumming.[23] He notes the different types of strokes and the tones that are produced and suggests a suitable notation for them, because he believed that notating African music which exists in oral tradition is one of the responsibilities of the African musician. African music must be accessible to other musicians not only through recordings but also through some kind of notation. His interest in this matter was not in descriptive notation per se but in the possibility that musicians could learn to play the music of Ewe drums through prescriptive notation.

The notation Cudjoe suggested was adventurous and innovative, for it was not staff notation but a combination of pulse notation and numerical notation in which each pulse of the standard Ewe bell pattern is assigned a number from one to twelve. The different drum strokes that occur on each pulse are then represented by symbols derived from the figure of a drum stick, the area of the drum head hit by the stick, and the type of stroke: that is, whether it is open, free, damped, or muted.

Being analytically minded, Cudjoe not only discusses his notation but also provides an exposition of cross-rhythms in Ewe drum music, particularly as exemplified in *agbadza* drumming. He resolves the rhythms into divisive groups in relation to the hand-clapping, while at the same time recognizing their additive nature by indicating the positions on the pulse line where the notes of each drum pattern fall.

As an art critic, Cudjoe was very much aware of the important role that the arts play in African societies. Hence, although his main interest was in the analysis of Ewe drumming, he also drew attention to the social importance of music in Africa. He did not, however, follow up his research interest in music or provide more expositions of Ewe drumming. He preferred to play the role of a catalyst and music critic rather than that of a musicologist, because his own profession did not give him sufficient time for systematic research in other fields.

Another contributor of this period who believed in making African music accessible to musicians through notation was Joseph Kygambiddwa. In his work *African Music from the Source of the Nile*, he provides examples of the scales and rhythms used by the Baganda as well as a discussion of various categories of songs—religious songs, work songs, play songs, war songs, and "dramatic" songs.[24] He devotes the greater proportion of the monograph to the music of the xylophones of the Baganda. He provides an analysis of its basic structure, the songs used as themes for each xylophone piece, the parts played by each of the three performers who squat around one instrument, and an exposition of the *miko*, a technique of transposition in Baganda xylophone music. The repertoire of the xylophones is then given in the form of scores, using Western staff notation. Although his pitch notation was an approximation by Western standards, this did not seem to have bothered him, for what he was providing was a blueprint for the musician rather than a descriptive score for the musicologist. It is also clear from this work that Kygambiddwa approached his study primarily as a musician, for what he had to say about history and culture was not as carefully thought out or investigated as the repertoire of xylophone music which he had learned to play from teachers at the Uganda museum in Kampala, to which he was attached for a two-year period as a student of African music. Nevertheless, as Wachsmann states in his review of this work, whose scholarly pitfalls worried him because "it hardly reflects credit on the advice given by his teachers," Kygambiddwa does make a notable contribution, for "there is no doubt that the publication of sixty-two xylophone scores and the discovery of the *miko* effect are major events in ethnomusicology."[25]

The third contributor of this period who deserves some notice is Ekundayo Phillips, an organist and composer from Nigeria. He approached his study of Yoruba music from a composer's point of view, his main interest being the creative use of Yoruba tunes in new religious music and the history of church music. While Kygambiddwa's monograph is mainly descriptive, the first part of the monograph of Ekundayo Phillips is historically oriented. As an organist, he was very familiar with Western church music, and he was naturally impressed by the apparent similarites between plain chant and Yoruba chant, a point made somewhat later by Father K. Carrol, who also points out the similarities and differences he noticed between the two.[26] In light of his impressions, Ekundayo Phillips postulates stages in the evolution of music from impassioned speech to songs with clearly defined scales. He sees a missing link between the Gregorian chant and later modes of expression and suggests that Yoruba music provides the missing link. Like other contributions of this period, his Yoruba examples are written in Western staff notation.

The evolutionary approach of Ekundayo Phillips is of course outmoded. Hence, his historical inferences can also be rejected as inconclusive. The significance of his monograph lies in the attempt he made at this time to find a comparative framework for interpreting Yoruba music. He made an effort to bring an African perspective into a way of looking at music that was current when he was a student of Western music at Trinity College of Music in London during the second decade of this century, and his monograph presents his own approach to syncretism as a compositional technique.

The last of the four major contributors of this period, Clement da Cruz, brings a different dimension to the study of African music. Whereas the other writers focus their attention on structure and give incidental information about the sociocultural background, Clement da Cruz focuses upon the ethnographic information on music in Dahomean society, paying particular attention to musical instruments and relevant oral traditions, no doubt because he worked as a museum scientist. His study considers the music of Dahomey (Benin) in four contexts: music and work, political life, worship (ritual), and popular entertainment.[27] He deals with the musical instruments of the Fon, Adja, Kotafon, Péda, and Aizo and provides relevant information on particular instruments wherever possible. He mentions the musical types performed in the areas of his investigation, giving in some cases the kings during whose reign they came into being and the social contexts in which they are used. The work is informative but not critical in its approach.

SCHOLARSHIP IN THE PERIOD OF
INSTITUTIONAL DEVELOPMENT, 1960-1970

Contributions to the study of African music by Africans continued to expand in the decade of transition from colonial rule to independence when many new nation states emerged in Africa, for the cultural revival that characterized the previous decade became institutionalized in many African countries. Culture assumed a new importance as an area of governmental action, and Departments or Ministries of Culture (or sometimes culture and youth, or sports and tourism) or Arts Councils were created to plan and implement cultural programs on a nationwide basis. The celebration of independence and its anniversary as well as other national occasions invariably featured performances of traditional music and dance in national capitals and other cities, while the formation of national dance companies became a common practice.

Pan-Africanism and African unity became important issues as the new nations tried to establish new political, economic, and cultural ties. Pan-African arts festivals and colloquia were organized to affirm the universality of the African cultural experience, to foster pride in the African heritage of culture, and to encourage its scholarly study as well as its promotion, preservation, and creative use. Emphasis was laid on preservation and continuity because of the colonial experience and the realization that some of the best exponents of culture belonged to older generations that may pass away without leaving their knowledge or expertise to posterity.

The long-term development of musical life (and the cultural image of each country) through the creation of appropriate institutions for promotion, education, and research in music and related arts also became a matter of national concern in cases where such institutions did not exist. The period 1960-1970 was, therefore, a period of institutional development, a period in which musicology came to be accepted not only as an academic discipline but also as something that could be of practical value to cultural development through its basic activities of collecting, recording, cataloguing, analyzing, interpreting, and disseminating information about music—thus contributing to its understanding, preservation, and promotion. Institutional support for programs of music, therefore, became a major concern during this period in some African societies.

Some countries such as Senegal and Upper Volta preferred to set up research units under the aegis of their Ministries of Culture or Education. Although the lack of trained nationals was initially a problem, foreign experts were hired as an interim measure solely for the purpose of collecting, documenting, and archiving "the national patrimony" of music, dance, drama, and the visual arts, ensuring of course that they had local assistants who would receive on-the-job training and eventually assume full responsibility for the task at hand.

Institutes and Centers of African Studies were established in this decade at the Universities of Ghana, Lagos, Zambia, and Nairobi for the interdisciplinary study of African history, culture, and the arts; and they provided avenues for music research. The research program developed in the Department of Sociology at the University of Ghana during the previous decade was transferred to the new Institute of African Studies, which from the very beginning functioned as a center for graduate studies. A diploma course in African musicology designed for Ghanaians who had diplomas in Western music from the various British schools of music and those who had taken Amu's specialist music course for teachers was established. Because the writing of a thesis formed part of the requirement for the diploma, the institute could involve students who took this course in its overall research program. In addition to the diploma, provision was also made for graduate students taking the interdisciplinary M.A. (and later the Ph.D.) degree in African Studies to specialize in African music by taking the relevant courses and writing a thesis or dissertation on a musical topic.

Another development which was perhaps unique to Ghana was the establishment and training of the National Dance Company of Ghana within the institute. This company consisted solely of young men and women who were recruited from the community, who had demonstrated an aptitude for dance, and who could be trained to perform traditional dances from different parts of Ghana. A team of master drummers and other musicians representing different ethnic traditions in Ghana was recruited to perform for the dance company and also to act as demonstrators, instructors, and resource people for the African musicology program. Although the objective of the training program was artistic and professional rather than academic, it enabled the institute to stimulate general awareness of the traditional arts on a university campus which had until then been Western oriented in respect to the arts.

Since the African musicology curriculum was primarily a graduate program, it was decided to establish a regular undergraduate School of Music, Dance, and Drama as another unit within the

Institute of African Studies. Courses in the school were, however, largely bicultural and included both African and Western materials, an approach necessitated by the colonial legacy which formed a part of contemporary Ghana.

A different approach was taken by the African Studies Institute at the University of Ife, for what seemed to be needed at that university was a creative arts center. The institute encouraged research but had no teaching program in the arts. Musicians who had already established themselves as composers (such as Akin Euba and Samuel Akpabot) were appointed as senior research fellows. Their task was to combine their research with creative work so that whatever original works they produced could be performed along with other items at the performing arts center in town during an annual arts festival that subsequently became an important event in Ife.

Having regard to the fact that the results of African music research could be of great educational value, some African universities linked their music research units to institutes in Departments of Education or to some educational project. Such a music research unit was set up at Makerere University in October 1961 with the support of the Rockefeller Foundation; it was run by Solomon Mbabi-Katana who had worked independently on African musical instruments while teaching in a secondary school in Uganda. The research at Makerere concentrated on the vocal music of East Africa. By the end of the third year of the program, one hundred and fifty songs had been collected and transcribed for use in the schools. Of these, one hundred were from different ethnic groups in Uganda, twenty-five from Kenya, and twenty-five from Tanzania.

A similar music research unit was established at the University of Ibadan in 1962. Fela Sowande, the eminent Nigerian composer who had had field experience in collecting and recording music for the programs and sound archives of the Nigerian Broadcasting Corporation, was placed in charge of this unit. He decided to concentrate on Yoruba religious music, in particular the music of Ife divination. This intimate contact with Yoruba music changed his perspective on musicology and, more especially, his own attitude toward African music and the approach that should be used in studying it. He became involved in problems of value and interpretation in symbolism, philosophy, and psychology. This led him to reject some of the Western values on which he had previously based his own work and to deemphasize abstract musicological analysis in favor of approaches which deal with meaning as a function of the African worldview.

Instead of setting up a small music research unit, the University of Nigeria at Nsukka took a bolder course and established a full-fledged university Department of Music for the teaching of degree courses in music and offering specializations at the undergraduate level in music education, composition, and ethnomusicology. To assist the department in developing a bimusical program which would include the traditional music of Nigeria, the university gave the faculty (which consisted of both expatriates and a few Nigerians—Echezona and Samuel Akpabot before he joined the University of Ife) grants for field research. This combination of teaching and funded research paid off handsome dividends. For example, William W. Chukudinka Echezona, whose previous research had concentrated on the musical instruments of the Ibo,[28] was able to study the ethnography of music in different parts of Iboland and to compile eight mimeographed monographs on music in Afikpo, Rivers area, Egede, Okpanam, Agukwu, Nnewi, Owerri, and Ibibio.

The faculty involved some of the music students majoring in ethnomusicology in their research. The program also required all third-year students to write a minor thesis, based on their own field observations and focused on some aspect of music in Nigeria. Until recently the music department at Nsukka was the only institution in Nigeria that provided a locally taught degree course in music. Many of Nigeria's musicologists who emerged in the 1970s and after (such as Lazarus Ekwueme, Meki Nzewi, Tunji Vidal, Mosunmola Omibiyi, Achinivu, and Okosa) received their initial training at this institution.

The need for professional training in music and related arts along conservatory lines led also to the establishment of a number of separate schools or institutes of fine arts in Sudan, Ethiopia (which established both the University's Center for the Creative Arts and the Yared School), Senegal, Ivory Coast, the Central African Republic, and Zaire. Kwanongoma College in Bulawayo, an off-shoot of the Rhodesian Academy of Music, also came into being in

1961. One of the objectives of the founders was to provide "a focal point for a new African musical scholarship."[29] Christian missions also joined in the institutional search for African musical values by encouraging not only their expatriate clergy but also Africans to record, transcribe, and study traditional music in their areas.[30]

Impact on Scholarship

Although the institutional development of the period 1960-1970 was intended to meet the cultural development needs of African countries, it also had a number of repercussions on the trend of musicology in Africa. It affirmed the need for musicological studies which focus on African materials but respond at the same time to the challenge of the African environment in respect to its formulation of theoretical concepts, modes of interpretation, and applications of research findings. Although the foundations for this development had been laid by pioneers such as Ballanta, Amu, and their successors, not enough progress would seem to have been made everywhere in maintaining a balance between scholarly studies and practical activities in music. Cultural awakening and cultural revival create enthusiasm for music and dance but not necessarily the scholarly orientation required for their study. It is the institutional arrangements for music research that provided the stimulus for the latter, so that African musicians would not only assert their consciousness of identity through their music but also be in a position to interpret it to their own people as well as to the wider world.

The demand for Africans who could meet these objectives encouraged those who had first degrees or diplomas in music to pursue advanced studies in music and to make musicology or music education a career goal, since musicians with these specializations were needed for a variety of programs in institutions of higher education as well as in Ministries of Education or Culture, national museums, broadcasting and television stations, and mission-related institutions. In some countries, graduate training was incorporated into manpower development programs. Governmental or institutional sponsorship was provided in this and the following decades for African musicians to pursue such studies wherever they could gain admission. A few turned to the University of Ghana; others went abroad—to the United States (UCLA, the University of California at Berkeley, Stanford, Yale, Columbia, Northwestern, Wesleyan, the University of Illinois at Urbana, Chicago, Pittsburgh, Michigan State, East Lansing, and Indiana), the United Kingdom (Belfast and London), or continental Europe (the Sorbonne and the Musée de L'Homme in Paris as well as the Universities of Metz, Hamburg, Cologne, Brussels, Rome, and Vienna).

While some Africans studied at institutions with ethnomusicology programs, others studied at institutions with programs in historical musicology, theory, and composition, or in music education and composition programs that allowed for substantial courses in ethnomusicology to be taken as part of their requirements. African musicology of this and the following decades would thus be enriched by the different perspectives that African scholars, exposed to a variety of Western approaches, brought to their work, along with the knowledge and insights gained through the analysis of their own African experience. For irrespective of the program, their doctoral dissertations were invariably on African topics—on the music of a contemporary composer or performer, the musical instruments of an ethnic group, the music of a selected society, traditional and contemporary choral music, drumming and other instrumental traditions, and studies of selected musical types. What seemed important at this stage was the discipline that enables people to approach the music of their own society as Amu did—"with a trained mind."

There was also a significant increase in the number and quality of other scholarly studies. In addition to the usual studies of musical instruments and ensembles, musical types, songs and song texts, and overviews of the music of single societies,[31] countries,[32] and sub-Saharan Africa as a whole,[33] theoretical and technical issues in African music engaged the attention of scholars—issues such as the factors that shape and maintain folk music, the role of music in society, the problem of meaning in African music, historical evidence in Ga religious music, sources of historical data on African music, compositional techniques of traditional music, the hocket technique in African music, and multipart structures and multipart relationships.[34]

New trends in music, including problems of acculturation, and traditional elements in African church music received attention.[35]

An annotated bibliography of music and dance in English speaking Africa and a catalogue of recorded sound also appeared during this decade.[36]

CURRENT TRENDS IN AFRICAN MUSICOLOGY

The formal links established with international scholarship during the period 1960-1970 continued during the next decade when the formulation of national cultural policies and the planning of cultural development became one of the central concerns of African governments. At the Inter-Governmental Conference on Cultural Policy held in Accra in 1974 under the auspices of UNESCO and the OAU, the need for the preservation, promotion, and presentation of traditional music was confirmed in a resolution passed by the conference for the formulation and implementation of a ten year development plan for music and the performing arts of Africa. Musicology, therefore, continued to be recognized both as an academic discipline and as an enterprise that could contribute to cultural development through its primary research activities of collecting (recording), archiving, analyzing, and building up a body of knowledge that could be applied constructively to nation building (especially in the training and education of future generations of musicians), to the education of the general public, and to the development of a new consciousness of personal and national identity. It was also believed that the results of musicological research could stimulate new directions in creativity and performance. These humanistic goals have continued to inspire research and to shape current trends in African musicology.

As Wachsmann observed two decades ago, in African musicology "music is the primary subject rather than one of the secondary ones."[37] This does not mean that considerations of the sociocultural context should be neglected. Later in the same article, he points out that "with music and musicology so strongly in the foreground it seems as if these pressures leave little room for anthropology. But this is deceptive. It is simply that anthropology has come to serve musicology rather than the reverse."[38]

It seems likely that this emphasis on music and musicology will continue to be a major trend in African musicology. Nearly all those who have turned to the scholarly study of music in Africa during the last three decades have done so from some field of concentration in music—as musicians with training in Western music theory who are rediscovering and systematizing a knowledge of music in their own societies, a music which had hitherto seemed inconsequential to some of them; as composers grappling with the problem of syncretism and the philosophies of African personality or *Négritude* in music; as performers who were trained in some area of Western music and desire to retrain themselves in other areas of performance in African music; as music teachers who need to rethink their philosophy of music education, methodology, and educational objectives when they confront the realities of the African situation; or as educators who themselves have to undertake the basic collection and analysis of traditional materials.

Thus, while all these musicians approach African music from a musicological point of view, each of them tends to see problems in African music from a particular perspective relative to his own specialization and interests. Composers like Akin Euba, Ekwueme, Akpabot of Nigeria, Najo, Mensah, and Ato Turkson of Ghana, Kygambiddwa of Uganda, and Kebede of Ethiopia take particular interest in searching for definitions of the African idiom, in categorizing creative output, in observing instrumentation, form, and structure in relation to creative processes, or, in the case of Ekwueme, also in formulating or applying Western music theory or models of analysis (such as the Schenkerian model) to African materials.

Similarly those with a background in performance, such as Nissio Fiagbedzi of Ghana, Olatunji Vidal of Nigeria, and Kazadi wa Mukuna of Zaire, tend to concern themselves with, among other things, the intrinsic value of African music or with problems of music communication and aesthetics or philosophy. Meanwhile music educators like Mbabi-Katana of Uganda, Mensah and Twerefoo of Ghana, Horton of Sierra Leone, and Mosunmola Omibiyi of Nigeria are concerned with musicological research that facilitates the transfer of musical knowledge and skills formerly acquired through socialization in the classroom and, in the case of Twerefoo, its application in continuing education and therapy. There are others like Mapoma of Zambia, Omondi of Kenya, Nzewi of Nigeria, and Mensah and Aning of Ghana who also look at a wide range of problems involving music, culture, communication, and the related arts, sometimes both synchronically and diachronically.

African musicology is thus a field of scholarly research that brings together composers, teachers, and others in the field of African music to pursue an advanced knowledge and understanding of the total musical scene in Africa. Its theoretical orientations and methods as well as its practical aims are related to the challenges presented by the nature and scope of African materials and their cultural, social, and political environment.

African musicology is, therefore, concerned with all aspects of African music in its social and cultural contexts; with the makers of music and the dynamics of music making in both traditional and contemporary contexts; with sound sources and the values that guide their selection and use; with the traditions (including myths and legends) associated with musical performance; with the art and technology of sound media; with creative processes, performance techniques, repertoire, modes of expression and presentation, and music as an object of aesthetic interest.

Current research programs also show interest in the study of the interrelations between music and language, music and dance, music and drama, music and the visual arts of Africa, music and various aspects of behaviorlike ritual. They are also concerned with religious, social, and political ideas and beliefs that inspire or guide aspects of music and music making as well as traditional and contemporary values.

The study of oral traditions related to internal and external factors of change and other historical processes and the musical confluence of Europe, the Americas, the Caribbean, Asia, and Africa in the musical scene of today are engaging the attention of some scholars. Meanwhile music educators focus on curricular materials, problems related to tradition and continuity, processes of enculturation, and the institutionalization of musical instruction and training.

Outlook for the Future

Although the prospects for developing African musicology as an integral part of music programs in Africa are bright, there are two major problems that need both institutional and individual attention: the coordination of research and the need for specialization. Inter-African cooperation in research has been minimal, while the choice of research topics has been generally random and, with few exceptions, not related to any kind of planning. Hence, the total picture that emerges when one looks at any single theme is rarely complete, not to speak of the gaps in our information about single societies, countries, and regions.

Closely related to this problem is the imbalance one finds in regard to research personnel. While some countries such as Ghana and Nigeria have a number of trained African musicologists, there are many countries which lack such personnel and have not yet seen their way clear to hire scholars from other African countries. Contributions to musicological knowledge in countries without local musicologists would have been nil but for the work of pioneer Western musicologists and their successors, a fact generally recognized by African scholars as they look at the positive contributions of the colonial era and the enrichment that comes from a synthesis of "insider" and "outsider" orientations and methodologies.

The second problem, the need for specialization, is one that has not been given much consideration in current training programs. Since specialization in different problem areas or branches of a discipline is often necessary for the advancement of knowledge, one hopes that this will develop in African musicology in view of the wide-ranging nature of the topics that fall within its scope. Included in this scope are the large number of ethnic traditions and linguistic groups, the vastness of the territories that must be covered, as well as the variety of problems whose investigation could be enriched by insights from cognate disciplines such as sociology and anthropology, history, psychology, linguistics, and aesthetics.

It is this need that has drawn many African musicians to ethnomusicology in spite of doubts about its nomenclature. As an area of specialization, it has grown out of its exotic preoccupations into a discipline that now synthesizes formal and contextual techniques of analysis into holisitic studies of music as a cultural phenomenon. In our experience, synchronic studies of the musical cultures of Africa as well as investigations into musical problems of immediate relevance to cultural development and nation building in Africa are greatly enhanced when they are approached from an ethnomusicological point of view, that is, as integrated studies of music, society, and culture. The supposition that an ethnomusicologist is someone who studies the music of another culture is rapidly becoming a myth, not only in Africa and many parts of the non-Western world but also in the West where younger scholars are increasingly turning their attention to music in their own environment. So is the supposition that objectivity is possible only when one works outside one's own culture, for it would invalidate much of the work of Western musicologists who study Western society and culture.

For the same reason, one hopes that a new generation of African musicologists will emerge and begin to specialize in other problem areas. We need scholars who will concentrate on historical approaches and make it a point to keep abreast with developments in methodology, sources, and modes of interpretation in the related fields of African history, archaeology, art history, and cognate studies. We need scholars who will develop lines of enquiry in historical studies of African music that will embrace the history of all music in Africa—the history of traditional and contemporary African music, as well as the history of Western and Arabic music in sub-Saharan Africa. We need specialists who will undertake intensive distributional and comparative stylistic analysis within the framework of historical studies. Similarly, systematic studies in aesthetics, psychology, and related fields should enrich the scope and quality of African musicology in the future; they should also enable scholars to contribute in a significant way and on the basis of their own field experience to all areas of scholarly studies in music.

It is important also that African musicology continues to be relevant and that it maintains its dual commitment to the discipline and the international world of musical scholarship on the one hand, and, on the other, to the society that cultivates the subject matter of its research. As the excitement of independence wears off and consciousness of identity becomes less and less of an issue, the inspiration that they provided for initiating relevant research might also wear off. Music, however, is such a practical and purposeful subject that one cannot lose sight of its role in society and the pragmatic issues that continually surround it or the creative impulse that continually revitalizes it. Response to the environment and the pressures exerted on it internally and externally and the world of scholarship to which Africa now belongs will give African musicology the versatility it needs to deal with music in the changing societies of Africa.

Because African musicology is a field of international scholarships, the need for dialogue cannot be overemphasized; for the African scholar and his colleague may be studying the same musical cultures, observing the same events, using the same teachers and informants, even though they may not always ask the same questions or seek solutions to the same problems. In this regard the initiative must lie not only with African scholars who are already disposed to engage in such dialogue but even more so with their Western colleagues who may need to modify attitudes inherited from the nineteenth century and the colonial era when scholarship was the exclusive concern of the West while other peoples and cultures merely provided field laboratories. There is certainly much that can enrich African musicology from the perspectives that scholars with different backgrounds bring to it. One can only hope, therefore, that collaboration similar to that established by Africanists in other disciplines such as history, archaeology, and linguistics will emerge in the near future in the field of African musicology, a relative newcomer in African area studies.

NOTES

1. Richard Schlatter, "Foreword" in *Musicology*, ed. Frank Harrison, Mantle Hood, and Claude Pallisca (Englewood Cliffs, N. J.: Prentice Hall, 1963), pp. vii-viii.
2. See, for example, Ruben Tolakele Caluza, "African Music," in *Southern Workman*, 60 (1931): 152-55; and Y. Bansisa, "Music in Africa", in *Uganda Journal*, 4 (1936): 108-14.
3. Sir Apolo Kagwa, *The Customs of the Baganda* (New York: Columbia University Press, 1934): chap. 28, pp. 140ff.
4. E. K. R. Sempebbwa, "Baganda Folk Songs," in *Uganda Journal*, 12 (1948): 16ff.
5. Mamadu Traore, "Une Danse Curieuse: Le Moribayasa," in *Notes Africaines* (IFAN), 15 (1942): 5-6.

6. Y. Q. Kintu, "Kisoga Music," in *Uganda Teachers' Journal*, 2, 2 (1940). With notes by K. P. Wachsmann.
7. "Biographical Note," *Musical America*, 84, 26 (1926), p. 6.
8. *Ibid.*
9. Nicholas George Julius Ballanta, "An African Scale," in *Musical Courrier*, 84, 26 (1922): 6; Nicholas George Julius Ballanta, "Gathering Folk Tunes in the African Country," in *Musical America*, 44, 23 (1926): 3-11; and Nicholas George Julius Ballanta, "Music of the African Races," in *West Africa*, 14 (1930): 752ff. The latter article was reprinted in the *Negro Year Book* (1931-1932): 441-44.
10. Ballanta, "Gathering Folk Tunes," p. 3.
11. *Ibid.*, p. 10.
12. See Ballanta, "Music of the African Races."
13. Edwin W. Smith, *The Christian Mission in Africa* (New York: International Missionary Council, 1926), p. 73.
14. Ephraim Amu, *Twenty-Five African Songs* (London: Sheldon Press, 1933), p. 1.
15. Ephraim Amu, "How to Study African Rhythm," in *Gold Coast Teachers' Journal* 5 (1933): 154-57, and 6 (1934): 121.
16. *West Africa* (1956), p. 871.
17. These papers have been collected in Malinowski, *Papers in Linguistics 1934-1951* (London, New York: Oxford U. Press, 1951).
18. J. H. Kwabena Nketia, *Funeral Dirges of the Akan People* (Accra: University of Ghana, 1955; rpt. Westport, Conn.: Greenwood Press, 1974).
19. Simon Ngubane, "Music North of the Limpopo," *African Music Society Newsletter*, 1 (1948): 19.
20. Fela Sowande, "Nigerian Music and Musicians: Then and Now," in *Composer*, 19 (1966) pp. 25-34.
21. Klaus P. Wachsmann, "Negritude in Music," *Composer*, 19 (1966): 16.
22. *African Music*, 1, 3 (1956), p. 75.
23. Seth D. Cudjoe, "The Techniques of Ewe Drumming and the Social Importance of Music in Africa," in *Phylon*, 3 (1953): 280-91; and Seth D. Cudjoe, "The Notation of Drum Music," in *Music in Ghana*, 1, 1 (1958): 70-80.
24. Joseph Kygambiddwa, *Arican Music from the Source of the Nile* (London: Atlantic, 1956).
25. Klaus P. Wachsmann, review of *African Music from the Source of the Nile* in the *Journal of African Music*, 1 (1963): 80-81.
26. Father K. Carrol, "Yoruba Religious Music," in *African Music*, 1, 3 (1956): 45-47.
27. Clement da Cruz, *Les Instruments de Musique Le Bas-Dahomey*

(*populations Fon, Adja, Kotafon, Péda, Aizo*) (Porto-Novo: Etudes Dahoméennes, 1954).
28. William W. Chukudinka Echezona, *Ibo Musical Instruments in Ibo Culture* (Unpublished Ph.D. Dissertation, Michigan State University: 1963).
29. *African Music*, 3, 2 (1963): 48.
30. See, for example, Benedicto Mubangizi, "Preliminary Report of Two Months Research in Ankole," in *African Music*, 4, 1 (1966): 77-78.
31. William W. Chukudinka Echezona, "Igbo Music," in *Nigeria Magazine*, 85 (1965): 45-52.
32. Akin Euba, "Nigerian Music," in *Nigeria 1960: A Special Issue of Nigeria Magazine* (1960): 193-210; and J. H. Kwabena Nketia, *Folk Songs of Ghana* (London: Oxford University Press, 1963).
33. J. H. Kwabena Nketia, "African Music: An Evaluation of Concepts and Processes," in *Music in Ghana*, 2 (1961): 1-35; and Francis Bebey, *Musique de L'Afrique* (Paris: Horizons de France, 1969).
34. See B. A. Aning, "Factors that Shape and Maintain Folk Music in Ghana," in *Journal of the International Folk Music Council*, 20 (1968): 13-17; Fela Sowande, "The Role of Music in Traditional African Society," in *African Music Meeting in Yaounde (Cameroon) Organized by UNESCO* (Paris: La Revue Musicale, 1970); J. H. Kwabena Nketia, "The Problem of Meaning in African Music," *Ethnomusicology*, 6, 1 (1962): 1-7; J. H. Kwabena Nketia, "Historical Evidence in Ga Religious Music," in *The Historian in Tropical Africa* ed. R. Mauney and Jan Vansina (London: Oxford University Press, 1964) pp. 265-83; J. H. Kwabena Nketia, "Sources of Historical Data on African Music," in *African Music* (Paris: La Revue Musicale, 1970), pp. 43-49; Wilberforce Echezona, "Compositional Technique of Nigerian Traditional Music," in *Composer*, 19 (1966): 41-49; J. H. Kwabena Nketia, "The Hocket Technique in African Music," in *Journal of the International Folk Music Council*, 19 (1967): 66-71; Atta Anan Mensah, "The Polyphony of Gyi-gu; Kudzo and Awutu Sakumo," in *Journal of the International Folk Music Council*, 19 (1967): 79-88.
35. The former is discussed in Samuel Eno Belinga, "Musique Traditionelle et Musique Moderne au Cameroon," in *Bulletin of the International Committee on Urgent Anthropological and Ethnological Research* (Vienna), 11 (1969): 83-90; Akin Euba, "New Idioms of Music Drama among the Yoruba: An Introductory Study," in *Yearbook of the International Folk Music Council*, 11 (1970): 92-170; Atta Anan Mensah, "Jazz—the Round Trip," *Jazzforschung*, 3/4 (1972): 124-72; J. H. Kwabena Nketia, "Traditional and Contemporary Idioms of African Music," in *Journal of the International Folk Music Council*, 14 (1964); 34-37; and Fela Sowande, "Nigerian Music and Musicians: Then and Now," in *Composer*,

19 (1966): 25-34. The latter is treated in Atta Anan Mensah, "The Akan Church Lyric," in *International Review of Missions*, 49, 194 (1960): 183-88; and Isaiah Mwesa Mapoma, "The Use of Folk Music Among Some Bemba Church Congregations in Zambia," in *Yearbook of the International Folk Music Council*, 1 (1960/1971): 72-88.

36. B. A. Aning, *An Annotated Bibliography of Music and Dance in English-Speaking Africa* (Accra: University of Ghana Institute of African Studies, 1967); and Agnes A. Ojehemon, *Catalogue of Recorded Sound* (Ibadan: University of Ibadan Institute of African Studies, 1969).

37. Klaus Wachsmann, "The Trends of Musicology in Africa," in *Selected Reports* (UCLA Institute of Ethnomusicology), 1, 1 (1966): 62.

38. *Ibid.*, p. 64.

Selected Bibliography

HISTORY

Ajayi, A. F., and Michael Crowder, eds. *History of West Africa*, Vol. 1. New York: Columbia University Press, 1972.
_____. *History of West Africa*, Vol. 2. New York: Columbia University Press, 1976.
Albertini, Rudolf von. *European Colonial Rule, 1880-1940: The Impact of the West on India, Southeast Asia and Africa*. Westport, Conn.: Greenwood Press, 1982.
Bennett, Norman. *Africa and Europe: From Roman Times to the Present*. New York: Africana Publishing, 1975.
Brooks, Lester. *Great Civilizations of Ancient Africa*. New York: Four Winds Press, 1971.
Ehret, C. *The Archaeological and Linguistic Reconstruction of African History*. Berkeley: University of California Press, 1982.
Freund, Bill. *The Making of Contemporary Africa: The Development of African Society Since 1800*. Bloomington: Indiana University Press, 1984.
Inikori, J. E. *Forced Immigration: The Impact of the Export Slave Trade on African Societies*. New York: Africana Publishing, 1982.
Olaniyan, R. *African History and Culture*. Lagos, Nigeria: Longmans, 1982.
Webster, J. B., A. A. Boahem, and Michael Tidy. *The Revolutionary Years: West Africa Since 1800*. London: Longmans, 1980.
Wilson, Monica, and T. Hunter. *A History of South Africa to 1870*. Boulder, Colo.: Westview Press, 1983.

POLITICS

Albright, David. E., ed. *Communism in Africa.* Bloomington, Ind.: Indiana University Press, 1980.
Bates, Robert H. *Essay on the Political Economy of Rural Africa.* Cambridge: Cambridge University Press, 1983.
Emerson, Rupert. *From Empire to Nation.* Boston: Beacon Press, 1969.
Cartwright, John R. *Political Leadership in Africa.* New York: St. Martins Press, 1983.
Chaliand, Gerald. *The Struggle for Africa: Conflict of the Great Powers.* New York: St. Martins Press, 1982.
Cook, Chris. *African Political Facts Since 1945.* London: Macmillan, 1983.
Foge, D. *Africa in Struggle: National Liberation and Proletarian Revolution.* Seattle: ISM Press, 1982.
Gailey, Harry A. *Africa, Troubled Continent—A Problems Approach.* Malabar, Fla.: R. E. Krieger Publishing Co., 1983.
Mazrui, Ali A. *The African Condition.* London: Cambridge University Press, 1980.
Mazrui, Ali A., and Michael Tidy. *Nationalism and New States in Africa.* London: Heinemann Educational Publishers, 1984.
Prosser, Gifford, and Louis Roger. *The Transfer of Power in Africa: Decolonization 1940-1960.* New Haven: Yale University Press, 1982.
Rothchild, Donald S., and Victor A. Olorunsola, eds. *State Versus Ethnic Claims: African Policy Dilemmas.* Boulder, Colo.: Westview Press, 1983.
Sithole, Ndabaningi. *African Nationalism.* London: Oxford University Press, 1969.

LAW

Comaroff, John L., and Roberts Simon. *Rules and Processes: The Cultural Logic of Dispute in African Contexts.* Chicago: University of Chicago Press, 1981.
Hay, Margaret Jean, and Marcia Wright. *African Women and the Law: Historical Perspectives.* Boston: Boston University African Studies Center, 1982.
Ogwurike, C. *Concept of Law in English Speaking Africa.* New York: Nok Publishers International, 1979.

RELIGION AND PHILOSOPHY

Clarke, Peter B. *West Africa and Islam: A Study of Religious Development From the 8th to the 20th Century.* London: E. Arnold, 1982.
Emefie, Ikemga Metuh. *God and Man in African Religion: A Case Study of the Igbo of Nigeria.* London: Cassell Ltd., 1981.
Hodgson, Janet. *The God of the Xhosa: A Study of the Origins and Development of the Traditional Concepts of the Supreme Being.* London: Oxford University Press, 1982.
Hountondji, Paulin J. *African Philosophy: Myth and Reality.* Bloomington, Ind.: University Press, 1983.
Kroger, Franz. *Ancestor Worship Among the Bulsa of Northern Ghana: Religious, Social and Economic Aspects.* Hohenschaftlarn bei Munchen: Klas Renner Verlag, 1982.
Lele, Boniface. *Family Spirituality in Africa.* Eldoret, Kenya: Gaba Publications, 1982.
Ottenberg, S., and W. Bascom. *African Religious Groups and Beliefs: Papers in Honor of William R. Bascom.* Meeaut, India: Folklore Institute, 1982.
Sanneh, L. O. *West African Christianity: The Religious Impact.* London: C. Hurst, 1983.

LITERATURE

Anozie, Sunday O. *Structural Models and African Poetics: Towards a Pragmatic Theory of Literature.* London: Routledge and Kegan Paul, 1983.
Chinweizu, Jemie, and I. Madubuike. *Toward the Decolonization of African Literature.* Washington, D. C.: Howard University Press, 1983.
Cope, Jack. *The Adversary Within: Dissident Writers in Afrikaans.* Cape Town: D. Philip, 1982.
George, Veronica. *Genres, Forms, Meanings: Essays in African Oral Literature.* Oxford: JASO 1982.
Gerald, Albert A. *African Language Literatures: An Introduction to the Literary History of Sub-Saharan Africa.* London: Longmans, 1982.
Irele, Abiole. *The African Experience in Literature and Ideology.* London: Heinemann, 1980.
Jan Mohamed, Adbul R. *Manichean Aesthetics: The Politics of Literature in Colonial Africa.* Amherst: University of Massachusetts Press, 1983.
Lawson, William. *The Western Scar: The Theme of the Been-To in West African Fiction.* Athens, Ohio: Ohio University Press, 1982.

McCulloch, Jock. *Black Soul, White Artifact: Fanon's Clinical Psychology and Social Theory.* London: Cambridge University Press, 1983.
Moore, Gerald. *Twelve African Writers.* Bloomington: Indiana University Press, 1980.
Okpewho, Isidore. *Myth in Africa: A Study of Its Aesthetic and Cultural Relevance.* London: Cambridge University Press, 1983.
Zell, Hans, and Carol Bundy. *A New Reader's Guide to African Literature.* London: Heinemann Publishers, 1983.

Index

Abraham, Willie, 154
Achebe, Chinua, 46
Achimota School, 225, 226
Activation de l'energie, L' (Teilhard de Chardin), 88
Adotévi, Stanislas, 100, 136, 166
Africa: bourgeoisie, 140; disease environment of, 21-22; doctrine of judicial precedent in, 190; as earliest civilization, 87-88; humanistic tradition of, 5; as conquered last, 28; progressive vision of, 155; and socialism, 49-52; stone-age technology in, 18; triple heritage of, 34-37, 40, 47, 52
African history: acceptance of, 14; as Cultural Essence, 33; study of, 13
African Music, 235
African Music from the Source of the Nile (Kygambiddwa), 237
African Musicology, 215
African musicology: current trends in, 245-47; function, 216; future of, 247-50; impact of institutional development, 243-45; individual research in, 235-38; from 1920-1950, 218-28; from 1950-1960, 228-38; and period of institutional development, 238-45; research methodology in, 230-32; research sponsorship for, 229-35; term usage, 215. *See also* Music
African philosophy, 146; as ambiguous, 89-90; Central-West shift of, 98; classifications of, 112-13; as collective world vision, 150-51; and culture, 142; definition for, 99-100, 103; diversity of, 112; and ideological school, 101-2; internal structure of, 98-99; 1956-1965 debate, 97; presentation of, 109-11; publications, 90-91, 97-98; scientific method in, 153. *See also* Ethnophilosophy; Philosophy
African problematic, 125, 135-36, 144
African religion: concepts of man

in, 58; defined, 55; and
knowledge of God, 57; and
levels of man's being, 59; and
nature, 65-67. See also
Christianity; Islam; Religion
African Studies Association, 13
African Traditional Religion: A Definition (Idowu), 69
Agblemagnon, Ferdinand N'Sougan, 97
Agbloe v. Sappor, 201
Agriculture, 18
Ahmed & anor v. R., 195
Akan, 71-73
Algeria, 138-40, 169, 170
Althusser, Louis, 100, 112, 152
Americas, depopulation of, 23
Amin, Idi, 51, 52
Amu, Ephraim, 222-28, 240
Anatolia, 19
Anthropology, 104, 142; and domination, 156 n.5; epistemological split, 92-93, 94; missionary, 92, 93-94
Aquinas, Saint Thomas, 112
Aristotle, 81, 100, 112, 149
Art d' afrique noire, L' (Mveng), 97
Asante, 71-72, 74
Assimilation, 161-62; and elites, 168-69; meaning of, 163-64; viability of, 165
Associated Board of the Royal Schools of Music, 219
Atal, Dosithée, 97
Australian Consolidated Press, Ltd. v. Uren, 194
Aventure Ambiguë, L' (Kan), 123
Chief Obafemi Awolowo, 51
Awonor-Williams v. Gbedeman, 202

Bacon, Francis, 79
Bacon, Roger, 79

Bahoken, J. C., 105
Baines v. Pick, 196
Balanced circulation of news, 176
Ballanta, Nicholas George, 220-22
Bambose v. Daniel, 201
Bantu Philosophy (Tempels), 91-92, 94, 97, 110, 116-17 n.9, 142
Batoula (Maran), 160
Bergson, Henri, 81-82, 83
Beti, Mongo, 160
Bipoun-Wum, Joseph, 167-68
Blyden, Edward Wilmot, 125
Bokassa, Jean-Bédel, 45
Boumedienne, Houari, 181
Boyd-Barrett, O., 175
Brazil, 24
Bronze Age, 19
Broome v. Cassell & Co., Ltd. & anor, 194
Buakasa, Tulu Kia Mpasu, 104
Busia, Kofi Abrefa, 228-29

Camels, 20-21
Capitalism, 27-30
Carrol, K., 237-38
Cartesian doctrine, 79, 80
Case-law system, 204-9
Catholic School of Theology, 98
Cereals, 18
Césaire, Aimé, 77, 137-38, 139, 165
Chandler v. Webster, 197, 204
Chariots, 19, 20
Child, naming of, 63
Childbirth, 61-63, 73
Christianity, 3, 185; indigenization of, 95, 96; and Islam, 36, 37; in Northern Nigeria, 38; from paganism, 96; and socialism, 51; and traditional religion, 36; and Westernism, 70
Church of England, 36
Circumcision, 63

Index

Civilization, 86, 88, 131-35
Civil law, 189
Clyde-Wiggins v. Maba Estates Ltd., 196
Coalescence, 42
Coker, A. C., 219
Cole v. Cole, 207
Coleman v. Shang, 207
Colonialism, 107; and identity, 122-24; impact of, 40-41, 184; as interlude, 133-34; psychiatric effects of, 139; rationalizations for, 124; resistance to, 160-61; tensions caused by, 124; as unquestioned, 92; vulnerability of, 4
Colonial Office Social Science Research Council of the United Kingdom, 219
Columbian Exchange, The (Crosby), 23
Communication: and integration, 41; as unidirectional, 184, 185; Western domination over, 176-77
Community, rituals of, 61-64
Composers, 246
Comte, Auguste, 80, 83
Conference of French and African Heads of State and Government, 165
Confrontation, 42
Congress of Black Writers and Artists, 110
Consciencism (Nkrumah), 107
Consciencism, 4
Crahay, F., 97, 108
Cromwell (Hugo), 80
Crosby, Alfred, 23
Cudjoe, Seth, 236
Cultural convergence, 18
Cultural diffusion, 45-49
Cultural divergence, 17-18

Cultural imperialism, 175
Culture: as choice, 108; erosion of, 185; as governmental action, 239; homogeneity of, 17-18; interdependency of, 184; manufactured, 175; originality of, 92, 93; and race, 126-27, 137; redefined, 140-41; and superiority, 16; symbols of, 225
Customary law, 206, 207-9

da Cruz, Clement, 238
Damnés de la Terre, Les (Fanon), 139
Danquah, J. B., 71
Death, 64
Delafosse, Maurice, 92, 104
Descartes, René, 78, 79, 81
de Sola Pool, Ithiel, 178
de Souza, G., 105
Des Prêtres noirs s'interrogent, 96
Destiny of Civilizations (Frobenius), 85-86, 87, 88
Diagne, A., 104
Dialectical materialism, 121
Didinga prayer, 65-66
Diop, Cheikh Anta, 83, 131-35, 145, 154
Diouf, Galandou, 161-62
Disease, 21, 23
Divorce, 208
Doctrine of judicial precedent, 189-90
Dodhia v. National and Grindlays Bank, Ltd. & anor, 202
Doguicimi (Hazoumé), 162
Domination, 168
Donoghue v. Stevenson, 198
D.P.P. v. Smith, 193
Dress, 46
Drumming, 236
Durkheim, Emile, 83

East African Music Research
   Scheme, 219
Eastern Nigeria, 38-39
Eboussi-Boulaga, Fabien, 97, 100,
   107, 110, 111, 113
Echezona, Eilliam W. Chukudinka,
   242
Education: for music students,
   219; for music teachers, 226-27;
   religious, 91; as Western-based,
   37, 38
Egypt, 19, 131-35
Ekpendu v. Erika, 201
Elder tradition, 43
Elites: and assimilation, 168-69;
   as functional, 167; schizophrenia
   of, 159, 163
Emotion, 127-28
Energie humaine, L' (Teilhard
   de Chardin), 88
English common law, 204-7, 210;
   attitude toward, 191-97; and
   courts, 189-91; foundations of,
   189; judicial independence from,
   192; post-reception date decis-
   ions, 197-200. *See also specific
   court cases*
English Indictment Act (1915), 195
Esan v. Faro, 201
*Essai sur la problématique philo-
   sophique dans l'Afrique actuelle*
   (Towa), 142-45
*Essai sur les Données immédiates
   de la Conscience,* 81-82
Essence of Christianity, The, 121
Ethiopia, 18, 34, 86, 88
Ethnicity, 33; as cultural congruence, 42-43; impact of, 41;
   and indigenous tradition, 40; vs.
   class consciousness, 50-51
Ethnocentrism, 5, 14, 96, 135, 205
Ethnography, 93, 94

Ethnomusicology, 248
Ethnophilosophy, 98, 142, 143,
   146, 147; classes of, 103-4,
   107-9; and cultural nationalism,
   147, 148, 153; Hountondju's
   critique of, 148-54. *See also*
   African philosophy; Philosophy
Eurocentrism, 83
Ezeani & ors v. Njikike, 193

Family, 59, 86
Fang people, 57
Fanon, Frantz, 137-40
Feuerbach, Ludwig, 121
*Feuerbach and the End of German
   Philosophy* (Engels), 121
Fibrosa v. Fairbarn, etc., Ltd., 197
Fichte, Johann Gottlieb, 80
Fidei Donum, 96
Filmmaking, 179-80
First Pan-African Cultural Festival,
   166
Firth, J. R., 229
Fleischman, E., 113
Folktales, 145, 146
Fote, Maurice Memel, 97
Fouda, Basile-Juléat, 166
France: independence from, 160-
   61; maintaining ties with,
   164-65; as neocolonialist, 165;
   Romantic movement in, 80
Franklin, Albert, 136
Free flow, 176-80
French Constitution, 168
French Revolution, 161
Freud, Sigmund, 94
Frobenius, Leo, 92; on civiliza-
   tion, 84-85; culture vs. race,
   86-87; and ethnography, 82;
   global perspective of, 83;
   methodology of, 84-88
Fulani creation story, 56-57

Index

Gérard, Albert, 110
Gerbner, George, 180
Ghana, 192; and common law, 206; national theatre movement in, 233-34; under Nkrumah, 140
Ghana Broadcasting Service, 235
Ghana Music Society, 235
God, 65, 71
Godelier, Maurice, 84, 85
Goethe, Johann Wolfgang von, 79
Gold Coast Teachers' Journal, 224
Gold mining, 24
Görres, Joseph van, 79
Gowon, Yakubu, 44-45
Griaule, M., 92, 104
Grimm brothers, 79
Guback, Thomas, 179-81

Habeas corpus, 189
Haley, Alex, 15
Hama, Boubou, 104
Hausa, 39
Hazoumé, Paul, 104, 162
Hebga, Meinrah, 97
Hegel, G. W. F., 33, 79, 100, 112, 146, 151, 156 n.5
Her Majesty's Judicial Committee of the Privy Council, 190
Herodotus, 83
Holmes, Oliver Wendell, 207
Hountondji, Paulin, 97, 100, 110, 112, 113, 141, 147-55
Houphouët-Boigny, Felix, 45
Hugo, Victor, 80
Hume, David, 70
Hungrier v. Grace & anor, 199

Idée d'une philosophie africaine, L' (Towa), 145
Identity, 141, 218; francophone search for, 165-68; global reality of, 135; integrated, 161; as intellectual problem, 122-25; media concern for, 179-80; problems of, 5; publications on, 167; Towa's view of, 144; as undefined, 173 n.21. *See also* Négritude
Ideologicophilosophical works, 105-9
Ideology, 49
Idowu, E. B., 69, 70-71
Imperialism, 27-30, 175, 176
Indépéndants d'Outre-Mer (IOW), 162
Independence, 13, 163-64
Indian Limitation Act (1908), 196
Indirect Rule, 38, 50, 51
Industrialism, 27-30
Industrial revolution, 18, 26
Indus valley, 17
Inferiority, myth of, 124
Information, 178-80, 182-86
Initiation, 63-64
Institute of African Studies (Ghana), 240
Institute of Musical Art (New York), 229
Integration: and continental cultural congruency, 42-45; and continental cultural diffusion, 45-49; cultural with national, 37-42
Intercommunication zones, 17, 19, 20, 21
Inter-Governmental Conference on Cultural Policy, 245-47
International Commission for the Study of Communication Problems, 176
Islam, 21, 34, 185; and Christianity, 36, 37; and socialism, 51, 52; and traditional religion, 36

Jahn, J., 108
John Chitenge v. The People, 198-99
Journalism, of music, 218-19
Journal of African Music, 215
Judge, role of, 209-10
Judicial precedents: African interstate use of, 200-3; and legal development, 204-9
Jurisdiction, 190
Jury system, 189

Kagame, Alexis, 91, 94-95, 100, 104, 112, 113; Hountondji's critique of, 149-50; on language, 130-31
Kalanda, Mabika, 107
Kane, Cheikh Hamidou, 123
Kant, Immanuel, 79
Kaoze, Stefano, 89, 104
Kasumu v. Baba-Egbe, 199
Kaunda, Kenneth, 44
Kenya, 40
Kenyan Parliament, 39-40
Kenyatta, Jomo, 40, 43, 45, 181
Kimoni, I., 106
Kinship, 59, 134
Kinyongo, Jean, 97
Kiswahili: as continental language, 46-47; impact of, 39-40; as second language, 39; and smaller languages, 41
Kygambiddwa, Joseph, 237

Labor, redistribution of, 25
Lakanmi & anor v. The Attorney-General (Western States) & ors, 202
Language, 166, 229-30; and being, 130-31; and cultural transformation, 37; demise of, 41; impact of, 3-4; and kinship terms, 59; and religion, 39, 72; Western conception of, 154
Laskin, Bora, 213 n.59
Law. *See* English common law
Leadership, 44, 182. *See also* Elites
Leibniz, Gottfried Wilhelm, 79
Lenin, V. I., 51
Lent, John, 184
Leopold Sedar Senghor: Negritude ou servitude (Towa), 141-42
Le Roy, A., 92
Levi Strauss, Claude, 82
Lévy-Bruhl, Lucien, 127, 156 n.5
Locke, John, 79
Loga v. Davordzi, 200
Lowenstein, Ralph, 182-83
Lufuluabo, F. M., 91, 104
Lugard, Lord John Frederick, 50, 51

MacBride, Sean, 176
MacIver & Co., Ltd. v. CFAO, 192
Maghreb, 169-70
Makarakiza, Andre, 91
Makerere University, 241
Malagache revolt of 1946, 172 n.10
Malinowski, Bronislaw, 229-30
Man: and God, 57-58; as individual, 61-64; mythological origin of, 56-57; and nature, 65-67; in society, 58-64
Maran, René, 160
Marketplace, 176, 178
Marriage, 61, 64, 208
Marx, Karl, 48, 70, 94, 100, 140
Marxism, 36-37, 107, 112, 121
Mascarene Islands, 24
Mass communication, 180
Mbabi-Katana, Solomon, 241
M'Bow, Amadou-Mahtar, 26
Mboya, Tom, 41

Mecca, 36
Media imperialism, 175, 184-85
Meditations (Descartes), 81
Memmi, Albert, 161
Mensah, Attah Annan, 235
Mentalité primitive, La (Lévy-Bruhl), 156 n.5
Merrill, John, 182-83
Messianic movements, 124
Mesopotamia, 17, 18, 19
Missionaries, 38, 90-91, 92
Mohammed, Murtala, 44
Monarchical tradition, 45
Monotheism, 69, 71, 75
Morphology of Cultures (Frobenius), 84-85
Mosengwo, Laurent P., 97
Mubarak v. R., 195
Mugabe, Robert, 33
Muhammad, 36
Muhammad Ali, 29
Mujynya, E. N. C., 105
Mulago, Vincent, 91, 105, 113
Multinational corporations, 177
Muntu (Jahn), 108
Music: for choral groups, 224; and evangelism, 222; information dissemination, 234; and institutional barriers, 221; and pan-Africanism, 46; and social change, 221, 228; status of, 223; students of, 219-28; teacher training in, 226-27; technical aspects of, 221. *See also* African musicology
Musical America, 220
Mveng, Engelbert, 97
Myths, 15, 56-57, 124

National Dance Company of Ghana, 240
Nationalism, 106, 129; as betrayal, 161; and ethnophilosophy, 147, 148, 153; in francophone Africa, 135, 160-61; francophone vs. anglophone, 163; opposition to, 155; pan-Africanism, 106, 107, 239; as retrospective, 156; and transformation, 143
Nationalist movements, 233
Nations Nègres et culture (Diop), 131-32
Nature, 65-67
Ndengue, Jean-Marie Abanda, 106
Négritude, 82, 86, 106-7, 111, 165-68; beginning of, 77; as black awakening, 125-26; as dominant ideology, 129; historical perspective of, 125; Hountondji's critique of, 147; as limiting, 156; music of, 233, 246; objections to, 122, 136-41; Senghor's formulation of, 126-29; significance of, 125; Towa's critique of, 142-45. *See also* Identity
Négritude et négrologues (Adotévi), 136
Neo-colonialism, 27
Neto, Agostinho, 181
Newbold, Sir Charles, 194-95
New International Cultural Order, 88
New International Economic Order, 88
News agencies, cultural invasion by, 177, 180
Ngugi wa Thiong'o, 46
Nguvulu, Alfonse, 106
Nichomachean Ethics, 81
Nietzsche, Friedrich, 81, 83, 94
Nigeria, 34, 50-52
Nigerian Broadcasting Corporation, 235

Nile valley, 17
Nkombe, Oleko, 98, 100
Nkomo, Joshua, 33
Nkrumah, Kwame, 4, 35, 44, 45, 107, 108
Nomadism, 134
Nonaligned Press Agencies Pool (NAPAP), 177
North Africa, 48-49
Northern Nigeria, 38-39
Nothomb, Dominique, 108
Ntedika, Joseph, 97
Nyerere, Julius, 34, 43, 181

Obote, Milton, 44, 51, 52
Ogbuagwu v. Police, 198
Oral tradition, 150, 247
Organization of African Unity (OAU), 245
Orude and Nwangi v. The Municipal Council of Kisumu, 194
Oyono, Ferdinand, 160

Paganism, 96
Pan-Africanism, 106, 107, 239
Parker v. R., 193
Patriarchy, 43, 86, 134
Patrice Lumumba University, 37
People's Republic of China, 37
Phillips, Ekundayo, 219, 237-38
Philosophers, 155-56
Philosophical Consciencism, 35
Philosophie Bantu Comparée, La (Kagame), 130-31
Philosophie bantu-rwandaise de l'être, La (Kagame), 91, 94, 130
Philosophy: as critical activity, 145; and culture, 142; definition for, 108-9; Hountondji's view of, 151-52; meanings of, 90; as metaphysics, 94; and oral tradition, 150; and realism, 103; role of, 146; and science, 152; and theology, 95-97; Thomist, 91, 94. See also African philosophy; Ethnophilosophy
Philosophy of History (Hegel), 156 n.5
Pius XII, 96
Plant, 86
Policy, and information, 182-86
Polytheism, 69-70, 75
Pompidou, Georges, 165
Positive tribalism, 41
Positivism, from rationalism, 77-80
Prayer, 65-66, 72-75
Prejudice, 132, 133, 205
Présence Africaine, 97, 110
Primitive monotheism, 71
Procreation, 61, 64

Queen (the) v. Sharmpal Singh, 193

R. v. L., 196
Race, and culture, 126-27, 137, 141
Racism, 14, 27, 48, 135, 141
Rashid Muledina & Co., (Mombasa) Ltd. & ors v. Hoima Ginners Ltd., 194-95
Rationalism, to positivism, 77-80
Rationality, and power, 144-45
Relativism, 93-94
Religion, 21; indigenous forms of, 34; labels for, 69; and language, 39; prayers in, 65-66, 72-75; and socialism, 51-52; as societal base, 185. See also African religion; Christianity; Islam
Religion des primitifs, La (Le Roy), 92
Revolution of 1889, 81
Rimbaud, Arthur, 82, 83

Index

Rituals, 61-64
Rivet, Paul, 82
Roman Catholic Church, 36, 90-91
Rookes v. Barnard, 193-94, 197
"Roots", 14-15
Rousseau, Jean-Jacques, 70

Sage tradition, 43-44, 45
Sahara region, 19
Sartre, Jean-Paul, 136, 139; on Négritude, 125-26
Scharfeneker v. Duley & Co., Ltd., 196
Schebesta, P., 93
Schlatter, Richard, 216-17
Schlegel, August Wilhelm, 79
Schlegel, Friedrich, 79
Schmidt, P. W., 92, 93
Schmidt, Wilhelm, 71
Scholarship, 5, 217
Schopenhauer, Arthur, 81
Science, and philosophy, 152
Season in Hell, A (Rimbaud), 82
Seclusion, 63
Secondary empire, 28-29
Sedentary life, 134
Seeger, Charles, 235
Self-determination, 160
Senegal, 239-40
Senghor, Léopold Sédar, 44, 93, 108, 122, 135, 154, 165, 181; on French colonialism, 162; on Négritude, 126-29; Towa's treatment of, 141-42
Shagari, Shehu, 44
Shang v. Coleman, 201
Ships, 20
Shukla, Vidya Charan, 177
Sidibe, M., 104
Slave trade, 15, 48, 107; explanations of, 22; impact of, 26-27; as migration, 23-26

Smet, Alfons J., 98, 100
Socialism, as transformation ideology, 49-52
Sociologie d'une révolution (Fanon), 138
Sociology, defined, 82-83
Southern Africa, 48
Soviet Union, 37
Sow, Ibrahim I. D., 110-11
Sowande, Fela, 219, 232-33, 235, 241-42
Soyinka, Wole, 46
Stereotypes, 181
Stowe, Harriet Beecher, 16
Structural Anthropology (Levi Strauss), 82
Sub-Saharan Africa: attitudes toward, 14; and Bronze Age, 19; elites of, 168-69; isolation of, 19-20; slave trade, 22
Sugar plantations, 24-25
Superiority, cultural, 16
Superman, theory of, 81
Sur la philosophie africaine (Hountondji), 110, 147, 149

Taine, Hippolyte, 80
Taiwo v. Dosunma, 201-2
Tanzania, 34
Tastevin, C., 93
Technology, 16, 17; impact of, 18; sharing of, 19; of Southern Africa, 47; uniformity of, 18; weapons, 28-29
Teilhard de Chardin, Pierre, 83, 87, 88
Television, 180-81
Tempels, Placide F., 91-92, 94, 97, 100, 101, 110, 112, 116-17 n.9, 128, 131
Theatre, 233-34
Theology, and philosophy, 95-97

Thiam, Doudou, 162-63
Third World: and disaster stories, 182; as media poor, 177, 178; and private information, 183
Tillich, Paul, 70
Touré, Sékou, 44, 49
Towa, Marcien, 97, 100, 106, 110, 112, 141-47
Trade: limitations of, 20; slave, 15, 22, 26-27, 48, 107; trans-Saharan, 21; West African, 28
Tradition, types of, 43-45, 86, 134, 150, 247
Transportation, 19
Trevor-Roper, Hugh, 14
Trinity College of Music, 219
Troeltsch, Ernst, 70
Tshiamalenga, Nt., 104, 111
Two-way circulation of news, 176

Uganda, 50-52
Uncle Tom's Cabin (Stowe), 16
Union des Populations du Cameroun (UPC), 172 n.10
Unité culturelle de l'afrique noire, L' (Diop), 134
United Nations Educational, Scientific and Cultural Organization (UNESCO), 26, 245; and free flow doctrine, 176; 1979 communications conference, 177
United States, 176
Universities, 13, 240-43
University of Ghana, 228, 229, 234, 235, 240, 243
University of Ibadan, 241
University of London, 228, 229

University of Nigeria (Nsukka), 242
University of Peking, 37
Un Visage africain du christianisme (Mulago), 105
Upper Volta, 239-40
Ursprung der Gottesidee (Schmidt), 93

Valéry, Paul, 78
Vallabjhi v. National and Grindlays Bank, Ltd. & anor, 202-3
Values, 4, 90, 123
Van der Linde v. Calitz, 196
Varis, Tapio, 180
Victoria College of Music, 219
Vienna School, 92
Violence, 139, 172 n.10, 181

Wachsmann, Klaus, 215, 219, 233, 245
Wallace Johnson v. R., 198
Warrior tradition, 43
Weltanschauung, 89, 90
West Africa, 47, 48
Western tradition, 34, 70
Winterbottom v. Wright, 197
Wire services, 178; and distortion, 181-82; significance of, 180; stereotypes from, 183

Yellow River valley, 17
Yonasani & ors v. R., 198
Yorubaland, 50, 51

Zaire, 90-91
Zamburakis & anor v. Rodussakis, 196

About the Contributors

NJOKU E. AWA received his B.A. and M.A. from Michigan State University and his Ph.D. from Cornell University. He is currently associate professor and director of graduate studies in the Department of Communication Arts, Cornell University. He has authored numerous articles on communication and national development, diffusion of innovations, and the cultural dimensions of the right to communicate. A former treasurer of the Society for Intercultural Education, Training and Research, Dr. Awa is active in professional organizations in his field. He is currently vice-chairperson of the Intercultural Communication Division of the International Communication Association. He recently edited a special issue of the *Journal of Black Studies* (Vol. 13, No. 1, Sept. 1982), devoted to mass communication and change in Africa, and is currently working on a book titled *Culture, Communication and Change in Africa.*

RICHARD BJORNSON received his B.A. from Lawrence University, his M.A. from Northwestern University, and his Ph.D. from the University of Paris, Sorbonne. He is currently professor of French and Comparative Literature at The Ohio State University, having taught previously at the University of Wisconsin and the University of Yaoundé in the Cameroon Republic. He has written extensively on European and American literature and is presently working on a study of the relationships among literature, culture, and the nation-building process in Cameroon. He is the author of *The Picaresque Hero in European Fiction* (Madison, Wisconsin: Univ. of Wisconsin Press, 1977). A former president of the American Literary Translators Association, he has translated René Philombe's *Tales from Cameroon* (Washington, D. C.: Three Continents Press, 1984) and Mongo Beti's *Lament for an African Pol* (Washington, D. C.: Three Continents Press, 1985).

PHILIP D. CURTIN received his B.A. from Swarthmore College and his M.A. and Ph.D. from Harvard University. He is currently professor of History at the Johns Hopkins University. He is the author, coauthor and editor of several books and the author of numerous scholarly articles. They include *Africa and Africans* (New York: Natural History Press, 1971), *African History* (Boston: Little Brown, 1978), and *Cross Cultural Trade in World History* (New York: Cambridge Univ. Press, 1984).

KWESI A. DICKSON received his B.D. (Hons.) from the University College of Gold Coast and his B. Lit., from Oxford University. He is currently professor of religion and director of the Institute of African Studies, University of Ghana, Legon, Ghana. Dr. Dickson, a Methodist minister, is the editor of *Biblical Revelation and African Beliefs* (New York: Orbis Books, 1969), and the author of *Religions of the World* (Accra: Ghana Publishing Corp., 1970).

TASLIM O. ELIAS received his B.A., LL.B., LL.M., and Ph.D. from the University of London between 1944 and 1949 and his LL.D. from the same institution in 1962. In 1947 he was called to the Bar at the Inner Temple, where he was a Yarborough Anderson Scholar. In the thirty-five years since 1949, he has held several positions and served in a variety of capacities. Among these have been the following: legal counsel (1949-1960); queen's counsel (1961); research fellow at the Universities of Manchester (1951-1953) and Oxford (1954-1960); governor of the School of Oriental and African Studies, University of London (1957-1960), corresponding member since 1970; visiting professor of political science at the University of Delhi (1956); professor of law and dean of the faculty of law, University of Lagos (1966-1972); attorney-general of Nigeria (1960-1972 except from January to October

1972); minister of justice of the Federal Republic of Nigeria (1960-1966); commissioner for justice (1967-1972); chief justice of the Supreme Court of Nigeria and chairman of the Advisory Judicial Committee (1972-1975). A member of the International Court of Justice at the Hague since February 1976, he served as its vice-president from February 1979 to August 1981, was appointed acting president in August 1981 and has been the president of the Court since February 1982. An internationally acclaimed advocate and legal scholar, Dr. Elias is the author of sixteen books on politics and law, as well as numerous articles in law journals.

ABIOLA IRELE received his B.A. in 1960 from the University College of Ibadan (in special relationship with the University of London) and his doctorate degree from the University of Paris. He is currently professor of French at the University of Ibadan, having previously taught at the University of Ghana (Legon) and the University of Ife. He is the author of numerous articles on African literature in English and French and on ideological movements in Africa. A collection of his articles has been published under the title *The African Experience in Literature and Ideology* (London: Heinemann, 1981). He has also edited a selection of the poetry of Léopold Sédar Senghor (published by Cambridge University Press) and is working on an edition of Aimé Césaire's *Cahier d'un retour au pays natal* as well as an essay on the novels of Chinua Achebe.

VICTOR T. LEVINE received his B.A., M.A., and Ph.D. from the University of California, Los Angeles. He is currently professor of political science at Washington University in St. Louis. He has held visiting appointments at several other universities, including the Universities of Ghana/Legon (1969-1971) and Yaoundé-Cameroon (1981-1982). Although his principal research interest has been politics in French speaking Africa, he has also examined political corruption, politics in the Middle East, and Afro-Arab relations. Author and coauthor of several books and numerous scholarly articles, his most recent book (with Timothy Luke) is *The Arab-African Connection* (Boulder, Colo.: Westview Press, 1979).

ALI A. MAZRUI received his B.A. from the University of Manchester, his M.A. from Columbia University, and his D. Phil.

from Oxford University. He is currently professor of political science and Afro-American and African studies at the University of Michigan and research professor at the University of Jos, Nigeria. He has held visiting appointments at over twenty universities in Africa, Europe, the United States, Asia, and Australia. He is the author or coauthor of several books and numerous scholarly articles. Considered as one of the leading commentators on African affairs in the world today, his most recent book (with Michael Tidy) is *Nationalism and New States in Africa* (London: Heinemann Educational Publishers, 1984).

JOHN MBITI received his B.A. from Makerere University, his B.Th. from Barrington College, and his D.Phil. from Cambridge. He is currently doing pastoral work in Switzerland where until recently he served as director of the Ecumenical Institute of the World Council of Churches. Considered by many as the leading authority on African religions in the world today, he is the author of *African Religions and Philosophy* (Garden City, N.Y.: Doubleday, 1970), *Concepts of God in Africa* (London: S.P.C.K., 1970), *Poems of Nature and Faith* (Nairobi: East African Publication House, 1969), and *The Prayers of African Religion* (Maryknoll, N.Y.: Orbis Books, 1976).

V. Y. MUDIMBE received his B.A. and D.Phil.Let. from Lovanium University. He formerly served as dean of the Faculty of Philosophy and Letters at the National University of Zaire and is currently teaching social science and philosophy at Haverford College, Pennsylvania. His numerous books include *Entre les eaux; Dieu, un prète, la révolution* (Paris: Presence Africaine, 1973), *Les Fuseaux, parfois* (Paris: Librairie Saint-Germain-Des Pres, 1974), and *O bel Imundo: Romance* (Rio de Janeiro: Atica, 1981).

ISAAC JAMES MOWOE received his B.S. and M.A. from Ohio University, his J.D. from Capital University, and his Ph.D. from The Ohio State University. He is currently assistant dean, College of Humanities, and associate professor of African politics at The Ohio State University. His research interests include comparative military behavior, political development and modernization, nation and institution building, political economy, constitutional law, civil rights law, jurisprudence, conflict of laws, and international law. He is the author of several scholarly articles and editor of *The Performance of Soldiers As Governors: African Politics and the African Military* (Washington, D.C.: University Press of America, 1980).

J. H. KWABENA NKETIA received his B.A. from the University of London. He subsequently studied at the Juilliard School of Music, Columbia University, and Northwestern University as a Fellow of the Rockefeller Foundation. His is currently Andre Mellon Professor of Music at the University of Pittsburgh and Professor Emeritus, UCLA. A former director of the Institute of African Studies, University of Ghana, he has held visiting professorships at the University of Queensland (Australia) and at Harvard University as the Horatio Appleton Lamb Visiting Professor of Music. He is a member of honor of the International Music Council (UNESCO), honorary fellow of the Royal Anthropological Institute of Great Britain, and a fellow of the Ghana Academy of Arts and Sciences. He is the author of several books in Twi and English and numerous scholarly articles on African music and related arts. He received the ASCAP Deems Taylor Award for his book *Music of Africa* and the UNESCO-International Music Council Prize "in recognition of distinguished service and leadership in music."

LÉOPOLD SÉDAR SENGHOR was educated at the Lycée-Le-Grand and at the École Normale Superieure of the University of Paris where he received the agrégation in 1934. In 1935 he joined the faculty of the Lycée at Tours. He was a member of the French Constituent Assemblies as a deputy for Senegal in 1945 and 1946, and in 1946 he was elected to both the French National Assembly and the General Council of Senegal. In 1948 Mr. Senghor was appointed to a professorship at the Ecole Nationale de la France d'Outre Mer in Paris. In 1955-1956 he served in the French government and over the next few years worked with others for the independence of Senegal. In 1960 he became the first president of an independent Senegal, a position he held until his retirement in January 1981. He is the author of several books and essays as well as volumes of poetry. One of the founders of the *Négritude* movement, he has received many awards for his literary works which include *Discours de remerciement et de reception: A l'Academie Francaise* (Paris: Editions du Seul, 1984), *Elegie des alizés* (Paris: Editions du Seul, 1969), *Nocturnes*, trans. John Reed and Olive Kleke (New York: Third Press, 1971), *On African Socialism*, trans. with introduction by Mercer Cook (New York: Praeger, 1964), *La Poesie de l'action: Conversations avec Mohamed Aziza Leopold Sedar Senghor* (Paris: Stock, 1980).